2001

RISOTTO WITH NETTLES

Portrait of Pasta
Good Housekeeping Italian Cookery
Pasta Perfect
Gastronomy of Italy
The Classic Food of Northern Italy
Secrets from an Italian Kitchen
Entertaining All'Italiana
Amaretto, Apple Cake and Artichokes

RISOTTO
WITH
NETTLES

A Memoir with Food

Anna Del Conte

Chatto & Windus

LONDON

Published by Chatto & Windus 2009

2 4 6 8 10 9 7 5 3 1

First published in Great Britain in 2009 by
Chatto & Windus
Random House, 20 Vauxhall Bridge Road,
London SW1V 2SA
www.rbooks.co.uk

Addresses for companies within The Random House Group Limited can be found at:
www.randomhouse.co.uk/offices.htm

The Random House Group Limited Reg. No. 954009

A CIP catalogue record for this book
is available from the British Library

ISBN 9780701180980

The Random House Group Limited supports The Forest Stewardship
Council (FSC), the leading international forest certification organisation. All our titles that
are printed on Greenpeace approved FSC certified paper carry the FSC logo.
Our paper procurement policy can be found at www.rbooks.co.uk/environment

Book design by Peter Ward
Typeset by SX Composing DTP, Rayleigh, Essex
Printed and bound in Great Britain by
CPI Mackays, Chatham, ME5 8TD

In memory of my husband
Oliver Waley

CONTENTS

INTRODUCTION

WHEN MY EDITOR suggested that I write a memoir, I was thrilled, flattered – and amazed. Who on earth would be interested in reading about my life? She explained: 'Anna, you were one of the first people in Britain to write about Italian food, and it is partly thanks to you that it is now so popular.'

My agent spurred me on with her infectious enthusiasm. 'Think what a fascinating life you had, brought up in one country and finishing your days in another. You went through a horrific war at an age when other generations just went to parties and dances and, frankly, I have never heard of another cookery writer who was machine-gunned and who went to prison twice.'

If I found it difficult to write this book, it was because I belong to a generation that was taught to be self-effacing. Vanity was the worst sin I could commit (it was taken for granted that I'd be unlikely to kill or even steal). I remember an aunt of mine once told me how pretty I looked in one of my favourite dresses, a white cotton dress with red poppies all over and a smocked yoke. My mother's words of caution were: 'Don't tell her that or she'll become too vain.' I was never praised for my work at school and seldom congratulated on any of my achievements. It was also assumed that I would behave well, love my parents and never utter a word of criticism about them. I was expected to be grateful for everything I had, and that was that.

So, when I was asked to write my memoirs, I began to think about myself, something I'd never really done before. True, I was born in one country and then lived mostly in another, so I am *né carne né pesce* – neither meat nor fish – as we Italians would say (neither fish nor fowl as we English would put it). That's why friends in Italy say I am no longer Italian but English, while, here in England, my friends find me very Italian, although, they say, I don't seem to gesticulate as much as Italians do, nor do I show my emotions as Italians are supposed to do. Though my parents – especially my father – would have deemed any outward display of emotion unsuitable for a 'nice' girl of my background, as would all their friends. It all sounds very Victorian England, but this was pre-war Italy and I am sure the way my parents brought up their children was no different from that of their middle-class, Catholic contemporaries.

The problem is that I am myself unsure whether I am Italian or English. I am – and feel – Italian when I say something complimentary about Italy or the Italians, yet I say 'We, in England,' when I want to praise the English. I don't intend to be opportunistic; it's just the way I am. Now, in my old age, I feel more Italian than when I first came to Britain some sixty years ago. But surely that's because as we get older we revert to childhood preferences, in our likes and dislikes, going back to our roots.

With me, this is particularly noticeable in respect of food. I am now a devotee of unfussy food as I remember it being served in my Milanese home. By that I mean ingredients – such as meat, fish or vegetables – of the highest quality dressed or cooked with a modicum of best unsalted butter or good olive oil. But there are two changes in my table appreciation: wine and fruit. I now drink wine regularly, and with great pleasure, though in moderation; excesses of any kind are not me. When I was a child, I didn't like the taste and wouldn't even drink the *due dita* – two fingers' worth – of red wine diluted with lots of water, which were administered to every Italian child from a very young age. I started drinking, as I started smoking, when I was seventeen, more for the impression it created than for the craving. As for fruit, I can only assume my dislike of it was simply a way of asserting myself against my mother, who believed that fruit was the provider not only of health and beauty but also of moral rectitude.

As a child, I was a finicky eater and, to a certain extent, I still am. I don't mean that I don't eat this or that – I eat absolutely everything from tripe to fish eyes and kid's head – but I am selective. I am not a gourmand, but I think I am a gourmet.

Writing about myself and my life was a challenge but as soon as I began to recall the tastes and smells of my childhood, memories came flooding back and I felt inspired. So here is my story, a memoir with food.

CHAPTER I

TOSCANINI

Marrons glacés

EVERY CHRISTMAS I get a box of marrons glacés, my favourite present. And year after year when I open the box, lift the paper, smell the first sweet-musty whiff and pop one in my mouth, I'm no longer in England but thrown back some seventy years to an elegant drawing room, full of beautiful furniture, the floor thick with layers of Persian rugs, the walls covered with pictures . . . and there I see a small man with a bright mane of white hair – the legendary conductor Arturo Toscanini. Marrons glacés always remind me of Toscanini and my childhood.

Meeting the maestro was my childhood ambition. Odd, I agree, for a child of eight. My elder brother Guido wanted to meet Charlie Chaplin; one of my cousins never stopped dreaming of Shirley Temple; and another was in love with film star Robert Taylor, but Arturo Toscanini was my pin-up.

At the time we were living in a flat in Via Gesù, an exclusive street in the centre of Milan that is now considered the best address in the world for couturiers, shoe makers, shirt makers and the like, and where the Four Seasons Hotel now takes up three of the oldest houses in the road. But before the Second World War, Via Gesù was a quiet residential street lined with elegant family houses and with only one unobtrusive shop – an antique dealer.

Our flat at Via Gesù was on the second floor of Number 3, a pleasant mid-nineteenth-century house divided into four large flats: two facing the street and two facing the courtyards. Ours was at the back, over the courtyards. Next door was the flat of the Clausetti, who were good friends of my parents. Margherita Clausetti, who must have been in her sixties then, was very beautiful, very amusing and very outspoken. She often recounted tales of her youth in Venice – the masked balls, the operas and the midnight rides in the gondolas. Apparently, Margherita had the most beautiful legs in Venice; she only had to lift her skirt to reveal her ankles and men would throw themselves at her feet. And then when rejected, they would throw themselves over the bridges – and *'così il fondo dei canali è coperto di cadaveri dei miei spasimanti ripudiati'* – 'so the bottom of the canals is covered by the corpses of my rejected admirers'.

Margherita's husband, Carlo, was a serious, distant man, devoted to music and musicians. He was a partner in the firm of Ricordi, the prestigious music publishing house. Everyone in the world of music went through the Clausetti's front door. I was so in awe of all those famous singers that, as a child, my ambition was to be an opera singer. Certainly I could sing, with a penchant for opera rather than popular songs, and I'd dream of treading the boards of La Scala Opera House to the echoing applause of an adoring audience. Sad to say, my inadequate musical talent soon put an end to that ambition, and I had to resort to adoration for those who trod the boards of La Scala in real life.

But I could still sing my favourite arias to myself, or to the unlucky members of my family. My repertoire was quite considerable for a girl of that tender age, and that was because I can truly say that I learnt many arias in the cradle. My father loved opera and I remember him singing his favourite arias to my younger brother Marco in his cot, to help him go to sleep, just as he'd sung them to me as I lay in the same cot some twelve years earlier.

Papà was proud of his baritone–bass voice that enabled him to sing some of the lowest notes in the opera repertoire – as in the famous line 'Sparafucil mi chiamo' from Verdi's *Rigoletto* and the aria 'Ella giammai m'amò' from *Don Carlos*. When, years later, I heard Boris Christoff singing that same aria in a spectacular production by Luchino Visconti at the Royal Opera House in Covent Garden, the memory suddenly flooded back of Papà leaning over Marco's cot singing that beautiful passage of unrequited love.

But why, I wonder now, was I so excited at the thought of meeting Arturo Toscanini? Perhaps it was because I had heard my parents talking about him with such reverence, so often heard their refrain after a night at the opera: 'It was good, but not as good as when Toscanini conducted it in 1928 . . .'

In 1929 Toscanini had resigned from La Scala, and in 1931, after refusing to play the fascist anthem before a performance, he was attacked and pilloried by fascists. He didn't conduct in Italy again until 1946, at the reopening of La Scala, which had been badly bombed in the war. So, I saw Toscanini as a paragon, not only of music but also of strength of conviction.

Not that I knew much about fascism and Mussolini at that young age, but I knew that Mamma was fiercely against Mussolini and that was enough for me.

So on that distant evening, when at last my dream came true and I was told I was going to meet the maestro, I put on one of my prettiest party dresses: a navy blue velvet number with Burano lace round the neck. White socks and patent leather black shoes completed the outfit of a typical bourgeoise girl of the Thirties. Mamma was looking radiant in a long champagne-coloured dress, one of her favourites. I remember the colour well as, that same evening, Papà had asked her, 'But why are you wearing that beige dress?' 'It's not beige,' she'd retorted, 'it's champagne.' And so champagne it was for me.

My mother was indeed a beautiful woman, her dark hair and dark eyes forming a vivid contrast with her light complexion. Always full of life, she captivated both men and women while remaining seemingly unaware of her charms. She retained her looks into her nineties, with her strong cheekbones and perfect nose – all features that can withstand the ravages of old age.

Mamma was always extremely nervous about meeting the maestro owing to an unfortunate experience some years earlier. One evening, during a performance of *La Traviata* at La Scala, she had accidentally pushed a box of chocolates too near the edge of the padded rail at the front of our box, which, as luck would have it, was directly over the timpani. As the chocolates fell from the box, one after another, onto the instruments below, they became the overture to the opera. Maestro Toscanini, already on the podium, was about to raise

With Mamma.

his baton; he stopped for a minute and turned to look up at my mother who wanted nothing more than to disappear from sight. Some days later, he sent a message via the Clausetti: the maestro would be very grateful if Signora Del Conte would try not to make her contribution to the musical evening with her chocolates.

It was no longer a time when people went to the opera as they would to their club – to meet friends, to exchange gossip, to munch sweetmeats and eat ice cream (Stendhal wrote that he'd had the best ice cream of his life at La Scala). Nor did they go to play cards, to flirt or even to engage in amorous rendez-vous, like the illicit lovers Andrea Memmo and Giustiniana Wynne at La Fenice Opera House in Venice, back in the eighteenth century. The opera itself, in those distant days, was incidental. But after the Great War, a more attentive audience was expected; certainly Toscanini would never put up with any distraction or lack of engagement from the audience.

So, on that long-gone night, we padded across the landing and rang the Clausetti's bell. Giuseppina, the parlour maid, opened the door in full uniform. The hall was a long gallery which opened up into the drawing room, and there I could see the maestro himself leaning over the grand piano and chatting. The hall had never seemed longer than it did that evening. The enchanting Signora Clausetti took me by the hand and led me towards my idol, saying: 'This is Anna, our little neighbour.' Toscanini looked down from his over-whelming height (or so it seemed to me as a child), said *'Che bella bambina,'* patted me on the head and handed me a dish of marrons glacés. I took one, said *'Grazie'* and turned away. Never before, or since, has a marron glacé tasted so good.

～

ANOTHER CHRISTMAS, many years later, I was in Milan and I had a sudden urge to see the house where I was born. It was a grey winter morning, so characteristic of Milan – rather foggy, rather wet, rather grey, rather indefinite – the sort of day that calls for reminiscences and *à la recherche du temps perdu.* There were not many people around and, as I turned the corner into Via Gesù, an image of the past appeared in my mind: walking towards me was a little girl in a grey tweed coat and tweed beret, holding hands with a lady in a black fur coat and a black perky hat . . . my mother and I.

We were going shopping – *fare la spesa*, the everyday grocery shopping, rather than *fare le commissioni*, the 'smart' shopping. We crossed over the road to Via Montenapoleone, and our first call was at Bianchi, a large panificio and patisserie, where all kinds of bread were sold at the back and, at the front, a long counter loaded with profiteroles, cannoli, petits fours, and tartlets extended as far as the imposing cash desk presided over by the even more imposing Signora Bianchi, her bosom resting majestically on the cash machine and her hair in tight crinkly waves. (Bianchi, alas, has long gone.)

Next stop, farther up Via Montenapoleone, was Zanocco, the *salumeria* – deli – bulging with salami and cheeses, where chubby Arturo used to cut a slice of pink and white prosciutto and present it to me on a piece of greaseproof paper. Zanocco had the best prosciutto in Milan, quite an accolade in a city famous for its food

At the corner of Via Montenapoleone and Via Borgospesso, two street vendors would be selling *calde arrosto* – roasted chestnuts – and roasted onions and beetroots from their tricycles, each with its burning drum for roasting on the front. Mamma always bought a few chestnuts, which the vendor would wrap in a cone-shaped newspaper parcel and hand to me. I'd quickly shell the nuts while blowing on my hands and popping them into my mouth, relishing two pleasures at once: the slightly burnt, delicious flavour of the nuts and the welcome heat on my frozen hands. Often, Mamma would buy the roasted onions and beetroots, too, to eat for dinner with boiled potatoes in the perfect winter salad. (I still make this salad today, but it's not the same, not as good, because, here in Dorset, I cook the vegetables in the oven rather than on an open fire.)

It was at Zanocco that I had my first independent shopping experience. Mamma was having a lunch party one day and needed some extra Russian salad. Russian salad is not Russian at all, actually; in Russia it is apparently called Italian salad. It was probably created in France when the Russian aristocrats arrived there after the revolution. In Italy in the pre-war years it was often served at smart lunches and dinners. Mamma used to make a delicious Russian salad: to all the cooked vegetables she would add simple ingredients, like hard-boiled eggs or anchovy fillets, or luxurious pieces of lobster, depending on the importance of the meal. That day everybody was busy, Zanocco couldn't deliver and somebody had to collect the salad. Looking back, it seems amazing that Mamma didn't have enough of any kind of food in the house. She always bought too much. Her fridge was forever bursting with food: you'd open the door and something would tumble out. Likewise, her bread bin was full of different packets of bread – the oldest, to be made into breadcrumbs or pancotto (bread soup), the not-quite-so-old bread, and the same day's bread which nobody was allowed to eat until the older bread was finished. (Much later, my poor husband, Oliver, was dismayed that in the country where you always eat *il pane di giornata* – today's bread – he had to make do with *il pane di ieri* – yesterday's bread.) Nothing was ever wasted in our house, and it's a thriftiness I have inherited and still practise today.

So I still cannot think why, on that particular day, Mamma

thought she did not have enough Russian salad – perhaps unexpected guests had turned up. Nevertheless, I felt honoured to be entrusted with the task of fetching it, so I brushed my hair – as I always had to do before going out – and darted off, down Via Gesù and across Via Montenapoleone. Cars were rare then, but one had to pay attention to the delivery boys on their tricycles. Arturo Zanocco gave me the usual slice of prosciutto and the parcel of Russian salad, exhorting me to take care crossing the road and to carry the parcel safely. When I arrived home, the Russian salad from Zanocco was mixed with one already made by my mother and then dished out, ready for the antipasto. There seemed to be a mountain of it and we ate the leftovers for two or three days afterwards.

That trip to Zanocco was the start of my passion for shopping – not for clothes or shoes, which I loathe, but for food. Zanocco has now disappeared, as has my favourite shop opposite, Parini the grocer's. Today there is still a grocer's, but a different one. No longer the big sacks of various lentils, of rice, beans, chickpeas, sugar, the rows and rows of jars of caramelle (sweets). No more the stacks of Marseille soaps, the bunches of black liquorice on the counter, the jars of different spices – the yellow saffron, the red paprika, the black pepper, the brown cinnamon – all lined up, and that incredible smell, both exotic and homely. The grocer's now, elegant as it is to the eye, is antiseptic, featureless and smell-less.

But still it conjures up in my mind a picture of Mamma and me continuing our round of the shops – she chatting and ordering the goods that were to be delivered – and eventually we are back in Via Gesù, where I'm standing so many years later looking up at the house where I was born.

Bomba di Panna e Marrons Glacés
Cream and Marrons Glacés Bombe

The bombe can be made and frozen up to 1 week in advance, although it will gradually lose flavour. Ideally it should be made 1 day before it is eaten.

SERVES 8–10

300g marrons glacés
5 tbsp dark rum
90g best bitter chocolate
700ml whipping cream
6 tbsp icing sugar, sieved
3 egg whites

Cut the marrons glacés into small pieces and put in a bowl. Add the rum and leave to macerate for half an hour or so.

Meanwhile, cut the chocolate into small bits. I do this by hand with a broad-bladed knife, as a food processor tends to reduce some of the chocolate to powder.

Whip the cream, then mix in the icing sugar, the marrons glacés with the rum, and the chocolate pieces.

In a clean bowl, whisk the egg whites until stiff and then fold into the mixture.

Spoon the mixture into a 1.5 litre (2½ pint) bombe mould, or other dome-shaped container of the same capacity. Cover with the lid or foil and put in the freezer for at least 6 hours.

Remove from the freezer half an hour before serving.

VIA GESÙ

Lemon granita

THAT VISIT TO Via Gesù, in the winter of 2006 – sixty-seven years after I'd left, in 1939 – was an unforgettable experience which left me both elated and drained. Our old flat is now occupied by Giulia Marzotto Caotorta, granddaughter of the Countess Vianson who had owned the house in my day. The sight of the courtyard, of the entrance hall and the grand staircase was enough to reawaken old memories. Ghosts came running to me and, with them, my childhood: there was Flora, the fat concierge, with Carlo, her emaciated husband, and Vanda, their granddaughter, who often came up to our flat to play with me. Vanda was two years younger than me and I used to boss her around in an unremittingly unpleasant way. I took advantage of my superior position in the household and the fact that, for a change, I was not the youngest around, which was my constant fate with most of my cousins.

In my mind's eye, I saw the Countess Vianson slowly descending the staircase, straight and imperious, in her long black dress, her black hat set firmly on her head like a tall flowerpot, her rows and rows of pearls dangling over her bosom and the fashionable black velvet collar kept in place by a large cameo. She was the Milanese answer to Queen Mary. My brother Guido and I used to hide behind the columns in the courtyard to avoid her. We were in awe of the grand lady – awe with a touch of fear, maybe. But the worst thing was that, if she saw us, we had to go to her: I had to curtsy and Guido had to kiss her hand. I didn't much mind the little bob, but Guido hated the ceremony of hand kissing. My father had never been too strict about that ritual, so Guido had to kiss the hand only of old and/or aristocratic ladies, and the Countess Vianson met both criteria.

I crossed the courtyard, with its doric columns and patterned, cobbled paving, and walked into the small garden at the back, which was dominated by a huge lime tree. The scent of its flowers, so strongly sweet, used to imbue every corner of our flat in June. The lime tree was even taller now, growing up and up in search of the sun, but the fig tree which had once flourished next to it was gone. I had loved that fig tree, with the statue of a young girl hiding among its fat green leaves. The statue was still there – like Alice in Wonderland with short hair and a bonnet. She'd been my imaginary friend and I used to dream of taking her by the hand and walking away with her along a beach, the backdrop scene to all my dreams.

I looked up to the first floor and noticed that the wisteria, too, was still there. It had always covered the terrace of the flat below ours, where Giulia and her mother and brothers used to live, but it was winter now and I could see only the naked twisted branches. I remembered it in full bloom in the early spring, when the scent at dusk was overwhelming, and then in summer when it became a green canopy under which Giulia's mother, the Marchioness Valdettaro, used to lie languidly on her chaise-longue, with Tabu her dachshund at her feet. Years later, when I visited the superb tomb of Ilaria del Carretto, in the Duomo di Lucca, suddenly in front of my eyes sprang an image of the Marchioness Valdettaro lying under the wisteria, dog at her feet, just like Ilaria and her dog.

The third courtyard used to be *il cortile di servizio* – the service courtyard – around which were the kitchens and some of the maids' rooms. This courtyard had been the realm of Gorini, the Countess Vianson's butler, and Lucia, the Clausetti's cook. Gorini also checked all the deliveries. He had a basket tied to a long rope which he'd lower so that the delivery boys could place their parcels in it. The boys would give a whistle, Gorini would let down the basket and then haul it back up. We used to play tricks on Gorini. If by chance the basket was down in the courtyard, we would put parcels in it – parcels of old newspaper, old rags, old bread.

Gorini always took our deliveries in the right spirit, while Lucia, who had her own descending basket, was not amused. She was a small, barrel-shaped woman with a long black skirt and a large white apron. 'Such a good cook,' my mother would say. I was too young to appreciate Lucia's food at dinner parties, but I recall that every autumn she made the most delicious cotognata – quince cheese. She used to store it, cut into small pieces and coated in sugar, in beautiful wooden boxes which came out for Christmas, when she'd call me into the big kitchen and let me choose one or two pieces. The cotognata had just the right amount of sugar to bring out that incredible flowery flavour of quince, and the right amount of moisture for the quince to fill my mouth with its celestial taste at the first bite. It is surely a flavour made in heaven for goddesses, as Paris knew when he gave Venus the perfect quince. I still make my cotognata from the fruits of the quince tree in my Dorset orchard, following Lucia's recipe.

~

THE FLAT WHERE WE LIVED has changed, of course. Walls have been removed and others built, doors have been shut and others opened, but there were some fixed points that evoked my childhood. The landing at the top of the staircase was the same, with its three doors, one of which used to be our front door. The landing was where I took refuge when I was cross with my mother, which happened very often. I used to 'leave home', as many children do. And for my departure, which I swore would last for ever, I took my beloved possessions: two chairs and one frying pan. The chairs, left to me by a great aunt, were nineteenth century and the frying pan was a gift from Zia Maria – Mamma's sister. I'd drag the two chairs out of my bedroom, across the hall and out onto the landing, fetch the frying pan, slam the door and sit there thinking how much my mother would cry when she realised I had left home.

Another place where I hid when I was cross was on top of a very tall bookcase in the study. First I had to stand on a chair, then on the radiator and, from there, climb on top of the bookcase where I'd lie in silence with my frying pan, though not the chairs, of course. Mamma and everyone else ignored my disappearance and, once I was back, the act was never mentioned.

Later, my eldest son Paul inherited a tendency to similar outbursts. The most unexpected was in France, on the way to

Italy. He was fourteen at the time. We had just spent the night in an hotel in Auxerre and Paul and I had a quarrel after breakfast, while packing the car. He got his sleeping bag and his holdall and stormed out of the hotel, muttering that he was going to walk to Italy! My younger son, Guy, and I, helped by little Julia, my daughter, finished the packing and drove off. About one kilometre down the road we saw Paul, who stuck out his thumb for a lift and climbed into the car. Nothing was said and we drove happily on to Italy.

~

STEPPING INSIDE THE FLAT at Via Gesù on that winter's day, was like stepping back into my childhood. Now one enters into what was once my bedroom. The pretty window is still there, as is the door to the hall where I used to run when I heard the noise of keys in the lock, to welcome my father home. My father was a tall, handsome man, extremely elegant in his hat – straw in summer and black homburg in winter – and always carried a cane. I would run to greet him and he'd lift me into his arms.

Papà would carry me around on his shoulders so I could look at all the prints hanging in the hall and corridor. He'd show me the horses, the dogs, the ducks and the birds, to all of which he gave fitting names. On Sunday nights there was the ceremony of winding the four clocks. I'd listen to the chimes while Papà turned the key. My favourite was an old English clock which had the chimes of Big Ben, as Papà told me. My father was a great anglophile. I remember quite clearly his answer to a friend who questioned his love of the English. The friend asked, 'But what about their arrogance?' to which Papà replied, 'Well, they would be perfect without it!' He admired, and liked to emulate, the aloof elegance of the English aristocracy who, at that time – in the Twenties and Thirties – were the leading international jet set.

Papà was a good sportsman. He played golf and tennis and liked to have a bet at the races, gambling also being one of his passions, often to the detriment of the family finances. On Sundays, as soon as spring arrived, he used to take us to the races at San Siro, or to the tennis club.

My mother, dressed in hat and gloves, would come along to the races – although I don't think she actually enjoyed them – but never to the tennis. She didn't like any sport except swimming. Unusually for someone of her generation, she'd stay in the sea for hours, slowly moving farther and farther with her funny side stroke.

They were like chalk and cheese, my parents; interested in different activities and different people. One interest they did share was playing bridge, at which my father was a deft hand, while Mamma played *sempre come una principiante* – always like a beginner – or so Papà used to say. There was also a marked contrast in their behaviour towards us: Papà loved me unconditionally when I was a small young child; later when we were older, he seemed to be unable to strike the right balance between his warm affection and the strict discipline he wanted to exert over his children. Papà was always affectionate, at least with me, yet also strict and authoritarian, while Mamma was a more complicated character, which I find very difficult to define. This is due partly to the fact that my generation was brought up with the principle that children should never appraise their parents, and partly because a mother-and-daughter relationship is such a sensitive one that, even now that Mamma has been dead for fourteen years, I cannot look at it with dispassion. At the time of writing, a spate of 'Memoirs' are being published, where the author, usually a woman, points her accusing finger at her mother. They seem to demand perfection from their mothers. I remember when my Zia Maria of Milan – Papà's sister – died, I told my cousin Sandro, her son, that I thought of her as the perfect mother. Sandro, a wise and perceptive man, said: 'But, Anna, there isn't a perfect mother, only ideal mothers, and she was one of them.'

My 'accusing finger' against Mamma is that she certainly much preferred boys to girls. This statement is not dictated by carping jealousy of my older brother (of whom I certainly was wildly jealous). It was confirmed by Nicholas, my brother Marco's son, whom she brought up along with his older sister after their mother left them and Marco for another man. Nicholas was well aware of her partiality towards him. Mamma had a steely hard shell. I am sure she built that cuirass around herself to fence off the tribulations of her life. Born into a wealthy family, she'd married a rich man, only to find herself, at the age of forty-five, homeless and penniless after the war. And, even before that, things did not always go smoothly for her.

She had to put up with the unfaithfulness of her husband, with whom she was very much in love. I only found out much later – after I was married – that Papà had a serious affair with an American woman who lived at the Hotel de Paris in Monte Carlo. This woman was famous for her louche life and her string of lovers and was once heard to say: 'Monte Carlo is the most wonderful place. You go to bed at night with one man, but you don't know who is going to be in your bed the next morning.' As a child, I'd been aware that Papà was not at home every night, but I never asked why, being only too pleased. For it meant that Guido and I could sleep in my parents' *lettone* – double bed – with Mamma; I in the middle, cuddling up to one or the other.

~

PAPÀ'S AFFAIR LASTED for two or three years, during which time he never came on holiday with us. Instead, we went with Zia Maria di Milano and my uncle, Zio Guido Peregalli, and their children Maria Teresa and Sandro, our favourite playmates.

I certainly did not miss my father much when we were at the seaside, at Forte dei Marmi, in northern Tuscany, where we'd take over the annexe of the hotel. We always travelled there in a caravan of two or three cars, full of trunks, baskets, nannies, dogs and the rest. The journey would take most of the day (today it takes some three hours, thanks to the motorway) and we'd stop for a picnic lunch high up on the Passo della Cisa.

Around midday, the spot for the picnic was chosen. White tablecloths were spread on the grass, and dish after dish of cold food was placed here and there. I always made a beeline for the *costolette alla Milanese* – fried veal chops Milanese style – which tasted even better cold. I'd pick up the chops with my hands and gnaw around the bone for the best bits. To finish, there were baskets of perfectly ripe peaches and apricots, into which we bit greedily, the juice dripping down our chins, while balia Teresa and balia Antonia (the nannies) ran after us with napkins to wipe away the juice which would spoil our pretty smock dresses and the white shirts of the boys. Then, back in the cars, we drove off in time to arrive at the hotel for dinner.

They were idyllic pre-war holidays, spent mostly on the beach, playing *pista* – a kind of marbles game – building elaborate castles with turrets and gargoyles and burying each other in the sand. We'd happily splash about in the shallow sea, with no cares in the world. It was at Forte where I learnt to swim. I was six years old and Mamma had decided the time was right. So one day she took me, on her back, out of my depth and then shoved me off. It was a radical approach, but I learnt to swim – and fast. Two strokes and I got hold of Mamma again and realised that swimming was fun.

In the afternoon, after a long rest, we'd play in the hotel garden or go for long walks in the pinewood, which was then luxuriant and void of all the hundreds of *villette* – holiday cottages – that dot it now. We seldom went to the beach in the afternoon, because our parents believed that *troppo mare innervosisce i bambini* – too much sea makes children irritable.

When I went back to Forte dei Marmi many years later, I realised that the families with young children still enjoy the same sort of holidays to those we had seventy years before. One of the few things in life that has hardly changed.

~

MAMMA NEVER talked about all the hardships in her life, except in a matter-of-fact sort of way. She lived looking straight ahead to the future and dismissing any unpleasantness of the past. Perhaps, that was the best way to stay sane.

After Papà's affair ended, things returned to normal at Via Gesù. Papà loved the flat, where he had first come to live years before with his mother and one of his younger brothers, Gino. My grandmother died in 1921, a year after my parents were married, and Gino stayed on, becoming part of it, although at times, I am sure, Mamma would have liked to see the back of him. We children loved our uncle Gino and called him Zio Tom – the nickname Guido gave him – after the hero of Harriet Beecher Stowe's *Uncle Tom's Cabin*.

Zio Tom was quite dapper and cared enormously about his appearance; his beautiful hands, always perfectly manicured, were his pride and joy. He loved to stick a flower or a feather in my mother's hats, he arranged the flowers in the house, he discussed menus for dinner parties with my mother and supervised the laying of the table and its decoration. His bedroom, dressing room and bathroom were, in theory, no-go areas for us children, although in fact we'd often sneak in there and throw his artistically arranged cushions at each other and use his loo – just to annoy him. Although Zio Tom had several lovers, he never married. He liked to gossip and also danced very well, attributes that made him a favourite of many society hostesses, to whom he was proud to be known as the 'Cavalier Servente'.

My younger brother, Marco, was born in 1937 and I was delighted with his arrival. He became my living doll. I was old enough, at twelve, to be able to carry him around, change his nappies and feed him. In spite of loving him deeply, I was extremely jealous as I saw my father transfer his predilection from me to my baby brother. Up to then, I had been Papà's little darling, who couldn't do much wrong. I was always shrewd enough to point the guilty finger at Guido whenever I'd been naughty. My father tended to believe me, my mother knew better, and good-hearted Guido took the blame. Papà also had the unfortunate tendency, like many men of his generation, to demand too much from his son. Guido was a boy, the older son and, as such, he must behave like a man. Even when very young, he was told that he should never cry (which I knew he often wanted to), that he should look after me, his little sister (who was impossibly bossy), that he should not be afraid of bangs (of which he was terrified), and a number of other unfeeling shoulds and should nots.

After Marco arrived, the flat at Via Gesù became too small and in 1939 we moved to a larger flat just around the corner in Via Sant'Andrea. It was an unfortunate move, because while Via Gesù is still standing, the house in Via Sant'Andrea was destroyed by an incendiary bomb in August 1943.

So it is in the flat of Via Gesù that most of my memories lie. When I went back that Christmas in 2006, I would have liked to walk down the veranda, the covered balcony that ran from the dining room to the kitchen, to recapture the memory of all the games we played there, such as *la corsa delle lumache* – the snail race which Guido and I enacted during the few days before Christmas. Christmas Eve is a *giorno di magro* – a meatless day – for Catholics. Oddly enough, snails are allowed on meat-free days, because they are fish not meat, as declared by a former Pope who loved them so much that he could not bear to go through the forty days of Lent without eating them. '*Cochleas pisces sunt*' he proclaimed, and so they are.

On Christmas Eve the traditional fare in my home was *capitone* – eels – for lunch, and pasta and bean soup followed by *lumache in umido* – snails in a sauce with polenta – for supper. Capitone is the big female eel. It was preserved in olive oil, then cut into chunks and eaten cold. That dish of snails was one of my mother's fortes – a *fortissimo*, I should say – and I don't think I've ever had snails to equal them. First, Mamma would cook them in boiling water for a short time until they died and could be taken out of the shell with a toothpick. That was a job I relished, although I couldn't really do it properly and often half a snail would be left behind in the shell. The snails were then washed in salted water and added to a little *soffritto* – a mixture of chopped parsley and garlic. A lot of garlic, in fact, which was unusual in my mother's cooking because, like all good Italian cooks, she used garlic with great *rispetto*. She'd chuck the shell-less snails into the *soffritto*, stir them around, then add a glassful or two of white wine and cook them in a beautiful earthenware pot for up to three hours. Lemon juice was added at the end and the pot was brought to the table. We just forked one or two up and put them in our mouths with some hot polenta, and we tasted heaven. Sadly enough, I have never been able to make them because in England I have never found live snails for sale.

But, even better than eating them was racing them. For Guido and me the snail race was the highlight of the week before Christmas. The snails were bought some days before they were cooked so that they could be cleansed in a zinc bucket full of bran and covered with a cloth tied up under the rim. For the race we'd choose the most lively ones and line them up at one end of the veranda. At the other end, seven to eight metres away, we put some lettuce leaves, having rubbed the race course with lettuce to entice the snails to get to the end. Guido and I would put bets on them and off they'd go for the slowest race ever.

~

In that winter of 2006, my wish to walk down the veranda couldn't be fulfilled because it now formed part of a separate flat, together with the attic. I would have liked to go up there, too, and look down once more on to the roofs of my childhood. The attic used to house the maids' bedrooms, icy cold in winter and sweltering hot in summer. But they had a spectacular view of the roof and chimneys of the house next door – the Palazzo Bagatti-Valsecchi – which is now a museum. This palazzo is a very large building, lavishly built in the nineteenth century in Gothic style – a bit of a mish-mash but quite attractive. Its roofs are splendid, all set at different levels.

I'd go up to the attic every October to see the swallows gathering in the sky before they left for warmer shores. I envied them, as I hated the cold and the grey of northern climes. But then the snow would come and the attic became so appealing again. I'd sprinkle breadcrumbs for the birds – the house martins and the sparrows. I did it religiously every day as soon as I got back from school, and I used to think how silly Hansel and Gretel were to sprinkle breadcrumbs in a forest as a route marker. No wonder they could not find their way home. It snowed a lot in northern Italy then; now, apparently, it seldom lies for more than two or three days. The roofs and the chimney pots of the Palazzo Bagatti-Valsecchi would become a good foot higher, thanks to that lovely crunchy white snow.

Another sortie to the attic was for our winter treat – lemon granita. Guido and I would get two tall glasses from the kitchen, pour quite a lot of freshly squeezed lemon juice into them, sprinkle in an even greater amount of sugar and mix and mix, and up we went to the attic. We'd open the window and fill the glasses with that cold white crunchy manna. Then back down to the kitchen, where we'd squeeze more lemon juice, sprinkle more sugar and slowly suck the granita up. The best drink ever, even in the depths of winter.

RECIPES

Granita di Limone
Lemon Granita

SERVES 2

180g sugar
400ml water
100ml lemon juice

Put the sugar and water in a small saucepan and bring to the boil. Simmer for 5 minutes, then mix in the lemon juice and leave to cool.

When cold, pour into a freezer container, seal and place in the freezer. Leave it there for at least 4 hours, stirring it with a fork every 20 minutes or so to break up any ice lumps that form.

Cotognata
Quince Cheese

This is not an easy preserve to make, because so much depends on the variety of the quince you are using and their ripeness. If, like me, you have a quince tree in your garden, you can learn by trial and error. It may be a lengthy and laborious performance but it is well worth the effort. However, this is definitely not a recipe for anybody in a hurry or for an inexperienced cook.

Equal weight of quinces (unpeeled) and caster sugar
Granulated sugar for dusting

Measure the same weight of caster sugar as the weight of the quinces, and set the sugar aside. Wash the quinces, cut them in quarters and place them in a heavy saucepan. Add some water in the proportion of 150ml per kilo of fruit. Bring to the boil and simmer until the fruit is tender. It is difficult to say how long this will take, but it will certainly take at least three-quarters of an hour. When the fruit is soft, press it down with a potato masher and then purée it through a food mill.

Wash the pan and put the purée back into it. Take a separate saucepan and put in the sugar. Heat the sugar, stirring constantly, until it turns a light caramel colour. Now pour the caramel into the quince purée and cook it until the purée becomes dry, stirring constantly, or almost constantly. This is the long and laborious process. The purée at the end should be quite thick and it should be hard to push the spoon through the paste, but again it is impossible to say how long this will take.

Line one or two baking trays with Bakewell paper and spoon the purée over it. Spread it out to a thickness of about 2cm, and press it down with the back of a hot metal spoon. Place the tray or trays in a hot cupboard or other warm place to dry.

When dry, which will take at least 24 hours, cut into rectangles of 5 x 3cm, dip them into granulated sugar and pack them into boxes, placing a sheet of rice paper between each layer. Cotognata lasts easily 2–3 months.

~

Pasta e Fagioli della Vigilia di Natale
Pasta and Bean Soup

SERVES 4

170g cannellini beans, soaked overnight
1 garlic clove, roughly chopped
1 celery stick, chopped
500g tomatoes, skinned and chopped or 1 x 397g can plum tomatoes, with their juice
2cm piece of fresh chilli, seeded and finely chopped
100ml extra-virgin olive oil
2 tbsp chopped basil or flat leaf parsley
100g ditalini pasta or other short pasta shapes
salt and freshly ground black pepper

Rinse and drain the beans.

Place the beans, garlic, celery, tomatoes and chilli in a large saucepan. Cover with 1.7 litres of cold water – do not add salt at this stage or the beans will take longer to become tender. Bring slowly to the boil and cook, covered, over a very low heat for about 2 hours, until the beans are tender.

Add the oil, the basil or parsley, the pasta and salt and pepper to taste. Stir well and return the soup to the boil. Cover and simmer for about 15 minutes, until the pasta is al dente, firm to the bite. The soup can be served either hot or at room temperature.

CHAPTER 3

MAMMA AND MARIA

Gnocchi, ravioli et al.

M Y MOTHER OFTEN claimed she did not enjoy cooking in spite of being an excellent cook. I think she considered it demeaning, an attitude shared by many ladies of her generation. Mamma was fundamentally an intellectual, however manqué, and preferred to focus her attention on interests that involved the mind. She never understood why I should want to write cookery books. Not once did she acknowledge my success in having them published. To her, they were just recipe books. Maybe she would have liked this one, but, alas, she didn't live long enough to read it.

Nevertheless, Mamma would go into the kitchen to supervise, discuss and also to prepare her favourite dishes, though she never liked the humdrum of everyday cooking and, at times, I can see her point. When, after the war, she found herself *sul lastrico* – on the rocks – as she used to say, and she had to go into the kitchen twice a day to prepare the meals, she complained bitterly. Yet, every day she would produce the most delicious meals and, despite her intellectual pretensions, she was deeply interested in food.

She used to make the perfect *manzo alla California* – beef

cooked in cream and vinegar – as well as succulent jugged hare and delicious *cassoeula*, the Milanese answer to the French cassoulet. This tasted so good that, every winter, my brother Marco's friends would insist on having *la cassoeula della Mamma di Marco*. And she went on making it for them until the day she died. Another speciality was *risotto alla Milanese* – a saffron risotto – which we always had on its own as a first course, rather than with meat, not even with *ossobuchi*, the traditional accompaniment, as Mamma always said that gremolada – the minced parsley, garlic and lemon zest garnish used on *ossobuchi* – was not good with saffron, instead preferring a plain *risotto in bianco*. And I agree.

MAMMA WAS MY first great influence in the kitchen, and the second was Maria, our cook. Maria came into my life when I was five and stayed until I was fifteen, the most formative years of life. It was Mamma who honed Maria's cooking skills.

Maria came from Friuli, in the north-east of Italy, as did most of the best domestic servants in Milan. Honest and hard-working, the Friulane girls were much sought after by the Milanese ladies. Up to 1960, Friuli was one of the poorest regions in the country. Agriculture, the only source of income, was in the hands of the big landowners, and so the peasants starved. Maria told me stories of how she'd go to school in winter with only a slice of polenta in her lunch box and, in summer, a slice of water melon. She and her seven siblings were always hungry and cold, with no shoes, only wooden clogs, and woolly rags around their shoulders. After leaving school, Maria had gone into service at the age of thirteen. First, she worked for a family in Udine who didn't treat her very well. For a pittance, she was expected to do all the household chores and wait on the family hand and foot. Then she moved to a family in Treviso, where she was employed as a tweeny – a junior servant – helping out in the kitchen. It was there that she learned to prepare food under the auspices of the head cook. After four or five years, she felt confident enough to take up a position as a cook herself and, at nineteen, ended up with us.

Maria was tall and strong, with curly black hair, which she wore tightly swept back into a low chignon on the nape of her neck, and black eyes as brilliant and dark as two ripe blackberries. She had the most irresistible smile, showing brilliant white teeth between generous red lips – the prototype of a beautiful Friulana, as Mamma used to say. Maria was quick and intelligent and, in spite of her limited education, she read beautifully. She loved reading to Guido and me, and I loved listening to her, curled up in her arms. But what she liked best was to teach us anti-fascist songs – or rather communist songs, which meant the same thing at the time. She made us promise never to sing them outside the house; she knew it was dangerous, but she couldn't resist her burning rebelliousness against fascism. As she polished the dining room floor with a heavy mop, up and down, up and down, at every stroke there was a new line: *'Avanti o popolo, / alla riscossa, / Bandiera rossa, / Bandiera rossa . . .'* ('Forward people, / to the revolt, / the red flag, / the red flag . . .'). Guido and I were fascinated, both by the secret pact between us and the implicit sense of danger.

In our household, there was a certain repetition in the daily menus. Monday was the day for that stalwart of northern Italian cooking, *bollito misto* – mixed boiled meats. This provided stock for the whole week: a delicate meat stock that became stronger and stronger each day. Every second day, the stock would be boiled for five minutes and then put in the *ghiacciaia* – a huge ice box, or ice cupboard (no freezers then). Blocks of ice were delivered every morning. (The refrigerator, another monumental affair, was installed some time later.)

The leftovers of the *bollito* were used on the Tuesday to make *polpette* and *polpettoni* – rissoles and meat rolls – at which Maria was the expert. The mixture was different every week and I'd help Maria to make the *polpette*, just as my grandchildren help me now. Maria was so clever at getting me interested. She'd ask me which of the ingredients on the table we should add to the minced meat. Apart from the usual eggs, parmesan and parsley, the other ingredients changed week by week and could be salame or mortadella, mozzarella or gruyère, garlic or onion and, in the autumn, a little white truffle, which transformed the humble *polpette* into a dish worthy of a king.

On Fridays – a no-meat day for us Catholics – my father liked to have his favourite fish dish, *polenta e baccalà* – polenta with salt cod. In those days, *baccalà* was considered a poor man's dish, but when it came to food – unlike clothes and suchlike – my father's tastes were very simple. Even when he went to smart restaurants he'd ask for *risotto con luganega* – pork sausage – minestrone with tripe, or polenta with *baccalà*. Papà liked a thick polenta, made with coarsely ground maize flour, and the *baccalà* had to have gallons of sauce. I hated *baccalà*; it was the only fish I couldn't swallow and my parents eventually came to terms with my adamant refusal. So I'd just be given a slab of polenta – a small yellow boat swimming in a red sea of sauce – and everybody was happy.

My gastronomic passion – inherited from Mamma – was truffles and they are still my favourite food. Often on Sundays, during the truffle season, the whole family would go to buy one or two from the small truffle market under the arcade in Piazza del Duomo. We always went to the same stall, run by a square, solid woman, with shiny brown hair neatly piled up at the top of her head in what looked like a chocolatey Danish pastry. She'd sit there, a thick rug around her legs, an emerald green crocheted shawl around her shoulders, with her small weighing scales and her 'jewels' lined up on the wooden table in front of her, just like a diamond dealer in London's Hatton Garden. My mother always maintained that the quality, and the price, of her 'diamonds' was better than that of the other dealers.

While in Piazza del Duomo, we'd go to the midday Mass in the Duomo instead of our parish church in Via Manzoni. I was allowed to carry the little parcel of truffles and I'd hold it under my nose all through Mass while looking extremely devout. Forget incense; truffle was my favourite smell. Looking back, I find it odd that I, a finicky eater, should be so passionate about these fungi with their peculiar smell of gas mixed with a touch of parmesan, garlic and armpit.

Back home, Maria would give me the soft little brush so I could gently scrub my treasure. I was not allowed to cut the truffles; she would do that herself and then give Guido and me the little bits of truffle to push inside the *polpette* mixture. 'Close the hole and pat, pat, pat,' she'd say, before flouring,

With Maria (from Friuli) and Guido.

then frying the *polpette*, and finishing them off with a little Marsala wine. Food for the gods, indeed.

When I started school, Mamma decided that she didn't need a nanny any more and she cut down her staff to a cook and a housemaid. So Maria became our nanny as well as our cook and playmate. As soon as I got back from school for lunch, I'd rush down the veranda to the kitchen, to say *Ciao* to Maria and to see what there was to eat. In the afternoon, after school, we'd have our *merenda* – afternoon tea – around the kitchen table or running up and down the veranda; in Italy, *merenda* is not a sitting-down affair, but a snack on the hop to break the afternoon.

We children always ate dinner with our parents, unless they were having a dinner party. On those occasions, we'd eat early, either in the kitchen or in the room next door. This was a large room with a Singer pedal sewing machine, a bed in a corner and a very big table on which another Maria, Maria Savoia who came twice a week to look after the linen and clothes, did the ironing. We used to tease her for having such an aristocratic name – she shared it with the wife of the heir to the throne of the oldest reigning family in Europe, the Savoias – and yet she worked for us.

Maria Savoia – we always used her forename *and* surname to avoid confusion with Maria the cook – came from the suburbs of Milan. A large, no-nonsense but warm-hearted woman, she'd busy herself lengthening hems, mending sheets and pillow cases, shortening sleeves, sewing buttons, darning silk socks, or ironing immense damask tablecloths, innumerable napkins, linen sheets and pillow cases, silk underwear, and the countless shirts of my father and of Zio Tom. I liked to sit with Maria Savoia as she sewed, and also with Mamma, an accomplished needleworker who would sit for hours embroidering small tablecloths or smocking a dress for me or a new-born baby, using precise, neat and even stitches. I still have a few of the things she made, as well as some tablecloths and linen sheets that were part of her trousseau. Things were made to last then and people looked after them.

Whenever I could, I'd help Maria – the cook – in the kitchen, mixing food or doing the *lecca-lecca* – lick-lick – of the bowl when it was emptied of the cake or biscuit mixture. Making sweets and cakes was more Mamma's realm, though. There was a cake I adored which Mamma often used as a base for other sweet concoctions, such as *zuppa inglese*, a custard-based dessert similar to English trifle, or *dolce squisito* – exquisite sweet, as we called it. The recipe for this, the Bavarese Lombarda, came from Pellegrino Artusi, who inspired generations of cooks with his book *La Scienza in Cucina e l'Arte di Mangiar Bene* (*The Science of Cooking and the Art of Eating Well*), which was first published in 1880 and is still in print today. Mamma would make the cake in a ring mould, and I'd be entranced by this golden ring with its light sponge and sugary flavour. I used to dip a slice into a hot crème anglaise, or cut it up in chunks then pour the custard over and eat it cold later.

Mamma made desserts for dinner parties, and cakes for her bridge parties or, very occasionally, for our *merenda*. Our *merenda* usually consisted of bread and perhaps salame, prosciutto, honey, jam or chocolate – although, surprisingly for a child, I never liked chocolate – and *caffè e latte*, a drink I usually hated and would throw down the sink, if no one was looking.

~

ONE *caffè e latte* I always drank with great pleasure was that made by my great-grandmother, Nonna Maria, who lived with her son, Nonno Giovanni, and his wife, Nonna Caterina (my maternal grandparents), in a large flat in Milan. Nonna Caterina had Parkinson's disease, so Nonna Maria was in charge of running the household, which she did with great competence. They lived in impoverished circumstances after Nonno Giovanni lost all his money, and most of Nonna Caterina's too, in the 1929 stock market crash. Nonna Caterina had been a rich lady, a descendant of the Prince Giovanelli of Venice who owned what was then the most important collection of paintings in Europe, only to see it gambled away by his son. Nonno Giovanni also lost most of his collection of late nineteenth-century paintings in that same crash. The two or three that he managed to keep were indeed impressive and I would love to have them now. Never mind, my ancestors seem to have been prone to losing everything – money and all.

Guido and I used to go to see *i nonni* once a week and have lunch or *merenda* there. We'd rush into the kitchen at the end of a long dark corridor to see what Nana, the cook, was preparing for us, and Nonna Maria was usually there too: two small ladies, ancient to our eyes, always dressed in black, the only distinguishing features between them being the spotless white apron wrapped around Nana's waist and the rows of pearls dangling over Nonna's bosom.

Nonna Maria made the most scrumptious lemony round biscuits, almond crescents and polenta cake, while *brasati* – braised meat dishes – were Nana's forte. One of these, which I later made with great success all my married life, was beef braised in wine flavoured with cinnamon and other spices. Nana would stand by the cooker for hours, cajoling the piece of beef with a wooden spoon in her hand, ready to add another drop of wine or a tablespoon of water, a pinch of cinnamon or another grating or two of nutmeg. That cooking was an act of love. She always served the *brasati* with polenta, another of her specialities. Polenta had been the staple food of Nana's childhood; she came from a region of Veneto where it was one of the few foods the peasants could afford. It was eaten with milk for breakfast and with boiled cabbage for lunch. Then, supper would consist of slices of grilled polenta, which were rubbed against the piece of *lardo* – pork fatback – hanging from a hook in the middle of the table. And Nana's *polenta pasticciata* – baked polenta layered with meat – which she covered with a rich, cheesy béchamel sauce, remains for me unsurpassed.

When Nana retired, she used to come and visit us in Via Gesù and always liked to busy herself at the cooker or the sink. She'd complain bitterly that our kitchen was too cold, since it led out onto the veranda, a covered veranda but with plenty of draughts for the cold air of Milan to blow through.

One day, Guido and his friend Carlino Valdettaro – who lived in the flat underneath ours – decided to warm Nana up. While she was standing at the sink they, slowly and silently, pushed a crunched-up newspaper under her long skirt and set fire to it. Thank goodness Nana's underwear was made of cotton, which was resistant to flame. Guido and Carlino were severely reprimanded and not allowed to play together for several days. Guido was also sent to bed without fruit for a week, his worst punishment, but one that I wouldn't have minded for most of the year, as I didn't like fruit except for the seasonal summer fruit, from strawberries to plums.

~

As an inveterate Friulana, our cook Maria also made excellent polenta. Actually, she made everything very well, even pasta, although she did not much care for it. Of course, she was perfectly capable of making a good *sfoglia* – pasta dough – but it wasn't part of the tradition of her region. In my home in Milan, tagliatelle were made probably once a week, and all kinds of ravioli, or tortelli, about once a month, if that, but always at Christmas when we'd have meat ravioli swimming in butter and sage. At Carnival we had the traditional *cappelletti* – hat-shaped pasta parcels – filled with all kinds of meats – then at Easter *ravioli di magro* – ravioli filled with cheese and spinach – and in the autumn the fabulous pumpkin tortelli. I was often involved in the preparation of all these pastas, especially the *cappelletti*, which Maria said I could shape so well round my little finger. A speciality of hers, though, was potato ravioli, a typical ravioli of Friuli, and she used to push a prune inside the stuffing of mashed potatoes.

Maria also made a delicious *fritto misto* – mixed fritters – not the usual *di mare* (seafood) but *di terra* in which she included different vegetables, sweetbreads, brains and slices of liver, all coated with egg and breadcrumbs and then fried. To accompany it, she made a *crema fritta* – chunks of cold crème pâtissière, again coated and fried. I liked the fried custard best, and Maria always gave me a small piece in the kitchen when she began to fry. What a feast it made: slices of aubergine and courgette, segments of fennel, florets of cauliflower, small bites of sweetbread, brains and sausages, all piled in a large dish and surrounded by squares of *crema fritta*. It's a recipe I've never attempted myself; the mere thought of it defeats even me, each ingredient needing a different cooking time, and then the essential last-minute frying. A fritto should be a *frienno e mannammo* – frying and eating – affair, as the Neapolitans say.

It was a tradition in Friuli to have *crostoli* on Giovedí Grasso, the last Thursday of Carnival. These are a kind of small lasagne fried in oil then sprinkled with showers and showers of icing sugar, and the ones Maria made were superb. The dish would arrive on the dining-room table, a mountain of hot *crostoli* to be shared by everybody, the last few fought over by Guido and me. I'd sink my teeth into those bubbles of air, coated with a sugar cloud, and my mouth would be filled with the lemony scent of an Amalfi grove or with the deep perfume of an Arabian night.

But the best staple dishes in Maria's large repertoire were the gnocchi: gnocchi of ricotta, of polenta, of semolina, of choux pastry, of spinach and, of course, potatoes. The last were definitely my favourite, though I still don't know if this was because I enjoyed making them as much as eating them. Maria would let me cut the long sausages into small bits and then flip each gnocco down the prongs of a fork. Flip, flip, flip and off they flew landing at random on the table covered with white teacloths. 'You are better than me,' she used to say, encouraging me, as I do now with my grandchildren who adore potato gnocchi just as much as I do.

After the war, Maria used to visit Mamma regularly, and she always made a point of coming when I was there, too. She still made gnocchi for us, but for me, at that time, the pleasure was not so much the gnocchi as the sight of Maria's cheerful, radiant face, such an intrinsic part of my childhood.

RECIPES

Cassoeula
Pork and Cabbage Stew

SERVES 6–8

---

2 pig's trotters, split lengthwise into quarters and then each quarter
into half
250g pork rind
2 tbsp olive oil
25g unsalted butter
2 large onions, chopped
750g spare ribs,
500g luganega, or other pure pork coarse grained sausage,
cut into 5cm pieces
2 large carrots, chopped
2 celery sticks, chopped
1.5kg savoy cabbage, cut into 2cm strips
salt and pepper

Cover the trotters and the pork rind with 1.5 litres of water, bring to the boil and cook for 45 minutes. Lift out the trotters and the rind and cut the rind into 4cm squares. Set aside. Leave the stock to cool.

When cold, put the stock in the fridge and leave until the fat has solidified at the top. Remove the fat and discard.

Put the oil, butter and onion in a very heavy, large stockpot (earthenware is best) and sauté gently, stirring constantly, until the onion is soft, but not brown. Add the trotters and the rind, sauté for 1 minute, still stirring, and then add the spare ribs. Fry for 10 minutes, then add the luganega and fry for a further 5 minutes, stirring all the while. Lastly, add the carrot and celery, then cover with the de-fatted trotters liquid, season with salt and pepper and place the lid on the pot. Cook very gently for at least 3 hours, adding a little water whenever the stew becomes too dry.

Blanch the cabbage. Drain thoroughly and add to the pot. Mix well and cook for a further 30 minutes.

~

Crema Fritta
Fried Custard

SERVES 4

For the crème pâtissière
3 organic egg yolks
100g icing sugar, sifted
75g Italian 00 flour
500ml full fat milk
Strip of peel from an organic lemon
2–3 drops pure vanilla extract
15g unsalted butter

For the coating
100–150g dried white breadcrumbs
1 organic egg, beaten
oil for frying
icing sugar for sprinkling

First make the crème patissière or *crema pasticcera*. Put the egg yolks and the sugar in a heavy saucepan, beat well with a wooden spoon and then slowly add the flour, while beating the whole time. Take the pan off the heat.

In a small pan, heat the milk with the strip of lemon peel and the vanilla extract until just beginning to boil. Pour the milk onto the egg mixture while beating hard. When all the milk has been incorporated, put the heavy saucepan back on the heat and bring to the boil. Simmer, stirring the whole time, for 5 minutes so that the taste of the uncooked flour has gone. The custard will gradually become quite thick. Remove from the heat, fish out the lemon peel, add the butter and mix well.

When it is smooth and velvety, pour the crema on a flat surface – a baking tray is ideal – and level it out with a wet spatula so that it is about 3cm thick. Allow to cool and then cut it into squares or diamonds. Coat each piece with breadcrumbs then coat it with the beaten egg and, finally, again with breadcrumbs, patting these firmly into the *crema*.

Pour some vegetable oil to come about 2cm up the side of a frying pan and heat. When very hot but not yet smoking, carefully slide in the *crema* pieces and fry until a deep golden crust has formed – about 3 minutes – and then turn them over and fry the other side until golden. Remove with a slotted spoon and put on kitchen paper. Sprinkle with icing sugar before you serve. Like any other fritters, *crema fritta* is better hot.

~

Gnocchi di Patate
Potato Gnocchi

This recipe is for the classic gnocchi made without eggs, which are the best gnocchi, although a little more difficult to prepare. My favourite dressing for these gnocchi is just good butter melted until it takes a hazelnut colour, flavoured with 5 or 6 fresh sage leaves, torn in 2 or 3 pieces and 1 crushed clove of garlic. Pesto is another good sauce for *gnocchi di patate*, as is a simple tomato sauce

SERVES 4

1kg waxy potatoes
1 tsp salt
170–200g Italian 00 flour

Boil the potatoes in their skins. When the point of a small knife can easily be pushed through to the middle, the potatoes are ready.

Drain the potatoes and, as soon as you can handle them, peel and then purée them through the smaller disc of a food mill, or through a potato ricer, straight onto your work surface.

Spread the purée around to cool it, then add the salt and some of the flour. Do not add all the flour at once. Gradually add a little more flour and stop as soon as you can knead the mixture into a dough, which should be soft, smooth and still slightly sticky.

Shape the dough into sausages about 2.5cm in diameter, and cut the sausages into 2cm chunks.

Now you have to put the grooves into the gnocchi, a more complicated operation. The grooves, by the way, are there for a reason, not just for beauty – they thin out the middle of the gnocchi, so that they will cook more evenly and, when cooked, will trap more sauce. So, keeping your hands, the fork and any surface lightly floured, flip each dumpling against the prongs of the fork, without dragging it, letting it drop on to a clean linen towel. Some cooks flip the dumpling towards the handle; others, like me, go from the handle to the point of the prongs. You will find your favourite way.

When all the gnocchi are grooved, bring a large saucepan of salted water to the boil.

Cook the gnocchi in 3 or 4 batches, not all at once. The gnocchi will first sink to the bottom of the pan, when you must give them a very gentle stir, and then very shortly afterwards they will float up to the surface. Count to 10 and then retrieve them with a slotted spoon. Pat them dry quickly with a piece of kitchen paper and transfer them to a heated dish. Dress each batch with a little of your chosen sauce. When all the gnocchi are cooked, pour the remaining sauce over them and serve at once.

CHAPTER 4

NICE

My first bouillabaisse

I NEVER ENJOYED THE best of health as a child, being thin and frail, with shadows under my eyes and pale cheeks which Mamma used to pinch to give them colour. Any cold, flu, cough, or infectious disease lurking around seemed to find a welcoming host in my little body.

When I was six, I caught diphtheria from my cousins Maria Teresa and Sandro and, apparently, I would have died were it not for the newly-discovered single vaccination. I was confined to two rooms: my parents' and my own bedroom. My mother and father, wearing white gowns, were the only people allowed in, and I was virtually bedridden the whole time – that was the therapy. I spent many long days playing cards with, or being read to by, Mamma or Papà. My favourite book was *The Adventures of Pinocchio*. We had the beautiful first edition, a large volume bound in blue leather with a picture of the puppet on its frontispiece. That volume of Pinocchio was lost when the house in Via Sant'Andrea was destroyed by bombs in August 1943, along with the far more valuable first edition of Dante's *Divina Commedia*, illustrated by Gustave Doré, and the first edition of *Le Memorie* by

Giacomo Casanova. An odd trio! Mamma mourned their loss very deeply, all her life, books being her greatest interest.

I remember the first day I was allowed out of those two rooms. I was peeping through the crack of the door between my parents' bedroom and the dining room, where the family was having lunch, when I saw on the floor one of the large tortoiseshell hairpins my mother used in her chignon. I asked if I could retrieve it, and '*Sí tirala su tu*' – 'Yes, you pick it up' – came the reply. I ran over that shiny parquet floor which Guido and I loved to slide along, picked up the hairpin and that was the end of my incarceration.

WHEN I got better, in the winter of 1931, Mamma took me to San Remo, on the Italian Riviera. She booked a room at one of the grand hotels on the promenade and off we went, leaving Guido behind with my father who, I realise now, must have been deeply involved with his American mistress at the time. Perhaps Mamma used me as an excuse to get out of the way?

I remember the mimosa tree, just outside our hotel bedroom, in full flower in February. Coming from foggy cold Milan, it seemed like a miracle, and I am sure my love for mimosa stems from those days, when every morning I'd rush onto our balcony and look at and smell those gorgeous yellow flowers dancing in the breeze at the end of their feathery green fronds.

In those days, San Remo was still an elegant resort. Queen Victoria used to visit nearby Bordighera, and in the nineteenth century both Bordighera and San Remo became *the* places to go, before the Côte d'Azur took over later that century. Quite a few English aristocrats used to spend the winter in one of the two towns; some even chose to live there, and many died there, as can be seen from the tombstones in the enchanting English cemetery. One of the first settlers was Sir Thomas Hanbury who, in 1867, bought the beautiful promontory of La Mortola, between Ventimiglia and Menton, where he created a large botanical garden with typical Mediterranean flora, as well as plants from hotter, dry areas such as Mexico, Australia and Arizona. My mother took me there one afternoon. She was extremely knowledgeable about plants and as we walked around she told me their names; they were all vigorous, luscious plants covered in thick green leaves at the time of year when, in Lombardy, I was used to seeing just bare sticks.

We had two other expeditions that left a lasting impression on me. The first was a visit to the Pallanca Exotic Garden in Bordighera, created by the Pallancas and an Englishman, Ludovico Winter. As we strolled round the steep, terraced garden I was mesmerised by the huge fleshy agaves and the gigantic cacti, and I remember standing in front of the famous, 300-year-old Copiapoa, the oldest tropical plant in any European garden. Mamma bought me a little cactus – a spiny, round blob with a small yellow flower on top – to add to my collection of tiny plants that I kept on one of the dining-room windowsills in Via Gesù. It was the window that caught more sun than any other, and it had a large radiator underneath it.

The second expedition was to Nice. Off we went on the train from San Remo. Two stops later, we crossed the border into France, showed passports and chugged and puffed into Nice. It was my first visit to France, although I had already started French lessons, after a fashion. My teacher was Zia

Zina – or Tante Zina, as she insisted on being called – who had lived in France for many years. My father had introduced a rule in our household that we must all speak French at mealtimes; after all, it was the language of the aristocracy. So I, normally a great talker, would sit at the table in silence, apart from the few essential phrases, such as '*Passe moi cela, s'il te plait*' and '*Merci beaucoup*'. However, the outcome is that I have always been able to speak and understand elementary French.

What I remember best about Nice is the food market in the Cours Saleya, in that glorious square surrounded by colourful old houses. Mamma and I happily browsed the market stalls with their array of fish, vegetables, cheeses, fruits – no tourist junk then. We also visited the flower market, with all its carnations for which the French Riviera was especially famous.

As we walked around, my first remark, in my first foreign country, was, 'But Mamma, here even the street sweepers speak French.' To me, French was the language of the upper class. Many times I had heard my father say that you must speak French to be able to mix with the right people. In Nice I was thrown into confusion: how could two men shovelling up the muck from around the market stalls speak the language of the aristocracy?

Afterwards, Mamma and I had lunch at one of those typical French provincial restaurants with white *brise-bise* curtains that prevented passers-by from looking inside. I was surprised to find that the tablecloths were paper and, no matter how much my mother tried to explain that lots of *trattorie* have paper tablecloths and napkins, I found it hard to accept. We sat down and Mamma ordered a bouillabaisse, the traditional fish soup of the region, for herself and for me. It was a dish I had never tasted before, but I'd always liked fish, so I enjoyed my bouillabaisse and ate it all up. I thought the fish soup was better than any I had eaten previously; but, I am sure it was because I was eating in a restaurant, a great treat then.

When I look back, I find that I had very odd tastes for the small eater that I was. My favourite foods, then as now, included truffles, brains and sweetbreads, *costolette*, artichokes and all sorts of fish, including squid, cuttlefish, octopus, vongole and mussels, but especially bouillabaisse – which I now have with the traditional rouille accompaniment, unlike that day in Nice, when Mamma judged rightly that a spicy garlic mayonnaise was not the kind of sauce a six-year-old would be particularly keen to lap up.

Those were the days when children had to eat everything that was put on their plate, at least that was the draconian rule in my family. (The only advantage of this is that, later on, I have been able to eat most things, with some notable exceptions, these being peanut butter – I only buy it now to put in my grandchildren's sandwiches – and porridge.)

~

I HAD TO WAIT twenty years to have a bouillabaisse that I liked as much as that one in Nice. In fact, it was a Ligurian *zuppa di pesce*, similar to a bouillabaiase but without the rouille. It was in 1951, in a trattoria near Recco. Oliver and I had not been married long and we'd gone to Recco for the weekend with my cousin Sandro, his wife Joan, and some other friends. Sandro and Joan gave Oliver and me a lift from Milan in their spanking new blue Fiat Topolino, which was a bit of a squeeze for the four of us. It was one of the most enjoyable weekends of my early married life. I was in my beloved Liguria, with old friends, doing things I'd always loved – mainly swimming and eating.

We had chosen Recco because we planned to go swimming in nearby San Fruttuoso, on the Portofino promontory, and then on to Camogli for dinner. For once, it was Oliver, instead of me, who was the odd one out among this crowd of jolly friends, and what struck him most was that, immediately after finishing lunch, at about four o'clock, we were earnestly discussing where to go, and what to eat, for dinner.

Camogli was where we had the memorable *zuppa di pesce*, in a trattoria down by the port. Frankly, I don't remember if the *zuppa di pesce* was really delicious in its own right, because it was enhanced by other delicious 'flavourings' such as the noise of the waves breaking only a few metres away, the silhouette of the church of Camogli against the darkness of the sky, the flowing of the wine and the company around the table. Whatever it was, it is one of my happiest memories. Dinner, the next night, was at Manuelina's, in Recco itself. It started with the famous *focaccia di Recco*, followed by *corzetti* – a kind of home-made pasta – with pesto, and a huge *fritto misto di pesce*. We finally got to bed at three or four in the morning, when the dark, dark sea was dotted with the small lights of the fishing boats, which would return to port in the morning, after the night's fishing. And the women of Recco would rush down to the port to buy the *rascasse* – scorpion fish – red mullet, monk-fish, sea bream and cuttlefish to make the *zuppa* once again.

RECIPE

Zuppa di Pesce
Fish Soup

This is my *zuppa di pesce*, which is really a Ligurian *ciuppin*, not a classic bouillabaisse, although the two are very similar.

SERVES 8

1kg assorted fish, such as hake, dogfish, whiting, John Dory, red mullet, rascasse and garnard, heads and tails removed
1 large onion, chopped
1 celery stick, chopped
1 carrot, chopped
1 garlic clove, chopped, plus a few peeled garlic cloves
120ml extra virgin olive oil
150ml dry white wine
400g tin plum tomatoes (with their juice), chopped
salt and freshly ground black pepper
8 thick slices good bread
3 tbsp chopped fresh parsley

Clean, if necessary, and wash the fish. Cut into thick chunks.

In a large saucepan, fry all the vegetables and the chopped garlic gently in 90ml of the oil for 10 minutes, stirring frequently. Add the fish, mix thoroughly and fry gently for 5 minutes, turning it over frequently. Pour the wine over and boil rapidly to reduce by half.

Pour over 2 litres of boiling water and add the tomatoes

(with juice) and seasoning. Return the soup to the boil and simmer for 20 minutes. Taste and check the seasoning.

Toast the bread for 10 minutes in a hot oven (200°C/gas mark 6). Rub with the peeled garlic cloves split in half and then place a slice of bread in individual soup bowls. Ladle the soup over the bread. Drizzle with the remaining oil, sprinkle the parsley over and serve.

CHAPTER 5

STRESA

Chicken consommé

As a child, my most precious toys were my soft dogs – at one stage, I counted twenty-six – plus one beautiful grey cat with piercing green eyes, and a blue ribbon around his neck. They lived, artistically lined up, on my bed. Each night before I fell asleep I chose a different one to snuggle up to. The dolls I was given, though, were largely ignored, save for two functions: first to strip them immediately of all their clothes and then plunk them in a basin full of water before proceeding to wash and cut their long, silky hair. Mamma became very worried, she told me later, not so much for the constant ruination of those beautiful dolls, as at the prospect of my ending up working in a hairdresser's salon.

I would have given up all those soft animals for one real, live dog. I begged and begged, but my father always refused to let me have one, saying 'It is cruel to keep a dog in a flat.' And now I can see he was absolutely right.

But once a year, for a whole month, I had not one, but two dogs to play with; they belonged to Mamma's friend, Olga de Fernex, with whom we spent the whole month of September in her villa at Stresa, on Lake Maggiore – one of the playgrounds of the rich Milanese and the equally rich tourists.

The de Fernex's villa was perched high above the town, overlooking the lake and its three jewels – the islands of Isola Borromeo, Isola dei Pescatori and Isola Madre. The villa was set in its own large parkland, with its banks of blue hydrangeas, always in full bloom when we were there. (If I still like that kind of overblown, oversized flower, it's only because they remind me of those distant holidays in the early 1930s.)

Not that I had a particularly exciting time there, as I had to make my own amusement. My brother Guido had his friends Nini and Gigi de Fernex, with whom he played tennis and croquet and bicycled around the garden. I had nobody except for two Pekinese dogs. Mamma was a typical mother of the Italian bourgeoisie; she loved us, yes, she saw that we were well fed and smartly clothed, but she certainly never thought it her duty to organise our entertainment. The villa was large, with plenty of toys and games; the garden even larger, offering all the distractions we could possibly want, so Mamma could allow herself to spend the day chatting and gossiping with Zia Olga, while making some elaborate piece of embroidery, or reading a book. She did, however, absolve this maternal oversight by reading me a story every day or playing a game of cards with me once a day.

(As I write this, it occurs to me that I was equally neglectful, if differently, of my children. Admittedly I worked, instead of chatting and embroidering, but generally they were left to entertain themselves; the difference being that in London, where we lived, my children were always surrounded by friends to play with after they returned from our long walks in Richmond Park.)

So there I was in that grand villa with nobody to play with save my two four-legged companions, Cio-Cio and Liù. I used to put them in my doll's pram and wheel them around, singing 'Non piangere Liù', the aria from *Turandot* that I'd heard my father sing. I'd dress them up, brush them and tie ribbons on their heads or tails. They were extremely good-natured and never complained, except once when Cio-Cio bit me on the nose.

Each morning, Zia Olga, Mamma and I would go down to the town in the de Fernex's Lancia – a splendid pale grey cabriolet – with Egidio, the chauffeur, in full grey uniform at the wheel, the two ladies sitting at the back and me and the dogs on the tip-up seats facing backwards. We'd do our shopping, then sit at one of the cafes and have an ice cream. Same routine, same ice cream but a different cafe every day, with me leading one of the pekes, usually Liù, because she was smaller and more obedient. Egidio would call at the shops later to collect our purchases, and then back we'd go up the hill, ready for lunch, where we'd all sit down at a large rectangular table for lunch, with Zia Olga presiding over the meal.

Zia Olga was not our real aunt, but any older lady who was a friend of the family was called zia as a mark of respect, just as often used to happen in Britain. A tall, blonde, rather grand lady, though extremely kind and gentle, she presented a Junoesque figure, her large, lace-covered bosom resembling a table draped with an elaborate tablecloth, and she dressed mainly in white in summer and grey or brown in winter. She always gave us the most marvellous Christmas presents. When I was young, children were never overloaded with presents, so we never became blasé and were always appreciative. My favourite was a miniature *drogheria* – grocery shop – consisting of three panels of white-painted wood and a counter at the front, on top of which sat a mini cash desk and a weighing machine with tiny, bright-brass weights. The *drogheria* was big enough to walk in and I used to stand behind the counter and help my pretend customers – usually Guido or one of my friends – to sugar, coffee, tea, rice, flour, or whatever, from the drawers of the counter which I topped up regularly from the inexhaustible supplies in the kitchen. There was a row of small jars for spices, another of the bigger jars of sweets, and on the counter I'd keep a small jar of cut-up liquorice sticks. It was indeed a miniature replica of any grocery shop of that period. I had such fun playing with it, sometimes all by myself, being the customer and the seller in turn. (Sadly, the grocery shop went up in flames when our flat in Via Sant'Andrea was bombed during the war. A pity, as I am sure one of my darling granddaughters would have loved it.)

Zia Olga often visited us in Milan, the strong attraction being our Zio Tom, her lover. She'd make her majestic entrance into the flat, followed by the faithful Egidio loaded with flowers and vegetables from her house in Olgiate, a village north of Milan, where the de Fernex lived during the winter. My greatest joy was in June, when Zia Olga brought us kilos and kilos of soft summer fruits that – strawberries apart – were hard to find in the 1930s in Milan. The strawberries were small and juicy – so different from the bloated, hard red blobs you see today – and we'd eat them with lemon and sugar, as we did the raspberries. The gooseberries were large and golden, like small Chinese lanterns. Mamma would sometimes put them in a pot with a glug of white wine and a few tablespoons of sugar; and when they went pop, they were ready. Then there were the red and white currants, which were simmered for a few minutes with plenty of sugar and a squeeze of lemon juice.

Zia Olga also brought beans – all kinds of French beans, as well as fresh borlotti to make minestrone. I loved the long, thin beans of Sant'Anna, and I liked the fact we shared the same name. And, when they were in season, she'd always arrive with bunches of courgette flowers, which I adored dipped in light batter then quickly fried plain, without any mozzarella, anchovy or other filling, just as Maria used to cook them. In the autumn, Zia Olga would turn up with braces of pheasants or partridges, a hare or a joint of a wild boar, all shot by her husband Zio Jean and his friends on the de Fernex estate in the Alps. Mamma would cook the hare *in salmi* – in a rich wine sauce – but even better was the wild boar which she prepared *alla Romana* – Roman style – as she called it, which involved marinating it for forty-eight hours in red wine and lots of spices. These were all dishes that Mamma liked to make herself – never Maria – taking great pleasure in their often lengthy preparation.

The de Fernex estate in Olgiate, where we often went on Sundays, was enormous, with a large vegetable garden, orchard, park and a tennis court where I played whenever I could find a willing partner. I'd spend hours gazing at the colourful, stripy carp and the big goldfish slowly swimming around the large pond in the grounds. Every year at Carnival, the de Fernex threw a party for the children. In customary style, we'd dress up in Harlequin costumes, such as

Guido and I dressed as Pierrot and Pierrette for a Carnival party
c. 1929.

Arlecchino, Colombina, Pulcinella, Pierrot, or one of the pirates from the popular Salgari books, which all the boys adored. The *merende* for these occasions were memorable, with mountains of meringues, profiteroles, *cannoncini* and an assortment of other *paste* – sweet pastries – oozing velvety-yellow custard, dark brown chocolate or fluffy white cream.

The de Fernex table was renowned for being rich and good. Zia Olga and Zio Jean entertained a lot, both at Stresa and at Olgiate. Mamma, a discerning food critic, always came back from their parties describing one or more of the dishes she'd had with great relish. I still remember the daily spread of antipasti at the Stresa lunches: the large platter of *affettato* – sliced meat – consisting of prosciutto, *cotto* and *crudo*, *coppa*, mortadella, two or three different salami, embellished with curls of butter; the platter of sliced melon; flaked tuna with beans; Russian salad; stuffed hard-boiled eggs; tortes of whatever vegetables were in season at the time; and the long green *sigarette* peppers. The latter, like most of the vegetables on the table, came from the vegetable garden and Giovanni, the gardener, brought them in every morning. The peppers were harvested very young and small so that they could easily be eaten in one mouthful. I didn't much care for peppers myself, but I loved watching the grown-ups eating these green 'cigarettes'. They'd cut away the top end, fill the pepper with olive oil, sprinkle a little salt over it, and in they went in one large mouthful. I regret that I never tried them.

In the evenings at Stresa, we children ate by ourselves, tucking into dishes such as pasta, chicken and *costolette*, which I always enjoyed, along with the company of the boys. After supper, I often went into the dining room to peep at the grown-ups' table. There, on the right of every place setting, was a cup and saucer, ready to be filled with the consommé that was drunk during the first course – a habit my mother often followed at her own dinner parties. I often heard Mamma say that the excellent consommé made by Giuseppe, the de Fernex chef, was better than hers or anybody else's. How did he make it? One year, one of our housemaids revealed the secret to my mother. 'Signora,' she said, 'he scrapes all the chicken bones from the plates when they are brought back from the table to the kitchen, puts them in a saucepan with all the usual flavourings and a little white wine and boils the whole thing up for some time. Then he strains the broth clear with egg shells and finishes it off with a generous glug of dry Marsala. And he charges Signora de Fernex for a boiler chicken for the stock.'

Years later, Mamma told me how disgusted she'd been on hearing this revelation. As I've said, she was a pernickety woman, a characteristic she picked up from her mother and one that I, in turn, have inherited to some degree. I remember her once dragging me into the chemist's in Milan and asking for some cotton wool and disinfectant, because a beggar to whom she'd given a little money had dared to stroke my cheek to show his gratitude. So the thought that, at Stresa, she was drinking a liquid obtained from food which other people had gnawed didn't please her at all. But I never did find out how she managed after that to handle the nightly drinking of the consommé.

When my maternal grandmother, a Venetian aristocrat, got married, she'd moved from Venice to Naples, where my grandfather was stationed in the Navy. They were living in a flat in one of the *palazzi* in Via Toledo, in the old part of Naples. The *palazzi* were surrounded by the *bassi* – slums. Horrified by the dirt and misery surrounding her, she wanted none of that inside her house: parquet floors had to be scrubbed and polished once a week, all outside windows and ledges were subjected to a scrupulous daily washing; fruit and vegetables to be eaten raw had to be gently washed with Marseille soap, rinsed under running water and dried. This continued later when she was in Milan, although there were certainly no *bassi* there. I remember quite well this ritual being performed on the tomatoes by Nana, her cook, in her kitchen in Milan. She did not want them peeled when eaten raw because she knew that most of the vitamins were in the skin. Mamma, in comparison, was far 'dirtier' – our parquet floors were not scrubbed – but her squeamishness vis-à-vis other people was noticeable nevertheless.

RECIPES

Costolette alla Milanese
Fried Veal Chops Milanese Style

This is by far the best way to prepare veal chops. It is not easy, but if you buy the right meat, and follow the method carefully, you will be amply rewarded by the result.

First you need a good and reliable butcher. When you buy veal chops for this dish, check that the meat is very pale pink

and the fat milky white. Ask the butcher to pound the chops
to a thickness of 1cm and to knock off the corner where the
rib joins the backbone, and to trim off the tail end of the chop.
(You can use these trimmings for stock or a *ragù*.)

I prefer to fry my costolette (and any other breaded food
which I fry in butter), by putting them in a cold pan together
with the butter, and then heating the pan. In this way the
butter is less likely to become too dark, and the chops cook
through while remaining golden on the outside without any
speckles of burnt.

SERVES 4

2 free-range eggs
sea salt
about 150g dried white breadcrumbs
4 veal rib chops
1 tbsp olive oil
60g unsalted butter

Beat the eggs lightly in a soup plate with a little salt
Spread out the breadcrumbs in a dish.
Dip the chops in the egg, coating both sides, then let the
excess egg fall back into the plate.
Then coat the chops with the crumbs, pressing them into
the meat with your hands.
Choose a large, heavy frying pan into which the chops will
fit easily in a single layer. Grease the bottom of the pan with
the oil and then put little knobs of butter here and there.
Only use about three-quarters of the butter. Lay the chops in

the buttered pan and only then put the pan on a low to moderate heat. Move the chops around all the time while they are cooking to prevent them sticking. Cook for about 4 minutes on one side, then turn them over and fry the other side. Add the rest of the butter in small pieces, placing them here and there between the chops. Continue cooking gently and moving the chops around for a further 3 minutes. The timing depends on the thickness of the chop. The meat should be cooked through to the bone, but still moist and succulent.

When done, transfer the chops to a heated dish, pour the sizzling butter over and serve at once.

~

Polpettone di Bietole
Swiss Chard Torte

SERVES 4–5

300g potatoes
7 tbsp extra virgin olive oil
1kg Swiss chard
1 small onion, very finely chopped
1 garlic clove, very finely chopped
½ tbsp chopped fresh tarragon
2 tbsp chopped fresh parsley
2 eggs, plus 1 egg yolk
6 tbsp freshly grated parmesan
3–4 anchovy fillets, chopped

Cook the potatoes in their skins in boiling salted water until soft.

Drain the potatoes and peel them, then purée into a large bowl through the small hole disc of a food mill or through a potato ricer. Dress the purée with 2 tablespoons of the oil.

Remove the green leaf part from the white stalks of the Swiss chard. (Reserve the stalks, to serve blanched and with a cheesey béchamel, on another occasion.) Wash the green leaves and put them in a pot with only the water that clings to them and 1 teaspoon of salt. Cook over a lively heat until tender. Drain and, when cool enough, squeeze out all the moisture with your hands. Chop the leaves coarsely.

Sweat the onion in 3 tablespoons of the oil for 7 minutes or so. Stir in the garlic, tarragon and parsley and sauté for 5 minutes, then mix in the Swiss chard and sauté for 5–7 minutes, turning it frequently. Transfer the contents of the pan to the bowl containing the potatoes.

Preheat the oven to 190°C/gas mark 5.

Add the eggs and egg yolk, parmesan cheese and black pepper to the vegetable mixture and mix very thoroughly. Add the chopped anchovy fillets and mix very thoroughly – hands are best. Taste and check the seasoning.

Brush an 18cm (7in) spring-clip tin with some of the remaining oil. Line it with greaseproof paper and brush with a little more oil. Sprinkle in the dried breadcrumbs and then shake out the excess crumbs.

Spoon the Swiss chard mixture into the prepared tin and

dribble the remaining oil over the top. Bake in the oven for 40–50 minutes, until set.

Allow to cool a little in the tin, then turn out and invert the torte onto a round dish. Serve warm or at room temperature.

CHAPTER 6

THE FASCIST YEARS

Mussolini and mussels

THE WHOLE OF my education was immersed in fascist culture from the first day of school, in 1931, until I finished in 1944. Mussolini had been elected prime minister in 1922, after his triumphant March on Rome, and in 1925 – the year I was born – he proclaimed himself Duce, a leader whom only the King could remove (as indeed the King did in 1943, but far too late, alas).

Our school day started with the morning assembly, when we sang the fascist anthem and other fascist songs. Every class had three images above the teacher's desk: a crucifix in the middle; a photograph of King Vittorio Emanuele III on the left; and a photo of Mussolini on the right. We had to greet all the teachers with the fascist salute and were supposed to attend the youth parades each Saturday afternoon. Actually, I didn't often go to these boring parades, because Mamma displayed her anti-fascist sentiments in this small act of revolt: she managed to convince our doctor to write a certificate saying that I was not strong enough to take part. Guido, however, looked, and indeed was, far too strong and fit to be excused. So I stayed at home, which, to be honest, I didn't mind. I hated the uniform I had to wear as a Piccola Italiana: black pleated skirt, black cloak, white blouse with a sticker of the Duce's face at the neck and another fascist sticker on the left bosom, *proprio sul cuore* – right on the heart – as our PE instructor used to point out; and then, horror of horrors, a sort of black stocking on the head. Dressed like that, we had to parade either in the schoolyard or, more often, in the stadium in town, doing boring PE exercises and singing patriotic songs about the glories of ancient Rome and the eventual end of *perfida Albione* – perfidious Albion – defeated by the sword of the righteous fascism.

We were taught not to use words of foreign extraction but the equivalents which had been created: *bidetto* instead of bidet, *gioco del ponte* for bridge (the card game), *palla a corda* for tennis, *palla ovale* for rugby, amongst others. (I wonder what Mussolini would have done with today's computer jargon.) Most importantly, we should never use *Lei*, the polite form of address for 'you', but the *Italianissimo Voi*. Furthermore, we were not to shake hands when we met in public, but to greet each other with the fascist salute.

~

FOR THE Christmas of 1936, the year before Marco was born, my father, who by then was happily reunited with Mamma after his affair, decided to take the family to Rome. He booked two rooms at the Hotel Principe di Savoia in Via Ludovisi, just off the elegant Via Veneto and close to the Villa Borghese, which was handy for walks. I was eleven and Guido was thirteen. It was a grand hotel in a smart street, with a doorman whom I thought very handsome in his green uniform.

My excitement in anticipation of seeing the Eternal City –
urbs Orbis – was at fever pitch. We had been relentlessly
indoctrinated at school that Rome was the centre of the
universe, the most beautiful city in the world and the most
powerful. In May that year, the war in Ethiopia had ended
triumphantly and Italy could proudly claim its Empire, consisting, admittedly, of only four African colonies, with Albania
joining later when it was conquered in 1938. Mussolini was
victorious, in spite of the sanctions that had been imposed on
Italy by Britain and France when the Italian Army invaded
Ethiopia in October 1935.

When I recently re-read a transcript of the speech delivered
by Mussolini to his worshipping subjects from the balcony of
Palazzo Venezia, announcing the Ethiopian invasion, I was
staggered to think how the Italians – intelligent, political and
shrewd people – could be led to believe all the bombastic
rhetoric that Mussolini proclaimed. The Italians had all rallied
round their Duce, ready to make the sacrifices they were
asked for. First came the demand to give to the glorious Patria
– Fatherland – all their copper pots and pans. My mother very
regretfully obeyed and the greater part of our copper *batterie
de cuisine* went for the glory of Italy: the splendid *paiolo* (the
polenta pot), the large pan for the *farinata* (chickpea focaccia),
and the pot for the risotto which Guido had often used as a
helmet – all beautiful old objects that had been in the Del
Conte family for decades.

Then there was the harder offering of gold. In a very well-
staged ceremony in Rome, the Queen walked up the steps of
the monument to King Vittorio Emanuele II – the so-called
'wedding cake' – took her wedding ring off her finger and

dropped it into a big barrel. Most women, and men, followed suit. Mamma stubbornly kept her ring, but my father gave his, together with all the other bits of gold he managed to convince Mamma to let go. At the time, Papà still believed in the Duce, who had brought prosperity and peace to a nation torn by the strikes and protests that followed the First World War. He was a dutiful party member, just as everybody who wanted to work had to be. Otherwise, he would have been struck off the register of stockbrokers, just as one of my uncles, Zio Carlo, had been from the register of engineers for not joining the party.

Zio Carlo was indeed one of the most principled people I have ever known. Later in life, I understood just how much the stance he'd taken had cost, not only to him, but also to his wife and his daughters, Mariella and Giovanna: he became unemployed and unemployable, and by the end of the war, his money was running out. His wife, Zia Renata, used to protest that 'high principles and rectitude don't fill your tummy'.

~

DURING THAT Christmas in Rome, in 1936, flags were flapping and people in fascist uniforms were everywhere. Mamma remarked sarcastically that 'Il Duce has managed to put a fascist uniform even on this beautiful city.' But Guido and I were ecstatic at last to be in the city whose glories we had sung every day at school. We ran around the Forum, visited Nero's Domus Aurea, walked in the Giardini del Pincio, went to the Vatican Museums and the Borghese Gallery, and many other museums that my mother was particularly keen for us to visit. She took the view that children must be trained early in order to appreciate art, and she certainly trained us.

We went to the Christmas Mass in Saint Peter's and, on New Year's Eve, we were out on the streets celebrating with the Romans, while trying to avoid being hit by objects falling from the sky. On New Year's Eve, it was a tradition in Rome for people to throw all their unwanted chattels – from old shoes to broken plates and small chairs – out of the window, a custom, I'm told, that has almost died out now.

I loved Rome, as I still do, passionately. I adored the expansive Romans and enjoyed eating out every day. As children we were rarely taken to restaurants in Milan. But in Rome, for two blissful weeks we went to a different restaurant for lunch every day and could choose to eat what we liked. In the evenings, we dined at the hotel. The large dining room had long, white tulle curtains to shelter the diners from the curious gaze of the passers-by. Here and there, next to the pillars, were enormous plants as tall as the pillars themselves. We had a round table in a corner and, soon after we sat down, the waiter would wheel the antipasto trolley to our table. This, and the sweet trolley at the end of the meal, offered everything I could possibly want to eat. I decided that I would try two or three new dishes each day so that towards the end of our stay I could hopefully go back to my favourites. But it wasn't easy to choose, because every day I couldn't resist at least one spoonful of the delicious Russian salad and a small portion of the heavenly chicken pâté dotted with a few shreds of truffle, and enveloped in a delicate, trembling layer of golden jelly. That didn't leave much room for the other options: sardines in a sweet and sour sauce; transparent slices of prosciutto and chunkier slices of *cacciatori* (my favourite salame); hard-boiled eggs lying in a pool of speckled mayonnaise; mussels stuffed with anchovy fillets, bread-crumbs and parsley; or the shrimps or lobster, both served with mayonnaise of which I was inordinately fond.

~

MY GODMOTHER, Zia Ester, had taught me how to make mayonnaise at an early age. I liked it with lemon, rather than vinegar, and not too solid. Zia Ester would sit at the kitchen table with me, a bowl in front of us and two eggs. I'd carefully break the two eggs, let the whites slide into another bowl and then start to beat the yolks with a small wooden spoon while she slowly poured the oil into the eggs. 'Adagio, adagio, and then you beat *svelto svelto*, always in the same direction, clockwise, and never stop not even if you want to do *pipí*,' she'd say. The mixture would get thicker and thicker and, when it was so thick that it was hard to mix, Zia Ester added a little lemon juice to soften it, and I had to keep beating and beating until she, the ultimate judge, decided it was time to add the salt and one tablespoon of iced water. And then the mayonnaise was ready and I could dip my finger in and lick it.

We often stayed with Zia Ester at her villa on Lake Como. Zia Ester was very amusing and slightly dotty. She had very strong opinions, not only on mayonnaise, but also on history. Her hero was Napoleon and she had embroidered quite a few cushions, dedicated to him, with the big N in the middle, and the dates of his birth, death, and the battles of Nile, Austerlitz and Borodino – but not Waterloo, of course. The cushions were dotted around the spare room where we slept, and where there was an ashtray with the message: 'A guest is like a fish; after three days it stinks'. I was so hurt when I first saw it that I burst into tears.

Not only did I learn to make mayonnaise and to admire Napoleon (living in England as I do now, I have been forced to renounce this admiration) from Zia Ester, but it is to her that I owe my fear of cows. During a walk on the slopes above Lake Maggiore, Zia Ester and I found ourselves facing some young heifers that started to run towards us. We beat a hasty retreat, but were soon confronted by a barbed-wire fence. I, small and thin, managed to wriggle through a gap at the bottom of the fence unscathed, but poor Zia Ester, a portly woman, tore her dress to shreds and ended up covered in scratches.

Another kind of food that Zia Ester taught me to love were *paste* – those little cakey concoctions you see in any patisserie in Italy. So in Rome at the Hotel Principe di Savoia, when the *dolci* trolley arrived at the end of the meal with its rich assortment of *paste* – profiteroles, *africani, cannoncini* oozing yellow custard, and little white meringues sandwiched with even whiter cream – I was again spoilt for choice. In 1936, fascism didn't interfere with the pleasure of eating.

~

MY EDUCATION continued, quite well actually, in spite of all the hours we had to spend learning about the greatness of Mussolini. And our lives went on as usual until that fateful September the 3rd, 1939. We were still at the seaside, almost at the end of our summer holidays, sitting at the bar and my parents were talking to some friends about the probabilities of Italy being dragged into another war. 'Mussolini would never make such a silly mistake,' declared my father, who was still convinced of il Duce's wisdom. 'I wouldn't be so sure,' rebutted a friend, 'I bet we'll be at war in a year's time.'

'But how could Europe have another war so soon?' some-one added, and this indeed struck me to the core. My parents' generation had gone through the most terrible war twenty years earlier and now they were facing a second one.

Papà used to tell me of the horrors of his war in the trenches of the Carso mountains where he fought for nearly four years. The Carso is a range of mountains dividing Italy from what is now Slovenia, but which then formed part of the Austro-Hungarian empire. (The mountains, which are full of caves and holes, later became notorious for the Foibe massacre when, at the end of the Second World War, thousands of Italians were buried in these caves, often alive, by Tito's Partisans. At the time, the Allies preferred to ignore the episode because they wanted to remain on friendly terms with Tito, leader of the Socialist Federalist Republic of Yugoslavia. So the whole matter was swept under the carpet where, to a certain extent, it still lies.)

Italy did not enter the war until June the 10th, 1940, five days after the Dunkirk evacuation, and at the time of the Fall of France. Mussolini had decided to go in then, in time to share the spoils, on the presumption that Great Britain would either ask for an armistice or be invaded, or both.

On that day, Mamma and I were on our way back to Milan after visiting some friends in Bergamo and, as we came out of the railway station, we saw a placard with Mussolini's declaration of war. Mamma was stunned, although she'd been fearful for months. We got home where we were welcomed by Papà and Zio Tom, both enthusiastically approving Mussolini's move, given the situation in France.

For the first two years, the war had little impact on our

daily routine, apart from a few disturbed nights during the early weeks, when we had some air raids. Wrapped in shawls, we'd trudge down sleepily into the cellar, candle in one hand and a piece of fruit in the other, Mamma being, as I've mentioned, a firm believer in its life-saving properties.

During those two years it became rather difficult to get decent meat in Milan. But Mamma had a very good relationship with her suppliers. One day, in the late spring of 1942, she was having a lunch party and had managed to buy a large joint of fillet of veal from our butcher in Via Borgospesso. She planned to cook one of her culinary specialities, *vitel tonné alla Piemontese* – thinly sliced roast veal in a sauce of anchovies, capers, tuna, lemon juice and mayonnaise. *Vitel tonné* is the old-fashioned Milanese name for the now familiar *vitello tonnato,* which was originally served without mayonnaise.

On the day of the lunch party, our housemaid, Augusta, all decked out with crest and white gloves, walked into the dining room triumphantly carrying a large oval dish of the sliced meat covered by a thin light mayonnaise and decorated with gherkins, lemon butterflies, olives and sprigs of parsley. But as she made her entrance, she tripped over the rug, the dish shot out of her hand and the *vitel tonné* finished up all over the floor. An utter mess.

Zia Ester, who was present, got up from her chair, her plate in one hand and a fork in the other. Kneeling down, she proceeded to help herself from the floor, saying: 'It's too good to waste and I'm going to eat it all the same.' Mamma decided to pick up the debris and ask the cook to cover it with fresh mayonnaise. The only lasting damage was to the Persian rug that forever after kept a few stains, but they seemed to fit in beautifully with the pattern.

The best story of salvaged food was that of Zia Maria of Rome, Mamma's sister – not to be confused with Zia Maria of Milan, Papa's sister. We didn't see Zia Maria of Rome during the five years of the war because, in 1944, Rome was separated from us in the North. Some time during the war Zia Maria lived on Lake Bracciano with two or three cats, next door to a woman who kept chickens. One day, one of Zia Maria's cats managed to kill a chicken. Unfortunately it happened to be the neighbour's favourite bird and the neighbour decided she couldn't possibly eat it, so she buried it at the bottom of the garden. During the night, Zia Maria crept down the path, desecrated the tomb and the next day had a feast. 'The best meal of my war years,' she told us later. 'I expect you forgot to add the wine,' rebuffed Mamma, who was always ready to criticise her older sister's cooking. Zia Maria was no good with pots and pans. 'She is always in contact with the dead,' Mamma used to say, 'and she can't be bothered to feed properly those who are still alive.' Zia Maria was indeed a dedicated spiritualist and she took that science far more to heart than that of cooking.

~

JULY CAME, and we left as usual for our summer holiday in Liguria. From 1939 to 1942 each year, we went to Cavi di Lavagna on the Eastern Riviera, on the Gulf of Tigurio, at the opposite side to Portofino. It had a long pebble beach which, at one end, gave away to rocks, which we used as a diving platform or we'd scramble over them to look for mussels, clams and crabs. We always rented a villa or a flat and stayed there for two idyllic months. Papà would join us for the two weeks of Ferragosto – the bank holiday in the middle of August – although he also came down from Milan every Saturday night in what was called The Bulls' train, because it was full of husbands.

We made many good friends there, some from Milan and some from Genoa, the latter whom we only met during the summer holidays. I always found my Genoese friends more fun than my fellow Milanese. I didn't even notice their thriftiness for which the Genoese are known, possibly because I share the same streak. (There's an old Genoese story of the woman who goes to the printers to arrange for the announcement of her husband's death to be printed on posters. She tells the man to print the words 'Mario Rossi scomparso' – 'Mario Rossi deceased'. 'Is that all?' he asks. 'You can have three more words for the same price.' To which the woman replies, *'Ah, va bene, allora aggiunga "Fiat in vendita"'* – 'Then add "Fiat for sale".' When I got to know the British later, I noticed that they shared the same dry humour, a rarer attribute in an Italian. The Italians, on the whole, are not able to laugh at themselves; they take life very seriously, with the Genoese and, to a lesser degree, the Neapolitans and the Venetians being the exceptions. Perhaps a sense of humour goes with sea-faring?)

Liguria is one of the most appealing regions of Italy. For me, its food represents the best of *la cucina povera* – peasant cooking. Because of Liguria's mild climate, herbs, flowers, vegetables and fruit flourish in profusion. Pesto, made with basil, has its origins in Genoa – its real name is *pesto alla Genovese*, because that's where the best herbs grow, and the locals have created the most delicious combinations of flavours in different herb-based sauces. For instance, I, a Lombard, have to acknowledge that the Ligurian salsa verde may be just a little better than the salsa verde from Brianza, the area north of Milan, where it is said to have originated. The Ligurians had the inspiration to add a small clove of garlic to the parsley, giving just the right touch. The wonderful local vegetables are stuffed in a myriad ways, and appear in endless variations of pies, tarts, *frittate* and *pasticci*.

Wagner, Verdi, Shelley, Nietzsche, Iris Origo, Byron, Keats and Dickens were all lovers of Liguria and its capital, Genoa. DH Lawrence used to 'disappear' to enchanting Tellaro, where he wrote a charming story about the local octopus which taunted the local priest by pulling the bell rope of the church that stands on the water's edge. All these people have appreciated and written about the paradise of this beautiful land- and seascape, of its art and its food.

Alas, the coast is now rather overbuilt, but nobody can ruin the hinterland. As children, in the afternoons we used to go for long walks up the hills where we scampered and played on the terraces shaded by feathery grey olive trees and dark green fig trees. That was the start of my love affair with the Mediterranean – the enclosed pool of water around which everything that is us began and, for me, everything finishes.

In September, just before we went back to Milan, the figs were beginning to ripen and there is nothing as voluptuous as a warm fig just plucked from the tree. We'd eat some and bring some home to form the perfect end to any meal. (Today, I still cannot bring myself to buy shop-bought figs, not even in Italy, let alone those hard, dark, round objects in England that

With Marco and Guido one golden summer.

pass for figs.) Figs shouldn't need anything doing to them; all that's necessary is to peel them and shove them in your mouth – no stewing in wine or honey or roasting in citrus juice, no silly pretentious recipes.

WHEN WE were a little older, in Cavi, we'd go for romantic midnight walks in the hills, where our passion was limited to affectionate hand squeezes and short, sharp kisses. There was not much else to do; by 1940 Mussolini had curtailed most of the activities of the young. Dancing smacked too much of Hollywood, so we saw the slow disappearance of those splendid *balere* – large open air platforms where live bands played and people danced. Sadly, I was too young to appreciate them.

But the sea and the beach and the boats made up for the lack of night life. We played water polo in the sea and basketball on the sandy pebbles. Being a very good swimmer, I was not bad at water polo but, but my lack of height rendered my efforts at basketball less effective, and I envied the long legs of my friends Millie and Noretta. It was my brother Guido who kept up the honour of the Del Conte family. He was an able sportsman and extremely good-looking. Most of the other boys were in awe of him, while all the girls were in love with him, and a little of that admiration reflected on me. Guido was well aware of his attraction, although he disguised it with an air of insouciance.

Those last summers at Cavi were full of unforgettable days that even Mussolini didn't manage to ruin. But then, during the summer of 1942, the war came closer. Some of our friends, only a few years older than we were, had been called up. Guido began to get worried – he would be eighteen in December, when it would be his turn and he certainly did not feel the urge to fight for anybody, least of all for the fascists and the Germans.

In spite of his physical toughness, Guido was the least belligerent man I have known, even less so than my gentle English husband. I remember when we were taken to the circus – we went every year with Mamma, her two sisters and Mariella, one of Zia Renata's daughters. We all loved the circus, the grown-ups just as much as us children. But there was one act I would have liked to eliminate, not for my sake, but for Guido's: when a man was shot from a large cannon. As soon as the cannon was pulled into the ring, Guido would start to fidget. The man, all bundled up like a mummy, got into the gun, and Guido would slowly bring his fingers to his ears. 'Siete pronti?' – 'Are you ready?' the ringmaster would ask.

'Sí!' we all screamed, except Guido, who by now was sitting with his head between his knees and his fingers pushed right into his ears. '*Uno, due, tre*', and, with the most almighty bang, the man was shot out of the cannon and landed on the net, to the applause and cheers from everyone – even from Guido whose agony was now over for another year. So, in 1942, the prospect of being surrounded by far more vicious bangs didn't please him at all.

The war dug in more deeply for me when I fell for a soldier who came to Cavi to join his family while on leave. That was the first time I fell in love. I was seventeen and Cicci was twenty-seven, a lieutenant who had already fought in the disastrous Balkan campaign. He was extremely serious about our affair, if I can call it that, since at that time well brought-up Catholic young men usually respected the virginity of young girls. We swam together, walked together, ate together, drank together, sat together, but we never slept together.

Cicci was a very pleasant man who I am sure would have made a good husband. Starting my married life in Genoa, where Cicci came from, would certainly have been easier than in London, if less interesting. After ten days, he had to say goodbye and rejoin his regiment, which was sent to the Russian front. I was desperate, but not for long. After six months or so, I decided I really could not be bothered to write these long letters. So, displaying that callousness of youth, I wrote and told him I did not love him any more. End of affair. How I could ever have written that heartless letter to a man who was fighting in the worst battle ever, at Stalingrad, I don't know. But I was young.

~

THOSE WERE golden summers and I still cherish the memories of carefree days spent on the beach or in the hills, or cycling along the then deserted Via Aurelia coastal road to Paraggi or Portofino. At Paraggi we'd stop for a swim in the emerald green water, so green that – or so the story goes – a herd of cows coming down from the hills thought it was a meadow, and went into it and drowned.

Once a year every summer we went on our San Fruttuoso expedition. We rode to Portofino, dumped our bikes there and walked up the promontory to go down the other side for a swim in that perfect cove and for an even more perfect lunch at Giorgio's, a small trattoria right on the rocks. We had huge bowls of *trenette al pesto* – Ligurian tagliatelle with pesto – and platefuls and platefuls of *fritto misto di mare* and mountains of *pesche da vigna* – vine peaches dripping with juice, peaches which seem no longer to exist. (Around three years ago, I went back to San Fruttuoso, which is just as beautiful as it was sixty or so years ago, because it is protected by Italia Nostra, the Italian equivalent to the National Trust. I was writing an article on Liguria for *Sainsbury's Magazine*. We went to Giorgio's – still there on the rocks – where we had *trenette al pesto* and *fritto misto di mare*. They were just as good as I remember them from my youth.) But the most delicious *pasta al pesto* was served at Santa Giulia, a tiny hamlet up on the hill some 500 metres above Cavi, with a church and a trattoria – the two temples of Italian society. We often went there for Sunday lunch with our parents, about thirty of us, young and old together, in the tradition of Sunday lunches. The pasta was not *trenette* but *picagge* – narrow sheets of lasagne – layered with a delicate yet flavoursome pesto of basil, pine nuts, and olive oil, all grown around the trattoria. The wine, too, was local – the rustic white wine of Santa Giulia, made from the vines right under our noses.

In September 1942, we said goodbye to Cavi, wondering when we'd be able to come back, if ever. We returned to Milan and its foggy gloom, and to the air raids which had now begun in earnest there. Turin had suffered quite a few air bombardments, and Genoa had fared even worse, with a terrible naval bombardment from the sea, which nobody had expected. Two of our Cavi friends from Genoa, a mother and daughter, were killed when their block of flats was cut in half. They happened to be in one of the rooms overlooking the sea, while the husband and two sons, who were in one of the rooms at the back, were spared.

We arrived in Milan to find that most people were leaving for the country. My parents decided that it was time for us, too, to go.

Muscoli Ripieni
Stuffed Mussels

SERVES 6

1.25–1.5kg mussels in their shells
10 tbsp dried breadcrumbs
10 tbsp chopped fresh flat leaf parsley
2 garlic cloves, finely chopped
freshly ground pepper
7 tbsp olive oil
salt
2 tbsp grated mature pecorino or parmesan cheese

To clean the mussels, put them in a sink and scrub them thoroughly with a hard brush, scraping off any barnacles with a knife and tugging off the beards. Make sure that you discard any mussel that remains open after you tap it on a hard surface and put the rest in cold water. Rinse until the water is clear, changing the water as many times as necessary. Most mussels are farmed now and quite clean.

Preheat the oven to 230°C/gas mark 8.

When the mussels are cleaned, put them in a large saucepan. Cover and cook, in their own liquid, over a high heat for about 4 minutes until the mussels are open, shaking the pan occasionally. Discard any that haven't opened. Shell the mussels, reserving one half of each empty shell.

Strain the mussel liquid through a sieve lined with muslin.

Mix together the breadcrumbs, parsley, garlic and plenty of pepper, then add the olive oil and 4 tablespoons of the mussel liquid. Combine well together. Taste and adjust the seasonings.

Place the mussels in their shells on 2 baking sheets. With your fingers, pick up a good pinch of the breadcrumb mixture and press it down on each mussel, covering it well and filling the shell. Sprinkle with the grated pecorino or parmesan cheese. Bake in the oven for 10 minutes.

~

Picagge al Pesto
Lasagne with Pesto

If you are making your own lasagne, turn to page 133 and follow the instructions, but remember that fresh pasta takes far less time to cook than dried pasta.

SERVES 6–7

For the pesto
60g fresh basil leaves
2 garlic cloves
30g pine nuts
pinch of rock salt
4 tbsp freshly grated parmesan
4 tbsp freshly grated pecorino
120ml extra virgin olive oil

For the lasagne
*500g top-quality Italian dried egg lasagne, or make
your own using 3 eggs and 300g Italian 00 flour*

For assembling
*120g ricotta cheese
60g freshly grated pecorino cheese
2 tbsp extra virgin olive oil
oil for greasing*

Preheat the oven to 180°C/gas mark 4.

Cook the lasagne in batches in boiling salted water. Drain, reserving 2 tablespoons of the pasta water, and set the lasagne aside on kitchen teacloths.

Now make the pesto. To make in a mortar, put in the basil, garlic, pine nuts and salt, and grind against the sides of the mortar, crushing with the pestle until the mixture has become a paste. Mix in the grated cheeses and pour the oil over very gradually, beating with a wooden spoon. Alternatively, to make in a food processor or blender, put all the pesto ingredients, except the cheeses, in the beaker. Process at high speed and when evenly blended transfer to a small bowl. Add both cheeses and stir thoroughly.

Mix the reserved pasta water thoroughly into the pesto. Brush a lasagne dish with oil and cover the base with a thin layer of pesto. Cover with a layer of lasagne, then a layer of pesto, followed by 2 tablespoons of ricotta cheese and about 2 tablespoons of grated pecorino. Repeat these layers, finishing with a layer of pecorino. Pour the extra virgin olive oil over the top and bake in the oven for 20 minutes.

CHAPTER 7

ALBINEA

Grappa

WE LEFT MILAN in the autumn of 1942, and evacuated to Albinea, in Emilia-Romagna. The village of Albinea lies in the foothills of the Apennines, south of the city of Reggio Emilia, where my parents had some good friends and there was also a good lycée for me. It is a rich agricultural region and Mamma, for whom good food was one of the most important priorities in life, was sure we would never go hungry in such a fertile area. She was right: we didn't, despite the perils and the horrors of being, in the last year of the war, too close to the front and in the middle of a raging civil war between the Germans and the fascists on one side, and the partisans on the other.

The house we first moved into, the Villa Viani, was a large, low, early nineteenth-century building, elegant in its simplicity, with a tranquil view over the valley of the river Crostolo. We rented one half of the villa, while in the other half lived the owner, Admiral Viani, and his family who had evacuated from Florence. (I went back there in 2006, to recapture the memories of those fateful years, and I was struck by the bucolic serenity of the place. The huge magnolia grandiflora, whose scent pervaded the whole house in early spring, was still thriving. We'd often sat under it reading, studying and chatting, or playing.)

Life went on quietly and monotonously for a year. Marco went to the primary school in the village, and I to the lycée in Reggio, some sixteen kilometres away. Some time in the spring of 1943 Guido, who was now in his eighteenth year, was called up and stationed in Veneto. Meanwhile, we played table tennis, boules and tennis at the tennis club, which some German officers had also joined. Everyone tried to avoid them, but there was one particularly good-looking officer who took a shine to me and I certainly would have liked to reciprocate. His name was Hans and he had piercing, pale-blue eyes that seemed to penetrate right through you. Not only did I find him handsome, but I discovered we had many shared interests. Hans spoke Italian very well, having lived in Milan for a few years when his father was working there. He told me he'd been to La Scala a few times, so we talked about our favourite operas. Like me, he loved Venice, and we said what fun it would be to meet up there after the war. We were young and attracted to each other; yet the war kept us apart. All we did was talk, and nothing else took place between us, not even a quick peck on the cheek. I desperately tried to keep a check on my feelings; he was a German and, although at the time Italy and Germany were still allies, any German was already persona non grata.

Marco, who was only six then and who often came to the tennis club to play with his friends, had noticed that I spent more time talking to Hans than to anybody else. One day at home, he was messing about, dancing around the sitting room in that childish, attention-seeking way, when he began to shout: 'Anna is in love with a German, Anna is in love with a German.' My parents looked startled and began to question me. Of course, I denied it and felt even more guilty. So, later, when Hans disappeared after the armistice in September 1943, I actually felt a huge sense of relief. I'd been terrified of succumbing to his charms. So I never ran the risk of having my head shaved after the war, as happened to all the girls who consorted with the Germans or the fascists.

OUR PEACEFUL LIFE in Emilia-Romagna was suddenly shattered a few days after the fateful 8th September 1943, when General Eisenhower granted an armistice to King Vittorio Emanuele III. We were ordered by the Germans to vacate the house in forty-eight hours. We moved into the *villino* – little villa – next door and shared it with another family.

That was when we began to feel that the war was precariously close. It became dangerous to talk to people we didn't know or to go on the larger roads, since all means of transport were potential targets of the Allied warplanes. Bombs could fall anywhere at any time, like the one that fell in the field behind our house. All the windows were blown out and the result was a few days of cold misery. It was said that those sporadic bombs were surplus ones, jettisoned by planes flying back after an attack. Nobody really knew or cared, as long as you were not underneath. In fact, no one understood anything of what was going on, or what to do.

IT WAS ONLY later, that we found out how this chaotic situation came about. In the events leading up to the armistice, the Grand Council in Rome, presided over by Mussolini, had met on the 24th July 1943 to sum up the catastrophic events of the war. The Grand Council voted for Parliament and its ministers to return to power, just as they had been before Mussolini assumed complete dictatorial control in 1925. Mussolini was present but, oddly enough, he never interfered. The next day, the King nominated Marshal Badoglio as prime minister and arrested a dumbfounded and humiliated Duce.

And this is where the behaviour of the King becomes implausible. Why didn't he declare Italian neutrality at the time? Some historians rightly blame the King for his incapacity to take decisions and, at the same time, his reluctance to let others take them. He was also afraid of the reaction of the Germans. Moreover he refused to accept the unconditional surrender demanded by the Allies and, worst of all, he chose the inept General Badoglio as prime minister. I was delighted when, having just reached the voting age, I was able to put my little cross alongside *Repubblica* at the plebiscite of June the 2nd 1946. This, by the way, was the first time women had a vote in Italy, the fascist regime having been in power since 1922 when women were not yet enfranchised.

During that summer of 1943, when Mussolini was no longer head of state, the Allies had launched their strongest air attacks yet on many Italian cities. In the space of four nights in August, the centre of Milan, where there was not a single military target, was destroyed and, with it, as we found out later, our flat in Via Sant'Andrea, along with most of my parents' possessions and all of their past.

Mussolini was eventually taken prisoner and held in an

isolated village high in the Apennines from where he was rescued in a German commando operation on September the 12th 1943. He was flown to a town on Lake Garda, where he was given command of the *Repubblica di Salò*, a new puppet state set up in northern and central Italy under German protection, the South having already been liberated by the Allies. So, by the time the armistice was granted, Italy was crawling with German soldiers, who had poured down the Brenner pass from Austria throughout the summer. Northern Italy was totally and irretrievably under the control of the Germans.

I am not a diehard patriot, but I clearly remember how I felt seeing my country invaded by a foreign power: a deep humiliation which gave rise to hate.

⌒

SEPTEMBER THE 8th 1943 had been a beautiful sunny day in Albinea. We were still on our school holidays and I, with my brother Guido and our great friends Marica and Carlo Saverio Balsamo and Giovanna and Nino Pellizzi were bicycling home after spending the afternoon playing tennis at a friend's house. When we got to the village of Puianello, we noticed people rushing out of their houses and the bar, talking excitedly. They had just heard the news of the armistice, which was spreading fast. We reached the Pellizzi's house just in time to hear Marshal Badoglio's broadcast to the nation:

> The Italian government, recognising the impossibility of continuing the unequal struggle against the overwhelming enemy power, with the intent of saving further and more serious disaster to the Nation, has asked General Eisenhower,

With Carlo Saverio, Giovanna, (Anna) and Marica.

General in Chief of the Anglo-American force, for an armistice. The request has been granted.

There were cheers everywhere and we jumped around with joy and excitement. At last the war was over.

Next day we began to realise that the situation was not that simple. The King and Badoglio had both left Rome to board a boat on the Adriatic to take them to Brindisi and safety, only a few miles from the advancing British 8th Army. The Italian Army was in disarray, left without any sort of leadership. The prisoner of war camp not very far from us was opened and the Allied soldiers walked out; they too, it seemed, had not been given any orders as to what to do.

About two or three days later we came to know what to

straight away and seek sanctuary nearby. That night was spent frantically rescuing the trunk full of silver which my mother had buried in the field next to the Villa Viani when we first arrived from Milan. The *contadini* – farmworkers – came to help us and, in the depth of the night, we all gathered round the burial site with spades and shovels, digging furiously. After that gruelling night Mamma swore she'd never bury anything again – a decision we all welcomed with great relief.

So at the appointed hour, on the appointed day, we piled all our possessions into the lorry the Germans had provided and made our way – Mamma, Papà, Marco, our maid Augusta and me, not forgetting the trunk full of silver – to the nearby house of the Crocioni family, where Signora Crocioni and her cook, Zerlina, were waiting at the front door to welcome us. The Crocioni had kindly offered to put us up until we found somewhere else to live. The Villa Crocioni was a large, late-nineteenth-century building with turrets and gables, countless rooms, huge cellars and a vast loft. It had to be, because during the fortnight we stayed there, it housed many occupants: eleven official inhabitants; three unofficial ones in hiding; and four German officers. The three in hiding were my deserter brother Guido, the deserter son-in-law of Signora Crocioni, an officer who – like Guido – never returned to his regiment, and her older son who was deeply implicated in organising the partisan resistance movement. They lived in the attic, awaiting orders. Only Signora Crocioni and her husband – and possibly Zerlina – knew they were there. (My parents also knew about Guido, but not about the other two.)

On the ground floor, four rooms had been requisitioned for the four German officers who were, in fact, remarkably polite and well-behaved. The Crocioni, however, would have dearly liked to see the back of them, as they were all too aware of the awful consequences – the firing squad – had it been discovered that they were giving shelter to three wanted men. When I think back to those terrible years, I realise how many people were risking their lives for the sake of others, but, at the time, it just seemed normal and none of us would have thought to behave otherwise.

Zerlina was a tall and skinny woman, with a rather thin-lipped mouth and eyes as devoid of expression as two fried eggs, but she was extremely kind, cheerful and an excellent cook. She and Signora Crocioni prepared all the meals in the kitchen, helped by our maid Augusta and my mother. Every day Zerlina was at the large kitchen table making pasta. In Emilia, at the time, fresh pasta was made every day from the local soft flour and plenty of local eggs. Dried pasta, made with the hard wheat flour of southern Italy, was considered esoteric. Zerlina also made delicious Italian sweet breads and *crostate* – tarts – that she covered with all the home-made jams stacked in jars in the cellar. My favourite *crostata* was the one covered with fig jam, which I still dream about.

But Signora Crocioni and Zerlina were involved in a more sinister occupation: making Grappa. They went down to the cellar at night where they had all the equipment they needed – the alembic for distilling the alcohol, the pure alcohol and the dregs of the Crocioni's best grapes. As liqueur-making was not allowed during the war, this was another well-guarded secret, punishable not by a firing squad but by the sequestration of all the Grappa-making paraphernalia and the precious alcohol.

One night, I was suddenly woken by a loud explosion. We

were quite used to bangs of all sorts but this was far too close for comfort. We all rushed downstairs while Signora Crocioni and Zerlina, her black hair singed, appeared from the cellar door shouting at the top of their voices, *'Non è niente, non è niente, è solo la Grappa'* – 'It's nothing, it's only the Grappa.' They kept shouting the same thing louder and louder and I couldn't understand why; it was only much later that I found out that they wanted the three illegal inhabitants of the attic to get the right message.

But the Germans, with their limited grasp of Italian, did not understand the Grappa message. In their pyjamas, revolvers to hand, they rushed out into the garden, certain it must be a partisan attack, and thinking this could be their moment of glory when the four of them would repel a regiment of heavily armed partisans. But they found only Rocky, the big Alsatian, prowling around the garden. Eventually they came back and the accident was explained to them. They examined the cellar, fascinated by the alembic, then the previous year's Grappa was taken out and handed round, and the evening ended in friendship and good humour.

I don't know if Signora Crocioni pursued her viticultural ambitions. She was certainly not a woman to give up easily, nor was her devoted Zerlina.

Crostata di Marmellata di Fichi
Fig Jam Tart

SERVES 6–8

For the pastry
225g Italian 00 flour
½ tsp sea salt
100g granulated sugar
grated rind of ½ organic lemon
120g cold unsalted butter
2 free-range egg yolks

For the filling
350g fig jam
juice of ½ organic lemon
1 egg yolk and 2 tbsp milk for glazing

To make this pastry, pile the flour on a work surface. Mix in the salt, sugar and lemon rind and rub in the butter. Add the egg yolks and work quickly to form a ball. If you prefer, make the pastry in a food processor. Wrap in foil and chill for at least 30 minutes.

Heat the oven to 200°C/gas mark 6.

Butter a 20 or 22cm (8 or 9 inch) tart tin with a loose bottom and sprinkle with 1 tablespoon of flour. Shake off the excess flour.

Remove the dough from the fridge. Put aside about one-third and roll out the rest into a circle. Line the prepared tin with the circle of dough and press it down firmly into the angle between the base and the side.

Put the jam in a bowl and mix in the lemon juice. Spread the jam over the circle of dough. Roll out the reserved dough and cut several strips about 1cm wide. Place these strips over the tart to form a lattice that goes right across. Don't worry if you have to make one or two joins in the strips: once the tart is baked the joins won't show. Brush the pastry lattice with the egg yolk and milk glaze.

Bake in the oven for about 10 minutes. Turn the heat down to 180°C/gas mark 4 and bake for a further 20 minutes until the pastry turns a lovely light golden brown. Remove from the tin and transfer to a wire rack to cool. In Italy, as indeed in France, tarts are served without cream.

Make the *crostata* on the day you want to eat it. The pastry can be made up to 2 days in advance and refrigerated, wrapped in foil. It also freezes well.

CHAPTER 8

MACHINE GUNS

Risotto with nettles

DURING THE FINAL year of the war, we witnessed some truly terrifying episodes. The first happened on the 3rd of July. That night, around eleven o'clock, four or five fascists went to Villa Calvi where our friends, the Balsamos, lived and asked for the Marchese Balsamo. He came to the door, he was ordered into a car – and that was the last the family saw of him.

Balsamo was a lawyer and a retired colonel from the First World War. He no longer worked, but just looked after his land around Albinea, and he was not, and never had been, politically involved. For the next four days his family and friends frantically searched the area, trying to find out where he'd been taken, but to no avail. Nobody knew anything. Five days later, his body was found not far from Albinea; he'd been shot soon after his arrest and left in a ditch. It was a hot July and the corpse had disintegrated so much that his sister-in-law recognised him only by his shoes. At his funeral in the local church, the sickly, sweet stench of his dead body in the thick mahogany coffin was quite overwhelming. No one ever found out why he'd been killed, although there was much speculation. Some people said it was class revenge; another, more likely explanation was that his name had been on a list, compiled by the fascists, of professional men accused of being Masons, although Balsamo had never been involved in freemasonry, which had been declared illegal by Mussolini.

His execution was one of the most shattering experiences of my life during the war. I was a close friend of his children, Marica and Carlo Saverio. Carlo Saverio was deeply in love with me, although I not with him, but after his father's brutal death, I felt the least I could do to help him was to return the sentiment, hoping that eventually I, too, would be able to fall in love with him.

My passion for Carlo Saverio might have been wanting, but my admiration for him was unbounded. He introduced me to Baudelaire and other French poets and novelists and he taught me to appreciate the poems of Ungaretti and Montale. Carlo Saverio was an intelligent, cultured man and great fun. He enjoyed life to the full, in spite of all the tragedies that punctuated it. He loved travelling and collecting vintage cars. (Once, in 1959, he came to see me in a magnificent green, pre-war Lagonda Coupé when I was staying with my two boys in a *pensione* in Bocca di Magra, which was then a sleepy and charming seaside place on the border between Liguria and Tuscany. The car created quite a stir in the village. Locals gathered round it, looked inside, stroked the bonnet and then looked at me in a new light.)

~

IN THE summer of 1944, we left the Crocioni's house and arrived at our final place of safety in the war: the farmhouse

of our friends the Pellizzis, in Puianello, around five kilometres to the west of Albinea, on the other side of the river
Crostolo. The Pellizzi's farmhouse was then a working farm,
a handsome, sturdy building topped by a square dovecote,
with no bathroom and no central heating, but it had the most
magnificent avenue of cypresses leading up to it.

In the last months of the war, we tried to walk everywhere,
rather than going by bicycle, especially after we were very
nearly killed on the road. One afternoon in October, Giovanna,
Marica and I had been cycling to a friend's house some ten
kilometres away. By that time there were few means of
transport, apart from bikes and horse-drawn carts. Most
military movements took place at night to avoid being bombed
or machine-gunned, or both. We were happily riding down the
road when we saw some fighter planes starting to dive in our
direction. Just further along the road, there was a house where
we knew we could take cover. But then we spotted a cart being
pulled by a donkey in front of us, giving us little room for
manoeuvre. Would we be able to get to the house in time?
Giovanna, a faster cyclist than Marica and I, overtook the cart at
full speed and pedalled furiously into the drive of the house. I
realised that Marica and I, only a few metres behind, would
never get there before the planes were on us. So I threw myself,
bicycle and all, into the ditch and Marica followed suit.

The four planes started firing at the cart, backed up with that
terrifying roar we knew so well, while a further four planes
began to dive towards us from the other direction. That
operation was repeated three times on each side, as was the
norm, which seemed quite unnecessary just to get a cart, a

donkey, an old man and three girls out of the way. Marica and I lay down as flat as possible without moving until the attack was over, and when we dared to raise our heads we saw Giovanna running towards us. We got up and there in the middle of the road was the poor donkey lying in a pool of blood. The old man who'd been driving the cart, who'd also taken shelter in the house, stood motionless. He was muttering, *'Era una brava bestia e lavorava bene'* – 'He was a good worker, and now what am I going to do?', followed by a string of expletives (of which the Emiliani are masters), the only repeatable bit being *'guerra puttana'* – bitch of a war. I can still see that man today, nearly in tears, his hat pulled down over his red face, cursing in that unmistakable sing-song of the local dialect and looking down at his miserable animal. It was indeed a *puttana* of a war.

We, three girls, got on our bicycles and rode back home, dirty and shaken, where we were met by Guido who, with great excitement, asked: 'Did you see the attack? I saw it from the attic window and I could even see the faces of the pilots.' No, we didn't see the pilots' faces because *our* faces were buried in the ground.

The next day three other planes began to machine-gun a target on the bridge nearby. I was quite a long way away, but as soon as I heard the noise of the planes diving, I immediately threw myself to the ground, which was covered with nettles – old nettles which have a powerful sting. My face, neck and hands were on fire, but it was nothing compared with the terror of the previous day. I often remember that burning sting when I go out, here in Dorset, to collect nettles to make one of my favourite spring dishes – risotto with nettles – but I remember even more those planes diving towards us as they spat their lethal fire.

~

ON THE night of March the 26th, we were awakened by the noise of heavy firing. Usually, once it was dark, we were surrounded by deep silence, apart from the occasional roar of an aeroplane, known to us as Pippo – a solitary plane passed overhead every now and then at night and was usually harmless, unless it decided to drop a bomb, which did sometimes happen. But providing you weren't underneath it, you just said 'Ecco Pippo' and forgot about it.

It was about two in the morning when the firing started. We grabbed our dressing-gowns and ran downstairs, quickly turning out all the lights, then threw open the door and rushed outside into the garden. In front of us, on the other side of the river, we saw the most dazzling display of what looked like fireworks, but was obviously gunfire. We realised immediately that it was a partisan attack on the Villa Rossi and the Villa Calvi in Albinea, opposite us on the other side of the river Crostolo.

The Villa Rossi was the headquarters of the German 14th Army where General Kesselring was a regular visitor. In the Villa Calvi, where the Balsamos used to live until the house was requisitioned, was the cartographic office and the telephone centre connected, so the rumour went, directly to Berlin. The firing went on for nearly two hours. The next day the *contadini* told us what had happened, although the report was very scanty.

But many years later, I found out the whole story after reading a book written by the leader of one of the groups of partisans who took part in the assault. The commander was an Englishman, Major Roy Ferran, who was parachuted into the partisans' zone with a dozen SAS men, to organise the attack and to train the partisans. The attack was successful: the offices in the Villa Calvi were destroyed and four Germans were killed, although Kesselring was not there at the time. But the British lost three parachutists, and six partisans were captured. These six were taken away to be shot and afterwards there was a heavy *rastrellamento* – cleaning up operation – in Albinea and in all the villages around. Farmhouses were burnt and civilians taken away, just as the Germans always did after a partisan attack.

The thing that affected me most about that attack was the shooting of the six partisans, which took place the next day. Giovanna and I were passing by the Villa Rossi on our way to our English lesson when we heard the spray of the firing squad's machine guns. Petrified, we stopped and looked at each other, knowing quite well what was happening. And then a few minutes later, the six single shots of the six coups de grâce rang out. Giovanna and I knelt down and prayed. It was the most chilling noise I have ever heard.

I RECENTLY MET James Holland, author of *Italy's Sorrow,* which described the horrors of that last year of the war. He told me how painful it had been for him to write that book, to hear of all the massacres of the civilian population and the suffering they'd had to bear. In comparison, we had been very lucky. We managed to live a sort of limbo life, kicked into harsh reality every now and then by horrible events. We went on knitting socks and endless scarves for the partisans, feeding the chickens and the rabbits, weeding the vegetable patch, doing our English homework, and helping out in the kitchen. I learnt, from Holland's book, that because of the difficulty in transportation, only about fifty per cent of the produce managed to get from the farms to the municipal depots for distribution. On the Pellizzi farm, flour was milled, grapes were crushed, cows were milked, calves were killed, hens were laying, vegetables were growing, pork and rabbits were raised . . . resulting in dishes of tagliatelle, bottles of wine, slabs of butter, blocks of cheese, slices of prosciutti, salami and *coppe* and heaps of greenery for us locals.

I still have the invitation to a party, written in verse, by Domenico Pellizzi to celebrate the end of a bridge competition in January 1944. Here are the last few lines:

> *A mensa si offriranno ai convitati*
> *antipasto all'usanza del castello,*
> *magnifiche reggiane tagliatelle,*
> *arrosti di pollastre e di vitello,*
> *torte, pan dolce, leccornie, ciambelle,*
> *vini nostrani vecchi e profumati.*

> At the table the guests will be offered
> antipasto as served in a castle
> splendid local tagliatelle
> roast of chicken and veal
> cakes, sweet delicacies and ciambelle
> local wines, old and scented.

In Rome, Milan, Florence and in most other cities, people

were starving while I had been eating some of the finest food of my life.

~

THE ALLIED advance was stopped during the winter of 1944 to 1945 at the Gothic Line, the German line of defence that crossed Italy from Pisa to Rimini. The air attacks on the cities of northern Italy became more and more frequent. Bologna, Parma and Reggio were all bombed, despite their well-known communist – anti-fascist – leanings which they had hoped the Allies would acknowledge. I remember vividly the attacks on Reggio, when the sky to the north of us became a mass of red vapours incessantly streaked by silver lightning. A magnificent yet terrifying spectacle.

At night we bolted ourselves in, worried about strips of light showing through the shutters or the doors and thus making us targets for the Allied planes. We gathered round the radio to listen to Radio Londra, when Colonel Stephens would broadcast what was really happening on the fronts. The Italian press was censored; we knew only what the fascists wanted us to know. Unbelievable rumours were circulating, such as one about a camp near Modena where Jews from all over northern Italy were said to be taken. As it turned out, that was indeed the notorious camp at Fossoli where Italian and Balkan Jews were gathered to board trains for Auschwitz and other concentration camps in Germany. But I don't think many people believed those rumours; they were far too ghastly to contemplate. Surely even the Nazis couldn't be *that* bad.

But there was one good thing I had to thank the war for. When I took my Baccalaureate in June 1944, my Ancient

Greek teacher told me, 'Del Conte, you will have the war to thank if I give you a pass.' But I got my pass. My Greek was shaky, to say the least, and there's no doubt that, in normal times, I would have failed the final exam and would have had to take the Baccalaureate again.

RECIPE

Risotto alle Ortiche
Risotto with Nettles

SERVES 3–4

300g nettle shoots
sea salt
2 shallots or 1 small onion, very finely chopped
60g unsalted butter
1 litre vegetable stock
300g Arborio rice
4 tbsp double cream
60g freshly grated parmesan

The sweet delicate taste of nettles is just discernible in this moist creamy risotto. Wearing gloves, pick a large bag of tender nettle shoots in April or early May. It will boil down as much as spinach does. Cooking removes their sting. The same recipe can be made with very young spinach or Italian spinach, but don't use the larger and older beet spinach as its taste is too coarse.

Pick the leaves and shoots of the nettles and discard the stalks. Wash in two or three changes of water. Put the nettles in a saucepan with 1 teaspoon of salt and boil over a high heat until cooked. You don't need to add any water; as with spinach, the water that comes from the leaves is enough. When cooked, drain, keeping the liquid. Set aside, keeping the nettles in a sieve placed over the bowl containing the nettle water.

Sauté the shallots or onion in half the butter, very gently, until soft.

Heat the stock and keep it at simmering point.

Squeeze all the liquid out of the nettles into the bowl. Chop the nettles coarsely and add to the shallots or onion. Sauté for a minute, stirring constantly, then add the rice and fry it until the outside of the grains becomes translucent.

Pour the nettle liquid into the simmering stock and then add about 150ml of the stock to the rice. Mix well. The rice will soon absorb the stock. Then add another ladleful of hot stock and continue cooking and adding more hot stock until the rice is done. Stir frequently, but not all the time. The better the rice, the longer it takes to cook: Arborio rice takes about 20 minutes from when it is put in the pan.

Draw the pan off the heat, add the cream, the rest of the butter and half the cheese. Leave it to rest for a couple of minutes and then stir vigorously to incorporate these final condiments; this makes the risotto *mantecato* – creamy – as any risotto should be. Transfer to a heated dish and serve at once, handing the remaining cheese round separately.

CHAPTER 9

PRISON

Salame

I WENT TO PRISON twice during the war, once in February 1944 and the second time in the following December. 'Weren't you terrified?' somebody asked me years later. No, I was not. Like bombs, and machine guns, prison was part and parcel of that war which was reshaping our lives. You went to prison and hoped to get out soon. I was lucky because, on both occasions, I was released very soon.

The first time it happened, I was out cycling late, just before the curfew, on my way to the house of some friends in Reggio Emilia where I was going to spend the night. I'd had a late lesson and didn't have time to go back home, all the sixteen kilometres to the Pellizzi's farmhouse in Puianello. Wearing my warm rabbit-fur coat, heavy boots on my feet and a rucksack strapped securely on my back, I was stopped by two fascists on suspicion of being a *staffetta*. *Staffette* were couriers, mostly girls, who delivered messages to or from the partisans and carried provisions to men in hiding. They were an invaluable army of people without whom the partisans wouldn't have been able to survive, let alone function. They went round by bicycle in the dark, and often after the curfew.

I was not a 'recognised' *staffetta*, although I had sometimes delivered messages, but only oral ones. But that night, all wrapped up, with a rucksack on my back and pedalling at full speed, in the eyes of the fascists, I was definitely suspicious. They led me to the barracks of the *Brigate Nere* – the fascist army paramilitary group – where all political prisoners were held, and pushed me into a room, where a *commissario* – officer – was sitting at a large desk. He had a low forehead over a hooked nose, eyes which were too close (my father had always told me never to trust a man with eyes like that), dark, wavy hair slicked down with masses of Brilliantine, a thin moustache over a mean mouth and two black lines for side whiskers cutting his cheeks in half. Perhaps my memory has exaggerated how villainous he looks, but I don't think so. I took an instant dislike to him, but I wasn't afraid.

One of his underlings threw my rucksack on the desk and the *commissario* began to interrogate me, while delving into my rucksack and fishing out the contents, one at a time – my heavy flannel nightdress, which he declared *deliziosa*, the toilet bag, and everything I'd packed for the night, including my precious salame, a present intended for my hosts. He looked at it with even more lust than he had the nightdress, then took out a penknife from his pocket and, ponderously, began to skin it and cut it into chunks, one of which he shoved in his mouth, before offering a piece to his underlings, who accepted with unctuous gratitude.

I was incensed. I put on my best sardonic tone and asked him if he liked it. '*É buonissimo*,' he replied, '*ma un po' troppo fresco*' – 'It's good, but a bit too fresh.'

The *commissario* asked me all the obvious questions and,

having demolished the salame, got up and left, barking orders for me to be escorted to my friends' house. My poor friends had been frantic with worry – by then I was some three hours late and well past the curfew hour. Soon after, though, we were celebrating my arrival with one of their salame and a bottle of Lambrusco.

~

I'D KNOWN that the salame the *commissario* had eaten was too fresh, because it had been made only a month earlier, in mid-January, when the Pellizzi's pig was slaughtered in the *contadini*'s courtyard.

We were woken up by the piercing shrieks of the poor beast, who'd been our friend until the previous day. I couldn't bring myself to watch the actual killing, but once the pig was dead, I loved watching the work that went into the making of all the divine pork produce at which the Emiliani are masters.

First the men scrubbed down the pig very thoroughly and then Pietro, the leader of the team, split it in half and opened it out like a book. He gave all the innards to the women, who proceeded to wash them in several changes of water, ready to be fried for lunch. Then Pietro got hold of both hind legs and started massaging them with salt for them to be hung in the attic later and eventually turned into prosciutto. Meanwhile, Maria, his wife, was scrubbing the trotters, in preparation for the *zamponi*, and then began to make *sanguinaccio* – black pudding – by adding garlic, salt, herbs, onion, and spices to the boiling blood. She had the reputation of being one of the best *sanguinaccio* makers in the area, quite an honour in Emilia. Some other men were sorting out the belly and the ribs for the pancetta. Meanwhile, the women collected all the remains to be washed, minced, flavoured and mixed for all the different salami – *cotechini*, *cappelli da prete*, sausages – and other goodies. The back fat would become *lardo*, that unappetising white slab which looks like white soap, but tastes heavenly after being salted and flavoured with herbs. Another woman was melting down more fat, which she poured into the washed-out bladder of the pig to make *strutto* – the traditional cooking fat of Emilia which gives the local cuisine such a deliciously rich flavour. Alas, it is very unfashionable now.

Marco and all the children were running around the kitchen screaming 'Viva i ciccioli, viva i ciccioli' and rhythmically clapping their hands. The old nonna chased them away with the long pallet she was using to turn over the *gnocco fritto* – a bread dough cut into diamonds and fried – which is the ideal accompaniment to *ciccioli* (crackling).

There's a saying in Emilia-Romagna: 'The pig is like Verdi's music; there is nothing to throw away.' So the next day it was time for the women to make the *coppa di testa* – brawn – from the pig's head. This was one of the most interesting dishes I learned to make during the war. I still make it today and the smell always takes me back to Puianello and the pig festivities. I buy my half head of pig and ask the butcher to axe off its teeth (I don't mind the eyes or the nose, but I cannot bear the teeth). Once it's marinated and cooked with all the flavourings, it transforms into a pièce de résistance.

~

THE SECOND TIME I went to prison, nine months later, was far more serious. The situation had worsened greatly during those nine months and we were constantly aware of the danger we were in.

Guido (reluctantly) in uniform.

At seven in the morning on the 1st of December we were awakened by a loud banging at the front door. I started to run downstairs and, halfway down, I met Guido, who whispered to me that he was going to hide in the attic of the adjoining farm, which he could reach via the attic of the farmhouse. That was the last I saw of Guido for five months, until the war was over. For the time being, though, he was wiped out of our lives. His name was never mentioned again, even between the four walls of our home, because we were afraid that little Marco might talk about him at school. We hoped that he would simply forget he had an older brother.

Gabriella Pellizzi, the owner of the house, opened the door. The house was surrounded by the *Brigate Nere*; a German officer and two or three fascists walked in, explaining they had to search the house. They had no warrant, but it was war and no warrant was needed, the officer told us. We were all gathered in the kitchen, apart from Mamma and Marco; Marco was in bed with diphtheria and he and Mamma were kept in my parents' bedroom with a fascist on guard outside.

Gabriella Pellizzi was asked to accompany the German officer and one of the fascists on the search. They went into each room where she had to open every drawer and cupboard. The German looked with suspicion at an eighteenth-century Neapolitan bureau. He knocked here and there on its surface, knowing quite well that many such bureaux of that period contained a secret drawer, which indeed the Pellizzi's did, but luckily he missed it. In the drawer, I later learned, there were compromising letters and documents belonging to Domenico, Gabriella's husband, who was in hiding.

I still have a copy of the account of the episode which Gabriella wrote after the war:

They opened all the drawers, read all the papers which they found in Giovanna's [Gabriella's daughter] desk and took her diary away. (I had warned her a few days earlier to tear out the pages in which she'd written about her father.) They also took her exercise book with some English translations, saying they would return the lot in due course. The minutes slowly ticked by. The German officer picked up a book of Grimms' fairy tales, a book I'd just bought to give to little Marco for Christmas, and slowly and pensively he browsed through it. I wondered if he was thinking of his home and his childhood. A local fascist came into the room and told them to hurry up. They asked all of us to get dressed and, when we were ready, they piled us into the lorry, leaving behind only Ernesta [Anna's mother] and little Marco.

MIRACULOUSLY, GUIDO was not found. He had hidden behind some branches and logs stacked in a corner of one of the attic rooms. The incredible thing was that one of the fascists found Guido's bicycle permit (a necessary document at the time) on the bedside table in his room. The fascist was obviously so pleased to get hold of a free bike that he never asked anything about its owner. Papà rushed to the store room and handed the bike to him, heartily relieved that it was only the bike and not its owner that was being loaded on to the lorry. Guido was a deserter as far as the *Repubblica di Salò* was concerned and, if found, would have been shot, as would Gabriella, too, for giving him shelter.

Guido had now been in hiding for months, but after that day in December he packed his toothbrush and immediately made his way up to the Apennines where few Germans would dare to go because the mountains were in the hands of the partisans. He was soon joined by Carlo Saverio, also a deserter. We didn't see Guido again, or even know where he was, until the end of the war, although every now and then we received a short message saying he was all right. As we discovered later, Guido never had to go into battle – he would have hated fighting even against the fascists or the Germans – but stayed up in the mountains and did ancillary work such as driving and cooking for the partisans.

MEANWHILE, THE lorry drove down to Reggio Emilia with all of us on board: Gabriella Pellizzi and her two children, Giovanna and Nino; my father and me; Maria, the Pellizzi's cook, and the maids Mafalda and Augusta; the *contadini* and their families plus two workers who had just arrived at the farm. We were taken to the barracks of the *Brigate Nere* where I had been questioned the previous February.

For everyone except the Pellizzis, our stay in that lugubrious place was mercifully brief; by midday we were loaded back on to the same lorry and taken home. The only question that Papà had been asked was if he knew Domenico Pellizzi – 'Yes, of course, I do; he is a friend,' he'd replied – and whether he had seen him recently, which he hadn't; none of us had. Why they took us all to prison was never clear.

But the Pellizzis were kept for twenty-three days and we were extremely worried about them, receiving only sketchy reports of what was going on. Here is my translation of what Gabriella wrote about her imprisonment:

Like Marie-Antoinette, I went to prison with my personal maid but, unlike her, I was pushed in a small room with twenty-three other women. At night they put a bucket next to my palliasse – mattress – to be used as a loo. Not very pleasant. At midday we went down to the ground floor with our mess tins and lined up to receive some soup and a piece of meat, which the soldier on duty fished out from the pot using the same fork he'd been eating with. At least we had all our own bedding from home, which was a real luxury – the only pleasant thing in that awful place.

The other women were all country girls, jolly and cheerful, singing and joking, apart from one emaciated woman and her young daughter. The fascists had brought the woman in because, when they'd searched her home, they could not find any men. To make her talk they had kept her in a tiny room with nothing to lie on. They fed her only very salty food and never gave her any water to drink. She was in a pitiful state.

After eight days, the Commandant came into our room, leading, as usual, a large Alsatian dog who used to belong to a partisan chief, in the hope that the dog would recognise his previous master and betray him. The Commandant had the reputation of being very cruel and he paid for it later by being killed in the most gruesome manner after the war. But, with us, he behaved very courteously. He told us that Giovanna and I and my sister-in-law and her daughter [who'd also been jailed] were to be moved to the barracks of San Tomaso. Just before we left, a young woman came in. She had been stripped and beaten to make her talk and she showed us the red wounds on her back. All the time we were there, we'd heard the stamping of heavy shoes up and down the stairs and the sound of muffled screams.

We said goodbye to our companions and walked in single file for ten minutes or so to our new abode where we were locked in a cell with two other women. They gave us some filthy bed covers and sheets. I thought, with regret, of the clean bedding in our previous 'hotel'. It was winter and terribly cold. After the evening meal, the light was switched off. We no longer had our knitting, which we'd had to leave in the other prison. Knitting had been a great distraction, but there were two great pluses. We had a proper loo with a basin and all our meals were personally delivered by the owner of the local restaurant, Cannon d'Oro. The very kind Signor Simonini cooked many delicious and varied meals for us, always ending with sweets and fruit – we had so much that we were able to give some food to the other prisoners. We were held there for fourteen days. And then, suddenly, we were free. We met Nino (he'd been kept in the men's prison) and for the moment this farce, which could have easily have turned into tragedy, was over. We borrowed some bicycles and rode home.

~

AND WE, the Del Conte family and the *contadini* – were anxiously waiting to welcome them back, safe and sound. After this episode, Domenico Pellizzi, who'd been in hiding nearby, cycled with Nino all the way to Milan (some 150 kilometres) for safety, where they stayed till the end of the war.

For us, life went on as normally as possible. My father

became extremely restless and worried, like *un leone in gabbia* – a caged lion – as my mother used to say. He'd not been able to work for the past three years and money was tight. He spent his days chopping wood for the fires and stoves around the house and walking incessantly up and down the sitting room and the hall. In the evening, we all played cards together, trying to warm ourselves around the stove. There was not much else to do. I was often in the kitchen, helping here and there and learning to make *sfoglia* – the pasta of Emilia – albeit without much success. Giovanna never came into the kitchen. She didn't like cooking, and still doesn't, but she was marvellous at weaving and taught me to spin the wool from the sheep. We knitted endless cardies and pullovers for ourselves, for Marco and for all the *contadini*'s children, as well as socks and scarves for the partisans. We went to our English lessons, hoping to be able to chat to our liberators soon. It was a hard, solitary existence for us young girls, but we were convinced that soon the Allied Forces would be able to break through the Gothic Line.

And then, one spring morning, we found that our endless wait was over.

Coppa di Testa
Pig's Head Brawn

SERVES 8

half a pig's head
3 tbsp coarse salt
3 bay leaves
a few parsley stalks
1 onion, unpeeled, stuck with 2 cloves
1 large celery stick
1 carrot
3 juniper berries, bruised
1cm cinnamon stick
7 peppercorns
generous grating of nutmeg
2 cloves
small piece of dried chilli
½ tbsp fennel seeds
1 garlic clove
1 tsp sugar
4 tbsp red wine vinegar, preferably balsamic
salt
rind of 1 unwaxed orange and 1 unwaxed lemon,
without any white pith
30g pine nuts
30g pistachio nuts, blanched and peeled

Ask the butcher to chop the half head into 2 or 3 chunks. Burn away all the hairs from the pig's head and scrape the rind thoroughly. Rub the coarse salt all over the pieces of meat and then then put them in a bowl with 2 of the bay leaves and the parsley stalks. Leave for 24 hours.

Rinse the meat chunks, put them in a stockpot and cover with cold water. Bring to the boil and boil for 5 minutes. Drain and then put the head back in the stockpot with the onion, celery, carrot, juniper berries and remaining bay leaf. Cover with cold water, bring to the boil and simmer steadily for about 4 to 4½ hours, until the meat comes away easily from the bones. Allow to cool a little.

As soon as you can touch the meat, remove all the meat pieces and set aside. Strain the liquid, reserve and cool. Remove the bones from the pieces of meat, cut the meat into bite-size pieces and transfer to a bowl.

Pound together in a mortar the cinnamon, peppercorns, nutmeg, cloves, chilli, fennel seeds, garlic and sugar, moistening the mixture with the vinegar. Stir into the meat pieces and add salt in generous quantity, remembering that when cold the flavourings will become much milder. Cut the orange and lemon rind into tiny pieces and add to the bowl together with the pine nuts and the pistachios.

And now the final preparation. It is difficult to say how much mixture you will have – it depends on the size of the head and on how much meat you have managed to get from it. Usually you will have enough to loosely fill 2 x 1-litre sandwich tins. Line the tins with clingfilm and spoon the mixture into them. Pour in some of the reserved cooking liquid until the tins are full. Mix well, then cover with clingfilm and place in the fridge to chill. Leave in the fridge overnight or longer, then unmould the shapes and cut into 1cm slices.

Serve with a liquid salsa verde (see page 268, but use proportionately more oil and vinegar and less parsley and breadcrumbs).

CHAPTER 10

LIBERATION DAY

An American feast

'MA COME MAI,' my father said, 'in the last two days we haven't heard a single plane, we haven't seen a single truck. Even our friend Pippo hasn't come to visit us at night.' This was the evening of the 24th of April 1945. Why so much peace around? Was it really the end of the war? Not a word was said about it on the radio; we knew nothing.

The next morning, at about eleven o'clock, we saw a military car driving along the avenue of cypresses up to our house. Down jumped a black soldier and that – more than anything – told us that the car contained neither Germans nor fascists. They were Americans. Three other soldiers got out of the car, and soon all of us – the Pellizzi, Del Contes and the *contadini* – surrounded them with broad smiles and open arms. Maria, one of the *contadini*, broke into sobs and started dancing around the yard with one of the Americans, shouting: 'Now he can come back, now he can come back,' the 'he' in question being her husband Pietro who had been up in the mountains with the partisans for the past year.

'They can all come back,' said Mamma, no doubt thinking that at long last she would see her beloved older son again.

The soldiers were invited into the house and sat around the table, and out came the wine and the glasses. And out of their jeep came bananas, tea, coffee, chocolate and packets and packets of cigarettes. They drank while we smoked and Mamma immediately ran into the kitchen to make the first decent cup of coffee in years. She loved coffee and the four years without it had been a real deprivation for her. She had tried to get used to the coffee made of ground roasted chicory roots, but to no avail, just as we tried to get used to smoking crunched-up dried mulberry leaves wrapped in what we called 'butcher paper'.

So the soldiers drank wine and laughed and laughed, and we laughed, too, in a natural outburst of joy rather than in response to what the soldiers were telling us, since we could hardly understand a word they were saying.

Marco, my eight-year-old brother, took a banana and, without peeling it, bit into it. '*Ma, non è buona,*' he cried, nearly in tears, and spat it out. So often he had heard us say how delicious bananas were. The black soldier, who we discovered was Brazilian, was killing himself with laughter, while Marco was getting more and more upset. After the disappointment, he had to bear the shame.

The soldiers told us the Germans were in full retreat and that the Allies had already arrived at the Po, the great river that cuts through the Lombard and Emilian plane from west to east. Signora Pellizzi decided that a celebration was called for. And in Emilia that means tagliatelle, the most festive of all food. She despatched her cook Maria to the kitchen and Maria got out her rolling pin and, in a few minutes, she was hard at work, kneading and stretching and pummelling with that rhythmic movement that the men from Emilia find so sexy, although I've often wondered why.

However, I do find the process of making pasta by hand absorbing, although I always make it with the hand-cranked machine. To stretch the dough by hand is a demanding job and, frankly, I'm not much good at it. The *sfoglia* – rolled-out pasta dough – should be very thin; so thin, the people of Emilia say, that if you lay it on a newspaper you can read the print underneath. You also have to work extremely fast because, if the *sfoglia* becomes too dry, you cannot stretch it any more.

Maria, Zerlina, Barberina, the Balsamo's cook, and all the other Emiliane I saw at work could all make a *sfoglia* of four eggs in half an hour. They were making pasta long before they could read or write, they said, if indeed they ever learnt to do that. The most fascinating part is the final stretching, when the hands seem to gently stroke the *sfoglia* as it is rolled round the *mattarello* – rolling pin – and pushed away. And then the turning of the *mattarello* where the *sfoglia* is rolled through 90 degrees, so that the same stroking and stretching happens all round the circle. The diameter of a four-egg sfoglia should be just under one metre, and as the rolling pin for pasta is eighty-five centimetres long, in the end the rolling pin disappears from sight. And for a happy life, the Emiliani say, you must have *conti corti e tagliatelle lunghe* – short bills and long tagliatelle.

Maria, however, was upset that day because the tagliatelle could not be dressed with ragù, as tradition demanded. She couldn't possibly make a proper ragù in one or two hours; she needed at least four. So she decided to dress the tagliatelle with prosciutto, butter and Parmigiano, of which there's always an abundance in every Emilian household, and threw in a few peas fresh from the garden. But a meal in Emilia is not complete unless it has at least three courses, so our maid Augusta was delegated to fetch two chickens from the *contadini* and to roast them with rosemary and butter, and the garden had a plentiful supply of vegetables – broad beans, peas, spinach, salads – to choose from.

So we all – the masters, the servants and the soldiers – sat around the large kitchen table and celebrated the end of that terrible war. Lambrusco wine was flowing, to the delight of the Americans. And Marco, at table, had his revenge. He looked at the Americans and exclaimed with disgust, 'But they don't even know how to eat pasta: they cut the tagliatelle!' Horror of horrors. As a little child he had always been told that tagliatelle must never be touched by a blade.

It was a jolly gathering of oddly assorted people who had only one thing in common: joy at the end of the war. And the food was superb. Mamma was staggered at the amount the Americans ate, while Signora Pellizzi was even more amazed at the amount of wine they drank. Some time in the afternoon, they packed up and drove away – full and drunk – and we wondered how long it would be before they ended up in a ditch.

In the evening, Giovanna and I decided to go into town to see what was happening. I put on my best dress – in fact my only dress – a navy little number, with short sleeves, a round neck, two buttoned-down pockets on the bosom and a skirt which was gathered at the hips. Apart from that, I only had a few, rather dull, skirts, some of which were made from my father's old trousers, and some cardigans which I'd knitted during the last year. Then I put on more than the usual amount of lipstick and felt quite pleased with the tout-ensemble.

We got out our bicycles and rode triumphantly to Albinea, across the bridge that for months we hadn't dared to cross. It was still passable, in spite of having been bombed eighteen times, as we were later told, but it was full of holes and it took a lot of effort to dodge them so as not to finish in the river, but we managed between one laugh and the next.

Albinea was *in festa*. Flags, sheets and cloths were hanging from every window. Some locals had put out tables and were dishing out food that they had saved for this occasion, delighted to share it with everybody. The band arrived and everyone started dancing. Yet somehow we couldn't really enjoy ourselves. I just stood and watched with a feeling of incredulity. It all seemed so unreal, and I got the impression that I was not the only one to feel like that. The struggle had been so long, and so hard and determined, that it had become our raison d'être and now we felt deflated and empty. After a few foxtrots, a plateful of *tagliatelle al ragù* and a glass of Lambrusco, Giovanna and I got back on our bikes, rode home and went to bed.

~

PEACE AT LAST and the dawn of a new life. My brother Guido and Carlo Saverio came down from the mountains some days later. I was delighted to see them and we sat down and talked and talked and talked. But somehow they didn't want to tell us anything about their life in the mountains and kept asking about our life down here, how we'd managed and what we did. I realised immediately that I didn't want to start my relationship with Carlo Saverio again. I had never really loved him and I was not prepared to pretend any longer just for the sake of being kind; in fact, I was sure it would have been more hurtful to him in the long run. He knew, and nothing was said about the matter.

One of the first things Guido did was to get hold of some soap – it was very scarce then – strip naked and stand under the hose in the garden. For the lack of a more private solution, the garden hose was our bath in spring and summer. As soon as the weather was warm enough, we took turns to go out and wash properly.

Slowly, everybody began to pick up the pieces and started to live again. Domenico Pellizzi and Nino came back from Milan, while my father left for Milan as soon as he could, anxious to meet all his friends and to start to gather whatever work he could. At the end of June, Mamma, Marco and I packed all our belongings onto a lorry and were driven to Cantù, north of Milan, to stay with Zia Renata, Mamma's younger sister. It was a very uncomfortable and slow journey, but a happy one. We picked up other people on the way and made friends with everybody we met. The 150-kilometre drive took two days. Bridges were down, roads were impassable and clogged with people, animals, carts, lorries. Everybody seemed to be on the move after months of enforced standstill. We spent the night in a run-down *locanda* where even my finicky mother did not mind the cockroaches which kept us company. We were alive.

We left that land blessed by the gods, where we'd found so many warm and hospitable friends and eaten some of the best food ever.

RECIPES

Pollo Arrosto in Tegame
Roasted Chicken in a Pot

SERVES 4

30g unsmoked pancetta, chopped
sprig of rosemary
10–12 sage leaves
3 garlic cloves, left whole
1 organic chicken, about 1kg
30g unsalted butter
1 tbsp olive oil
125ml white wine
salt and pepper

Put the pancetta, 1 sprig of rosemary, 5 or 6 sage leaves, 1 garlic clove and salt and pepper into the cavity of the chicken. Close the opening with a skewer and tie up the bird.

Heat the butter and oil in a flameproof casserole, then place the chicken in it and fry on all sides until brown. Pour the wine over and allow it to bubble away for 2–3 minutes, then add another sprig of rosemary, a few sage leaves and the remaining garlic cloves. Cover the casserole and cook over very gentle heat until the chicken is cooked through, which should take about 1¼ hours. Turn the bird over once or twice during the cooking.

Transfer the chicken to a dish and keep warm while you make the gravy. Remove the sage leaves and garlic cloves from the casserole and discard. Tilt the casserole and remove as much fat as you can with a spoon. Add 4 or 5 tablespoons of hot water and boil rapidly, scraping the bottom of the dish with a metal spoon. Pour these cooking juices over the carved chicken.

~

Tagliatelle al Prosciutto e Piselli
Tagliatelle with Prosciutto and Peas

If you are making your own tagliatelle, follow the instructions in the recipe for home-made pasta on page 133, but remember that fresh pasta takes far less time to cook than dried pasta.

SERVES 3–4

50g unsalted butter
½ small onion, very finely chopped
100g prosciutto, cut into matchsticks
100g cooked peas
250g dried egg tagliatelle, or make your own using 2 large eggs and
approximately 200g Italian 00 flour
3 tbsp double cream
50g freshly grated parmesan cheese
salt and black pepper

In a large frying pan melt the butter and fry the onion for about 5 minutes until just soft. Mix in the prosciutto and the peas and cook for 5 minutes, stirring frequently.

Meanwhile, cook the tagliatelle in boiling salted water.

Drain, reserving 1 cupful of the pasta cooking water, and add the tagliatelle to the frying pan with the prosciutto mixture. Stir well, then add the cream and half the parmesan. Toss gently for 30 seconds, season with plenty of pepper and, if necessary, add 1 or 2 tablespoons of the reserved pasta water. Serve at once, with the remaining parmesan in a separate bowl.

~

Home-Made Fresh Pasta

Here is my recipe for making the traditional pasta from Emilia-Romagna. It is a pasta you can bite into and one that holds its cooking point well. It is not possible to give an exact quantity for the flour because it varies according to the flour's absorption capacity, the size of the eggs and the humidity of the atmosphere.

MAKES ENOUGH PASTA FOR 3–4 PEOPLE

2 large free-range eggs
approximately 200g Italian 00 flour

Put the flour on the work surface and make a well in the centre. Break the eggs into the well. Beat them lightly with a fork and draw the flour in gradually from the inner wall of the well. When the eggs are no longer runny, draw in enough flour to enable you to knead the dough with your hands. You may not need all the flour; push some to the side and add only what is needed. Alternatively you might need a little more from the bag, which you should keep at hand. Work until the flour and eggs are thoroughly amalgamated and then put the dough to one side and scrape the work top clean. Wash and dry your hands.

Proceed to knead the dough by pressing and pushing with the heel of your palm, folding it back, giving it half a turn and repeating these movements. Repeat the movements for about 7–8 minutes if you are going to make your pasta by hand, or 3–4 minutes if you are going to use a machine. Wrap the dough in clingfilm and let it rest for at least 30 minutes, though you can leave it for up to 3 hours.

Rolling out pasta by machine
The hand-cranked type of machine is very good and inexpensive. I strongly advise you to buy one and you will be amply repaid within a few weeks. You will be able to produce good tagliatelle for 6 people in half an hour at a quarter of the price of shop-bought fresh pasta and of a quality you could never find in a shop. I prefer the old fashioned hand-cranked machine to the sophisticated but noisy electric ones, of which there are several at various prices.

Follow the manufacturer's instructions, but do remember to knead the dough by hand for a few minutes, even if the instructions say that the machine can do that for you.

When making tagliatelle, lasagne and *tagliolini*, the *sfoglia* – the rolled-out dough – must be allowed to hang a little to dry, or the strands will stick to each other. It is difficult to say how long it needs, as it depends on the temperature and humidity of the atmosphere, but it should be dry to the touch and just beginning to become leathery. Stuffed pasta must not be left to dry.

CHAPTER II

AFTER THE WAR

Champagne and gin

O NE OF THE FIRST things Mamma and I did when we finally arrived in my native Lombardy, was to go and see our flat in Via Sant'Andrea, or rather the site where the house had been. There were mountains of blackened stones and stumps and debris of every sort in between the columns of what had been a beautiful courtyard. I looked across at the Senato palace – our house had been at the corner of Via Sant'Andrea and Via Senato – and tears filled my eyes as I thought of all the times I had enjoyed the sight of that stunning seventeenth-century building of perfect Lombard Baroque from the window of our sitting room just opposite. My mother had already been back with my father in 1943 a few days after the bombing. They travelled from Albinea, a difficult and long journey, to try to rescue the things – plates, glasses, books, paintings and other chattels – that were stacked in the cellar. She told me of her and Papà's rage when they went down, opened the door of the cellar and saw that it was virtually empty. Almost everything was looted and that was that – actually that was war. A few things of value that were saved, were later stolen by one of our maids, Augusta.

Augusta was a very good maid and an extremely shrewd woman who managed to gain my mother's trust completely and to take advantage of that trust.

Augusta's stealing career started when I was a child, with her pinching my beautiful Longines watch, a gift from my godmother, Zia Ester, for my First Communion. I still remember Augusta saying to Mamma: 'Oh, la Signorina Anna has fallen in love again and she is always losing things.' I knew perfectly well that my Longines had disappeared from within the house. Then Augusta progressed to a small Cartier brooch I'd inherited from my grandmother. It was shaped like a cock's head with a small diamond eye and a crest made of tiny rubies. Augusta was eventually caught by my father, in flagrante, walking out of our flat after the war with a small Persian rug under her arm. 'Augusta la Bella' – a sobriquet that Guido and I had given her, more because of what she thought of herself than by way of aesthetic judgment – became 'Augusta la Ladra' – Augusta the Thief – and disappeared from our lives. My parents were unable to sort out what had been stolen by her or what was destroyed by the bombs that hit the house, or what had been looted. It was the war, and we were lucky to be alive.

At the end of the war, my parents received damages from the government for the losses they had sustained during the bombing of our Via Sant'Andrea flat, but these were based on their value in 1943. The inflation between 1943 and 1946 was staggering; suffice it to say that, in 1946, my parents received just enough money to buy two mattresses. Mamma was a natural home-maker and the loss of her house and all her possessions must have been devastating.

~

THE FOLLOWING October, I enrolled in the faculty of History and Philosophy at the Università di Stato in Milan. In Italy, even sixty years ago, it was expected that girls would go to university and have the same type of higher education as their brothers. I could be a student, but I also had to work to earn money. University students of the Humanities did not, and still don't, need to go to lectures regularly, just enough – say, six or seven times per term – to get the signatures of all the lecturers and to be recognised by them. That was easier to achieve if you had a pretty face, since most of the lecturers at that time were male.

I also took a course in shorthand and typing, at the end of which my typing speed was snail-like and my shorthand was abysmal. But one of my uncles took pity on me and gave me a job as his secretary in his firm which manufactured syringes, phials, vials and other boring things of that nature. That was *real* nepotism, the Italian word *nipote* meaning a nephew or niece.

My parents and Marco were still living with Zia Renata north of Milan. But straight after the war, Guido became involved with Bibi, an extremely attractive married woman. Soon enough a baby boy, Luca, arrived. Bibi's father gave them a small flat in Milan and I went to live with them, sharing Luca's room.

Friends slowly returned to Milan and we began to live the kind of normal life that young people do, albeit affected by the disasters of war. I even acquired a boyfriend who was studying engineering. The faculty building, the famous Politecnico, was quite close to my office, so I used to go there and eat at the canteen with him and other friends. The food in the canteen was good, homely and cheap, offering meals such as pasta al pomodoro, followed by meat or fish with a vegetable or a salad, and fruit. (Jamie Oliver would have approved.) Looking back, I think it was the food and the convivial atmosphere that attracted me most, rather than a yearning to be with Mario. It was hardly a passionate affair and I certainly wasn't too distressed when he eventually dumped me in favour of a very rich girl from Florence. A dowry was a very important asset and mine was nil. The only distressing part for me was that he was rich and titled. I was moving in a circle of wealthy young people and I found it difficult to keep up with them. They were smart, I wasn't; they gave parties, I didn't; they had villas in the country, while I had only a room which I shared with Guido's new baby. But I still enjoyed their company and I went to parties, the theatre and the cinema with them.

I remember one particular dance party on a steamer on Lake Como in the summer of 1945. I'd gone with a great friend of mine, Joan Allen Tuska, who later married my cousin Sandro. Her mother and a group of society ladies had organised the dance for some American officers stationed around Como. The steamer was decked with the Italian tricolour and the Stars and Stripes. We, the girls, chaperoned by a handful of mothers, were already on board when the Americans arrived all spruced up in their smart uniforms. And the music started. I hadn't really danced for three years, nor, I expect, had most of the other girls on that romantic night-time sailing across Lake Como. The war had robbed us of our youth. So there we were, twenty or so pretty girls, all dressed up to the nines, as eager as 14-year-olds at their first dance.

My gaze fell on a tall, handsome American, but I soon realised that he already had his eye on Joan who, being half American, had the advantage of being able to converse in English, rather than just bat her eyelashes and smile. I soon found a willing partner in a rather small but charming man who seemed to understand my elementary English. And so we danced and danced to the music of 'In the Mood', 'Georgia on my Mind', and 'Stardust' – songs we hardly knew, Mussolini having forbidden the playing, showing, or selling of American or other foreign music, films, books, everything. For the previous ten years, since the invasion of Ethiopia, we had lived in a fascist cocoon, where we heard and learnt only about the things on which Mussolini had put his stamp of approval.

The buffet on that boat was another new experience. I had eaten many excellent dinners in Albinea during the war, where the food was without doubt better than that on the boat on Lake Como. But the drinks were something else. In our feasts during the war, we drank mainly wine, albeit very good local wine, and the occasional local liqueur, such as *Nocino* and *Grappa* – so rough that they took your breath away – or one of the home-made herb liqueurs. But on that beautiful evening, as soon as we got on board, we were offered gin – gin with tonic, with orange juice, with French vermouth, with Italian vermouth, pink gin, gin with this, gin with that, gin with anything. Then there was the champagne – proper French champagne, not Asti Spumante or other sweet Italian bubbly. Oddly enough for me, an inveterate lover of food rather than drink, I don't remember anything about what we ate that night. I can only recall a long table covered with dishes, but not the food itself. Perhaps it wasn't worth remembering, or maybe I'd simply been too entranced with the romance of that night?

~

Sixty years later, in 2006, I attended another party on Lake Como. This time we were celebrating Joan's eightieth birthday at a lunch in her late eighteenth-century villa at Moltrasio, on the shores of the lake. The perfectly proportioned villa was built in the age when baroque had all but disappeared in favour of a return to classicism, but a classicism softened by the lapse of time. Now it has also the commercial advantage of being near George Clooney's villa.

There were seventy of us at the birthday party, most of us elderly, but with a sprinkling of young, and a few children to liven things up. And while, at that first party on Lake Como in 1945, the food had been unmemorable, at this second one it was unforgettable. The first course was set on the large table and, by the time I got to the buffet to choose from the antipasti, I just managed to scoop out the last three *gnocchetti* of spinach, which everyone at my table agreed were first-rate. The pasta salad was also exemplary, demonstrating that cold pasta can be seriously good – as long as it is not smothered in thick mayonnaise. The *risotto in bianco* was served, in traditional Lake Como style, with fillets of perch – the local fish – coated in egg and breadcrumbs and fried in butter.

To our surprise, there was more to come, and the table was reloaded with *i secondi* – the second course – which consisted of all manner of summery dishes, my favourites being a spicy hunk of roasted tunny fish and *vitello alle erbe* – veal with herbs – the delicate flavour of the meat, and its rich cooking juices, enhanced by a perfectly balanced mixture of fresh herbs.

And on we ate and chatted and drank, until a waiter – followed by a string of children – walked through the terrace to the garden carrying the most splendid birthday cake which he placed on a round table. The cake, some forty centimetres in diameter, consisted of a pastry case filled with crème pâtissière and topped with concentric rows of raspberries, each stuffed with a drop of crème pâtissière. The white candles simply formed the figure of 80.

Joan, surrounded by her grandchildren and grandnephews and nieces, was overwhelmed. We sang *Tanti auguri a te* – happy birthday – and drank to her health. No speeches; they are not part of the Italian tradition at such events. Instead, from across the lake a large boat slowly came into view and anchored just in front of the villa. And then . . . music. A brass band on the boat played the Drinking Song from *La Traviata*, followed by the Toreador song from *Carmen* and the Anvil Chorus from *Il Trovatore*. It was a beautifully timed surprise.

The theme of that party was 'memory lane'. I met people I hadn't seen for fifty years, and a few I didn't recognise and didn't dare ask whether they could see in me the faintest traces of the pretty dark girl I had been.

~

IN 1946, AGED twenty-one, I was indeed pretty, although it is a period of my life I would have preferred to forget. I moved back in with my parents, who had eventually found a small, sad-looking, ground-floor flat in Via Kramer, which, compared miserably to the noble Via Gesù and Via Sant'Andrea of the pre-war years. There was a little yard at the back, where Marco played tennis against the wall and my mother, a keen gardener, grew some herbs and tomatoes. She also planted a jasmine, in the hope that its scent would mask the smell of the zuppa di cavoli – cabbage soup – which the neighbours seemed to cook every day.

My parents' life was radically different from the one they'd led before the war. Most their money had been spent during the last three years of the war, and the little they still had was now worthless because of the inflation of 1945. During the war, the Milan Stock Exchange had been shut and, when the war finished, there was little trade at the beginning. While some stockbrokers traded in foreign currencies, my father for some reason felt it was unethical and unpatriotic. And Mamma was not the type of woman who could go out to work. Anyhow, what would she have been able to do? So she stayed at home, cooking, cleaning, washing, ironing and helping Marco with his homework, the latter being a laborious task since Marco was not a brilliant student.

In the autumn of 1945, my father had started working again, resurrecting his stockbroking career, slowly and with some difficulties at first, but gradually things became easier and money started coming in again, though by that time he was in his early seventies. He loved the stock exchange, the bustle, the ups and downs of the market, and the gamble, which even in his old age he couldn't resist. He died, aged eighty-three, after a morning's work in his office. In that respect, he was lucky.

But the earlier Via Kramer days were very tough for everybody. I went on working for my uncle and doing my university course. I passed all my exams, if not exactly with flying colours. I met new people, mostly in the art world, thanks to my dear friend Lalla Ramazzotti who was taking a degree in Art at the Accademia di Belle Arti di Brera. We went to the bars and pizzeria near Brera where we'd sit and talk into the small hours about the philosophy of Karl Marx or the paintings of Max Ernst or the films of Pasolini, Rossellini and De Sica. Despite our backgrounds, we all held left-wing views. We had that youthful ideology of hoping to change the world, wanting a world where equality could coexist with freedom.

Sometimes we were joined by the playwright Dario Fo, who was just at the beginning of his successful writing career which, in 1997, earned him the Nobel Prize for Literature. We went to the Piccolo Teatro, which Giorgio Strehler had just started and where he organised avant-garde performances – another of my Italian contemporaries who gained international fame.

Although the evenings were fun and my friends interesting, I couldn't help feeling that my life was banal. So, when I met Vanna Orefice, who was planning to work as an au-pair in England, I joined forces with her and two other friends, the Arton twins. All three girls were Jewish and had spent the last years in Switzerland to escape the racial war Mussolini had launched to assuage Hitler. Their parents had been far-sighted enough to leave Italy before Mussolini began to gather up the Jews and send them to Germany. In Switzerland, the Arton girls had made friends with a woman who, in 1947, set up an au-pair agency placing Swiss girls in England. We put our names down and she found us all places. I'd had enough of my boring job, enough of always being short of money, enough of living at home and enough of having to work and study at the same time and doing neither properly. Anything, I decided, would be better.

My parents took my decision quite well in spite of the fact that in Italy at that time, girls were supposed to live at home until they married. The irony was that, about ten days before I was due to leave, I fell passionately in love with a man called Franco, who was charming, *simpatico* and fun. We had a whirlwind affair and then I had to say goodbye. We promised each other that we'd be together again when I returned from England, but, as often happened in my life, things turned out differently. Franco came to the Stazione Centrale in Milan to see me off and we had one of those emotional farewells, *Brief Encounter* style, with him holding my hands while running alongside the train, and me with tears streaming down my face.

So in January 1949, with a heavy heart, I said goodbye to Franco and to my life in Italy. It was indeed goodbye, as it turned out – not *Arrivederci*, but *Addio*.

RECIPE

Tonno Arrosto con Senape
Roasted Tuna with Mustard and Three Peppers

This simple yet excellent recipe was given to me by Signora Maestri, who prepared the eightieth birthday lunch party for my cousin.

1kg fresh tuna
2 tbsp French mustard
2 tbsp ground green, pink and black pepper
2 tbsp plain flour
sea salt
2 tbsp extra virgin olive oil

Preheat the oven to 200°C/gas mark 6.

Wash and dry the tuna.

In a small bowl, mix together the mustard, ground peppercorns, flour and 2 pinches of sea salt. Add the oil using a fork, then spread this mixture all over the tuna, patting it firmly with your hands.

Lightly brush an oven tray with oil and place the tuna on it. Bake in the oven for 20 minutes.

Remove the tuna from the oven and let it cool. When cool, carve into thickish slices, about 1cm thick.

The tuna should be quite pink inside, just like a perfectly cooked roast beef.

CHAPTER 12

MOLESEY HOUSE

Puddings and pies

O N THE 24TH OF JANUARY 1949, I arrived at Victoria
Station in London, feeling tired after twenty-five hours
on a train. But the journey had been fascinating for us four girls
after years of not being able to go anywhere. Later, I was asked
how it felt travelling through that part of northern France
which had been devastated by the war. And I realised that I had
not even noticed. I'd been so used to seeing towns in ruins
during the last few years that it had barely registered with me.

At Victoria Station I walked down the platform with my
large Gladstone bag and there, at the end, was a gentleman in
a pin-striped, double-breasted blue suit, a bowler hat, carrying
a rolled umbrella. It was my host, Joss Staveley-Hill, a rotund,
sprightly figure who could have stepped straight out of the
pages of *The Pickwick Papers*. He came towards me with a
broad, welcoming smile, twinkling dark eyes and his bowler
hat in his left hand. I said goodbye to my friends and followed
him to a different platform where we got on the suburban
train to Hampton Court.

In that first half-hour in England, I realised that my limited
knowledge of English might have been of some help in

talking and reading, but it certainly left me high and dry when it came to understanding what people were saying. I had learned English first at school for three years and then, when I was fourteen, I had to drop it and start ancient Greek which was part of the curriculum at the classic lycée where I was studying. I continued to learn English privately, but my lessons had often been interrupted by the accidents of war, such as bombs, machine guns and difficulties in transport.

At Hampton Court, Joss put my bag into his car, a pre-war blue Ford known as the Blue Bag. Then we drove to East Molesey and turned into the drive of Molesey House, the home of the Staveley-Hills. He opened the door and I entered the world of a typical upper-class English family. His wife, Kitty, in cashmere twin-set, pearls and tweed skirt, came to welcome me, followed by Penny and Henry, the six-year-old twins – the reason for my becoming part of the family – and a barking, black-and-white dog called Whisky. 'What a lovely dog. What is it?' I asked. 'Oh, nothing,' answered Kitty, 'it's just a mongrel.' Mongrel was a new word for me, so I asked her to explain. 'Ah,' I said, 'a bastard.' 'Oh no,' she replied, laughing, 'bastards are men, mongrels are dogs.' And that was the first English lesson Kitty gave me. My new life in England had begun.

⁓

FOR THE first weeks, I missed Franco desperately, or so it seemed. We couldn't even talk on the telephone, because there weren't as yet any international telephone connections. I wrote, he answered, he wrote, I answered, but . . . what the eye does not see, the heart does not bleed over. Slowly at first, and then with gathering momentum, memories of Franco and my Italian life receded and I started to enjoy this new adventure.

I had been lucky to land in the midst of a charming family who did their best to make me feel at home. But I didn't really feel at home for quite some time. In spite of my twenty-three years, I had always lived with my family. I'd been through a violent and bloody war and been able to cope and survive in very difficult situations, and yet now I felt as I had at five years old when Guido and I were sent for a few days – which seemed like weeks to me – to stay with the Peregalli family in their villa on Lake Como. For the first few weeks in East Molesey I missed my family and my 'habitat'. Still, here I was for the next eleven months and here I stayed, apart from a brief weekend in Cambridge in June with my friends the Cavalli-Sforza.

Pupa Cavalli-Sforza was the sister of my old schoolfriend Lalla Ramazzotti Morassutti. Lalla and I attended the Liceo Parini state school together until 1942 when we left Milan because of the bombings. The Parini was – and still is, I have been told – the best lycée in Milan, with high academic standards, and all the children from wealthy Milanese families vied to go there where they mixed with bright working class children. (My husband Oliver later called it the Italian Eton, since wherever we were – in a restaurant, on a beach or in a smart shop – someone would come up to me and say, '*Ma tu, tu non eri mica al Parini?*' – 'Weren't you at the Parini?' The difference is that the Parini is a state school.)

Pupa had married Luca, a budding scientist from Pavia University who was currently doing some research at Cambridge. Luca, who spoke perfect English, was a great anglophile and liked to model himself on the English academics. He smoked a pipe, wore brogue shoes and tweed jackets with leather patches at the elbows. But he was far too soigné in his casualness, to be convincingly British.

As I entered the Cavalli-Sforza's small terraced house in Cambridge I was overwhelmed by nostalgia – the smells, the sounds, the gestures were all Italian – and for two days it felt as though I was in Italy again. I can still remember the *pollo arrosto*. The chicken was roasted in the Italian way, with the addition of white wine which made the gravy so flavoursome. And, to finish the meal, we had real coffee made in the Napoletana, the old-fashioned machine that you turned upside down as soon as the water boiled to allow the water to filter through the coffee grounds. There was even a bidet in the bathroom, a portable one, but a bidet nevertheless. (A year later, when the Cavalli-Sforza were leaving Cambridge, I asked Pupa if I could have her bidet, the best souvenir she could leave me. To the English, bidet was still a dirty word, associated with unmentionable sex rather than its original purpose, hygiene.)

Pupa and Luca took me for a walk down the river Cam, pointing out all the colleges, and introduced me to the Early English architecture of King's College chapel. I fell in love with Cambridge (although a year later I had to change my allegiance when I married into an Oxford family).

The following Monday, I was back in Molesey House and its unpretentious charm. I liked my little room at the front of the house, with its pretty, flower-patterned bedcover and curtains, a comfortable small armchair and a large wardrobe, but I mainly sat and studied in the large nursery overlooking the garden, until the twins got back from school at four o'clock. Kitty Staveley-Hill was a real home-maker and every room spoke of her good taste. We had family meals in the pantry, next to the kitchen, where there was a gas fire against which I used to toast – or rather burn – the slices of bread, held at the end of a long fork, for breakfast (no toasters then). The laying of the breakfast table was baffling in its complexity: jars of marmalade and jelly, honey and Marmite, jugs of milk and coffee and tea, dishes of butter, packets of cereals, egg cups, different forks and spoons for all the variations of the cold or cooked breakfast, and cups and plates and toast racks. In Italy, I was used to a plate and a cup and saucer.

Not only was there no toaster but, far more regrettable, no central heating. In Milan, a city with a comparable climate, every house or flat I'd been in had central heating. In our flat in Via Gesù, it had been installed in 1922, shortly after Guido was born. And here I was in a house full of antique furniture, beautiful paintings and eighteenth-century porcelain, shivering as I got up each morning or when I went from one room to another during the day or took a bath in the freezing bathroom.

But the comparative lack of creature comforts at Molesey House was largely compensated by the warmth of its inhabitants and the pleasantness of its atmosphere. Kitty reigned undisputed in two rooms – the kitchen and the sitting room – the latter being a large room with chintz curtains, floral-patterned sofas and armchairs and a grand piano on one side. She'd sit there by herself in the afternoons, if she was not gardening, until after tea when Henry and Penny were allowed in to spend some time with her. Then, when Joss came home from work, the sitting room would come alive with his presence and his music. He played on the piano all the popular songs from the musicals of the time, and the ones from *Oklahoma*, which had just opened in London, were his favourites.

The large kitchen was light and sunny with a rectangular table in the middle and all manner of types and sizes of cupboards around the walls. There was a big Aga at one end and, in front of it, on the table, an old newspaper would be spread out every day for collecting the cooking debris.

Kitty, who prepared all the meals herself, was an accomplished cook and I scarcely noticed the strict food rationing that was still in force. Meat, butter and sugar were all scarce, but somehow Kitty was able to make her food taste good. She went shopping every morning, in the high street, with Whisky on the lead, or in Bentalls in Kingston, and then proceeded to make the kind of dishes I had never tasted before: meat pies, fish pies, fruit tarts, tartlets, steam puddings, trifles, custard and other creamy concoctions. Most of the vegetables came from the vegetable patch, which took up a good section of the large garden. It was cared for during the week by the one-legged Mr Russel, husband of the cleaning lady, and by Joss at weekends.

I was amazed at Kitty's ingenuity in the kitchen, given the food shortages in England in 1949. She made an excellent béchamel sauce, and endless variations thereof, to make the main ingredients go further. She rolled out the crispiest short pastry and the airiest flaky pastries; she baked cakes and biscuits in which even the margarine tasted good. The result of all these pies, puddings and custards was that, in the eleven months I lived at Molesey House, I put on more than a stone, an alarming amount for my diminutive height of five foot three inches. Luckily, one stone didn't sound as much to me as six kilos would have done.

I was fascinated by Kitty's dexterity with flaky pastry, a new experience for me. She used lard – that white block which bore no resemblance to the Italian *lardo*, and she was extremely quick at folding and turning. The flaky pastry was transformed into jam puffs for our tea, filled with the superb jam made from the raspberries in the garden. The pastry would break up as soon as you sank your teeth into it and then you tasted the divine raspberry flavour.

I didn't help much with the cooking, usually remaining a spectator. But there was one occasion when Kitty's parents were staying with us and Kitty had to go out for lunch. She asked me to warm up the meat casserole and boil some potatoes and carrots. Plain boiled vegetables were not in my repertoire and were the only part of Kitty's cooking that I never really enjoyed. So I made a potato pureé, with margarine of course, but adding plenty of rich, creamy milk as it was then, and stewed the carrots in a little soffritto of onion, as I'd always done at home. Both vegetables went down very well with the rather grand Sir Dudley and Lady MacCorquodale, who declared the carrots the best they had ever eaten.

It is to Kitty that I owe my knowledge of good British cooking and to both her and Joss my knowledge of properly spoken English (although I never mastered the accent). Kitty, in true upper-class fashion, taught me never to utter the words toilet, notepaper, serviette or pardon, and introduced me to the works of Jane Austen, the Bronte sisters and Nancy Mitford.

When I first arrived in England, I'd joined an English for Foreigners course at the Adult School of Education in Kingston. I dutifully went twice a week for the first few weeks, but soon found the pace too slow for me, so I decided to follow my own course, which involved reading *The Times* every day, writing down the unfamiliar words and then learning them by heart. Penny and Henry were also a fount of information, in spite of their youth.

Twice a week I took the train to Waterloo and then the tube to Piccadilly Circus, which was the meeting place for all foreigners. Even in 1949, I was thrilled to be in London, that huge metropolis which had fascinated me since hearing a song, as a child, which started with 'Piccadilly, Piccadilly, paradise of illusion, Piccadilly, your kisses are passion' – or at least that was my translation. In fact, Piccadilly and the whole centre of London was drab then, with bomb damage, dirty and crumbling buildings and dreary shops with only a few miserable items inside. At 5.30 p.m. everything shut down and everybody scuttled home to their uneatable high teas. I was used to Milan, which came to life in the evenings. After finishing work, people would meet up for an aperitif and for the traditional *passeggiata* – stroll – in Via Montenapoleone, up and down, up and down.

In London, though, people looked miserable and still dressed in grey, melancholy austerity. No cheerful restaurants, no bars, no cafes then, only pubs, which were strange territories for us foreigners. We did go into a pub in Soho once. Everybody stopped talking and turned round to stare at us, three girls looking lost and uneasy. A minute later, every-one forgot about us and started up their loud conversations again regularly broken by peals of intoxicated laughter. (Even after more than fifty years of anglicisation, pubs are not my favourite haunts, although I quite enjoy an occasional beer and a sandwich at my local in Dorset.)

Soon I met a group of young people, all Italian of course, with whom I went to the cinema, mostly to the Curzon to see Italian and French films in their original language, and to the theatre and the Proms, the latter being an amazing discovery for us.

~

THERE WERE many social evenings at Molesey House, too, where Kitty often held dinner parties, and it was from her that I learnt the art of entertaining *à l'anglaise*. Kitty was a very good hostess and her dinner parties were more formal than the ones I was used to at home. What I found strange was the 'withdrawing' of the ladies at the end of the meal. I am sure no English woman wanted to 'powder her nose' and if she did would have preferred to do so singly and not *en masse*. Was it really, as I was told, because the men wanted to go on drinking and telling each other stories too risqué for the delicate ears of a lady? In Italy men and women 'withdrew' together, to have their coffee and liqueurs in the drawing room to talk, or flirt, with whom they chose. I also found it disconcerting how very few English women of my generation went to university. The girls here were supposed to get married, after a secretarial course and that was that. Was this male chauvinism the Anglo-Saxon version of the Italian 'machismo'? While the British male felt intellectually superior, the Italian male felt sexually superior. But I am talking of sixty years ago, of course; now no British man would dare to think himself intellectually superior, while I feel sure that Latin machismo still exists; I am equally sure it exists because the women do not mind.

The other custom of the English upper class that I found and still find incomprehensible, and far more objectionable, was that of sending their children away to boarding schools at a very young age. After the summer of 1949 when the Staveley-Hills, plus me, motored around Brittany in the Blue Bag, eating oysters and mussels and Breton Far – a thick baked custard to which prunes are sometimes added – and crêpes, we returned to Molesey House at the beginning of September. A large trunk was hauled down from the attic in preparation for Henry, aged seven, leaving home for his new school. Kitty began to pack, with tears in her eyes, folding all the new shorts and socks and pants and vests, while Henry and Penny looked on, pained and perplexed. Joss didn't show any tears, although I'm sure he was suffering, too.

It was the first time in their lives that the Staveley-Hill twins were going to be separated, and I felt deeply sorry for that blond, dreamy boy who had to venture into life on his own. And I felt equally sorry for Joss and Kitty. Henry was quite miserable at school at first, but 'it's all for his good,' Kitty said. Certainly Henry ended up with a successful career as a stockbroker, following in his father's footsteps, and now lives in a beautiful house in Dorset with his wife and two daughters. Penny stayed at home until she was ten, long enough to learn how to cook from her mother so well that she is now reputedly the best cook in Northamptonshire, where she lives. No doubt, her fish pies are even better than Kitty's, but then she doesn't have the challenge of producing excellent dishes from a limited supply of ingredients, as in 1949.

RECIPES

Elephant's Turd
(Aberdeen Sausage)

I still have Kitty's original recipe in imperial measures and it is officially called 'Aberdeen Sausage'. The children, Henry and Penny, called it 'the elephant's turd' because of its appearance. In the original recipe the meat is 'steak' and I cannot remember what Kitty used at the time. I have made it with minced beef and/or pork and it works. Kitty used to grind the bacon and the meat together in that old-fashioned mincer with the handle that you screw on the table. The meat was ground just at the right texture. She served it with chutney or pickles and, having tried it with different sauces, I too like it best with chutney or pickles, *à l'anglaise* as it should be, served with a green salad *à l'italienne*, dressed with extra virgin olive oil and vinegar, which here I prefer to be balsamic. In spite of being a 'war dish', or just post-war, it is very good. Johnny, my greedy grandson, loves it 'especially in a sandwich', as Henry and Penny often had it.

225g smoked bacon, rind removed
225g best minced beef or pork
50g breadcrumbs made from 1 or 2 days old white bread
½ onion, chopped
1 lightly beaten egg
a generous grating of nutmeg
1 tsp mustard powder
a generous grinding of black pepper
3 tbsp grated mature cheddar
pinch of sugar
pinch of salt

For the vegetable stock:
1 onion cut in ½ and stuck with 2 cloves
1 carrot, cut into pieces
1 celery stick, cut into pieces
half a dozen peppercorns, crushed

Cut the bacon into pieces, put into the food processor and whiz until just ground, but not reduced to a paste. Scoop it out into a bowl and add the mince, breadcrumbs and all the other ingredients. Work the mixture thoroughly together with your hands and then place it on a board. Shape the mixture into a large sausage 20–25 cm long. Pat it hard and roll it backwards and forwards to get rid of any air pockets. Put the sausage on a plate in the fridge while you prepare the stock.

Put all the vegetables and the peppercorns into a saucepan in which the sausage will snugly fit, half fill the pot with water and bring to the boil. Simmer for 30 minutes.

When the stock is ready, remove the sausage from the fridge and place it on a board. Put a muslin cloth under a hot tap and then squeeze out all the water.

Lay the muslin next to the sausage and roll the sausage over it. Wrap the sausage tight into the wet cloth, tie both ends with cooking string and lower it gently into the simmering stock. Cover the pot with a lid and cook, over low heat, for 1¼ hours. After that, lift the sausage out, place it on a board and put a weighted plate over it. Leave it to cool still in its muslin. When it is cold, remove the weights and the plate, and place the sausage in the fridge overnight. The next day, pat it hard all around, unwrap it and cut into thick slices.

~

Crispy Apple Amber

In the garden there were a few fruit trees – apples, pears and a very prolific cherry tree. The apples provided puddings for months and this was my favourite. The fat that Kitty used was, of course, margarine but I've replaced it with butter here.

SERVES 4–6

5 large slices white bread
75g unsalted butter
675g cooking apples, peeled, cored and sliced
2–4 tbsp granulated sugar
grated zest and juice of ½ organic lemon
2 eggs, separated
50g caster sugar

Preheat the oven to 200°C/gas mark 6.

Cut the crusts off the bread.

Melt the butter, then dip the bread slices into it, coating them on both sides.

Cut each slice of bread into 3 strips and use to line the bottom and sides of an oven dish (20cm diameter and 7cm deep is perfect). Bake in the oven for 20 minutes.

Meanwhile, in a large saucepan cook the apples with 2–3 tablespoons granulated sugar (depending on the sourness of the apples), lemon juice and zest, and 3 or 4 tablespoons of water. When the apples are soft, beat them to a pulp, then taste and add more sugar if necessary. Beat in the egg yolks. Return to a very low heat and cook for about 1–2 minutes, stirring constantly, then spoon into the prepared dish.

Whisk the egg whites until stiff, then fold in the caster sugar and pile on top of the apple mixture. Place in the oven and bake for a further 10–15 minutes until the meringue is set and just golden.

CHAPTER 13

OLIVER

Lyons Corner House tomato soup

'NEXT WEEK, AT this time, I shall be at home.' That's
what I was thinking as I crossed the square in front of
Westminster Abbey one Wednesday afternoon in December
1949. And, the next moment, I came face to face with a young
man in a smart camel-hair coat, maybe a bit frayed, but still
smart. We exchanged glances and I went into the Abbey.

I had caught an earlier train than usual from Hampton
Court and arrived at Waterloo far too early for my
appointment with some friends at the Lyons Corner House in
Leicester Square. So I decided to go, for the last time, to see
Westminster Abbey, which always gave me pleasure and
peace.

I went through the door and walked down the right-hand
aisle to the cloisters, which I particularly liked. It was a clear
winter's day and I thought it would be pleasant to wander
around them. Then I noticed that the young man with the
camel coat was following me. On I went, and on he went,
stopping here and there, when eventually he said, 'It's
beautiful, isn't it?' I burst out laughing; I thought his opening
gambit was a bit lame after he'd had a good five minutes to

think what to say. (Later, I realised that it was also the most untypical act in all Oliver's life.)

He had just started his Christmas holidays and was walking home to his parents' house behind the Abbey, in Lord North Street, when he spotted me and was struck by the classic *coup-de-foudre*. Twenty-five years earlier, my mother and father had been hit by a similar bolt of 'lightning'. It happened at Salsomaggiore, a prestigious spa resort in Emilia-Romagna, which, before the Great War, was where the rich and famous went for their mud baths and to drink its famous spring waters. (After the First World War, all the finest fin-de-siècle hotels had reopened for the elegant clientele of Florence, Rome and Milan.) As my mother was coming down the stairs of the Grand Hotel with her mother, sisters and brother at the end of their stay, my father, who'd just arrived, was going up the stairs. They took one look at each other – and that was that. My father made enquiries at the reception and, back in Milan, managed to find a friend who would introduce him to the 'Tonello' family (my mother's maiden name). Not, maybe, as unconventional as my meeting with Oliver, which was certainly not out of the etiquette textbook. It was so outlandish, in fact, that Oliver didn't dare tell his parents, saying instead that we'd met at a party in Oxford. I, on the other hand, did tell my parents, who had the good grace not to flinch.

Oliver was in his last year at Oxford university. He'd started there, at Balliol College, in 1943, but a few months later he was called up and sent to Arizona to learn to fly. In 1947, he was demobilised and went back to Balliol to finish his degree in English literature. As we walked around the cloisters, he told me the only Italian he knew were the words from the song 'Là ci darem la mano', so we started talking about opera, about which I knew far more than I did about English literature. He loved Mozart and Handel and didn't much like Puccini; I loved Mozart and Puccini and hated Handel. We eventually said our goodbyes and arranged to meet up again in a few days. And so it was that, purely by chance, I'd taken an earlier train that day and ended up spending the rest of my adult life in a foreign country.

When I look back I am always amazed at the part fate plays in one's life. Because of that chance decision, I have become a hybrid, fitting properly neither here nor there, being neither English nor any longer Italian, always missing something when I am here or something else when I am there. Even now that I am old, I have the dilemma of where I should be buried: here in the lovely churchyard of this picturesque village in Dorset, where I now live, or in my family tomb in the grand Monumentale cemetery in Milan. Even dead I will not settle. In Italy we have a saying, *'Moglie e buoi dei paesi tuoi'* – wife and chattels from your own country. I find it an alarmingly wise saying, which I ignored. One might have a less dull life, more interesting experiences, broader education, but the price is high. It demands a lot of goodwill to bridge the gap that separates two people who have grown up in different countries. You certainly learn to share most things, but the baggage of anecdotes, proverbs, everyday allusions remain incomprehensible to the other person. In many cases the partners can make the most of this situation, but it can also create an abyss that tends to widen.

~

I FINALLY ARRIVED in Leicester Square that day in 1949, thinking about the irony of it all. I had been in England for eleven months and had sometimes been painfully homesick. I had been looking forward to going back to my family and starting a new life . . . and now, the week before I was due to leave England, I didn't want to go home any more. Once again, I had fallen in love with a man at the last minute, and I was determined not to let the fire die this time.

Oliver and I met again the following week, in Soho, where we had a passionate farewell. We promised to keep in touch with each other, which we did by writing long, regular letters. (Sadly, all those letters disappeared later during one of my all-too-frequent moves.)

Another goodbye, another sad train journey. Back in Italy I didn't bother to enrol at the university again, but decided to look for work. Soon afterwards, I landed a very good job as the secretary of Edoardo Visconti di Modrone, managing director of the Carlo Erba pharmaceutical firm. Edoardo Visconti, a handsome man, was the descendant of one of the ruling families of Milan during the early Renaissance, and the brother of Luchino Visconti, the film-maker, who by 1950 was already famous for his neo-realistic films. I'd got the job on the strength of knowing the right people, and for my knowledge of English, even though that was still fairly elementary. But I could translate well enough as long as I could read the shorthand hieroglyphics I made while taking dictation.

But, in spite of my well-paid job and attractive boss, five months later I packed my Gladstone bag once again and got on the train at Milan's Stazione Centrale to start my journey back to Victoria Station. The following October I married Oliver.

~

OLIVER HAD wanted to do things properly. So, first, he asked me to marry him after a May ball in Oxford, he in dinner jacket, I in an eau-de-Nil empire-line satin dress with puffy sleeves and a row of pearls at my neck. The second task was to go to Italy to ask my father for my hand in marriage, and the third was to do the family round in Italy.

The first two were relatively easy. I was ready to be caught, and my anglophile father – whatever his misgivings – was not going to object. Oliver was a nice young man from a very good family and with an Oxford education – and that was a very good pedigree. But I think he was far less happy than my mother to see his beloved daughter leaving home to live in a another country. Mamma had already made up her mind that I was going to be a *zitella* – spinster. She and her two sisters were all married by the time they were twenty-one, and she saw my single status at the age of twenty-four as a bad omen. So, since I'd missed what she'd thought was my last chance with Franco, she was determined that I should hold on tightly to this young Englishman.

But the last of Oliver's tasks, the family round, could have been trickier. One or two of my aunts were stiff, upper-class ladies, who sat on equally stiff upright armchairs, as they examined their 'prey' through golden lorgnettes. Oliver had improved his Italian beyond *'là ci darem la mano'*, but his vocabulary was still extremely limited, and not enough to make polite conversation. So he sat there, smiling and my aunts said, *'Ma che simpatico che è'* – 'But what a nice man he is' – and he passed their scrutiny with full honours.

The most demanding test he had to undergo was dinner at

Our engagement photo.

Zia Gengia's house. Zia Gengia, imperious and forbidding, sat on one side of the very large table, with Zio Alfonso opposite her, and the rest of us – their daughter Mariella, me, Oliver and my parents – on either side. The second course was *vitello tonnato*, the popular summer dish. My mother had cooked that very same dish just days before and Oliver had loved it. So that evening at Zia Gengia's he started eating and declared, in his best French, *'Mais, il est bon comme le vitel tonné d' Ernesta l'autre jour.'* That was indeed a great compliment, as my mother had the reputation among her sisters-in-law of being the best cook. On the way home Mamma, not impressed by the suggestion that my aunt's cooking skills were on a par with hers, cattily declared that Zia Gengia's *vitello tonnato* was probably from the *salumeria* in Corso Magenta, which often supplied the food for Zia Gengia's dinner parties.

After this tour de force within the tour de la famille, Oliver and I had three blissful days in Venice which, ever afterwards remained the place we most loved to be. Then we returned to London to find a house and arrange the wedding.

Unfortunately, we could not get married in Italy because Oliver was unable to live there for the stipulated four months prior to the wedding. In September he was due to start work in the advertising department of International Paints, a large firm manufacturing paints and varnishes. So we planned a simple ceremony in London at the Catholic Church of Our Most Holy Redeemer and St Thomas More, the parish church of Chelsea, where I was au-pairing at the time with another family. Oliver had to receive Catholic tuition from the church's parish priest, Father De Zulueta, and promise that our children would be brought up in the Catholic faith. Oliver, who had no religious upbringing, never complained; he was so in love with me he would have done everything he could to marry me.

We got married on the 5th of October 1950, I in a proper, boring grey suit with a blue beret and Oliver in a suitably dark blue suit. Weddings were small affairs in those post-war years and there were only a few guests in the church: our parents, Oliver's brother Stephen, his best man David Williams, and my friend Cetto Bianchi. There were two hiccups during the ceremony. First, I repeated after the priest 'my awful wedded husband', forgetting to pronounce the important 'l'. The second was when Oliver had problems pushing the wedding ring onto my finger. Was that an ominous warning? I doubted it, because Oliver loved me too much to doubt, even unconsciously, his desire to make me his wife. But it was certainly odd, since I can still take off my wedding ring now, even though my fingers are knobbly and arthritic.

After the ceremony, my parents-in-law gave a cocktail party in their Georgian house in Lord North Street where I, in a stylish green and gold brocade dress, met many of Oliver's English relatives. After the party, we got into Oliver's pre-war Morris Coupé and drove to Bath for a five-day honeymoon in a smart, but rather stuffy hotel in the Circus. All of this had happened eight months after that first encounter at Westminster Abbey.

~

I WAS STILL feeling somewhat stunned when I recounted the story of that first whirlwind romantic encounter to my friends, the three girls with whom I'd originally come to England, and whom I was on my way to meet that fateful day in London. We met as always at the Lyon's Corner House in Leicester Square, where, at the self-service counter, I took the usual two bowls, one of tomato soup and the other of salad. These were the only two items on the menu that I could eat, not exactly with pleasure, but certainly without distaste. The tomato soup, I expect, was Heinz and the 'rabbit' salad, as we called it, was undressed. The lettuce itself was quite good, since that awful hard Iceberg had not yet been invented. It was proper lettuce grown in real fields, with a few slices of cucumber, radishes, tomatoes, onions or whatever was in season at the time. But I've never liked 'naked' salad (still common in Dorset pubs today), so I always drowned it in salad cream – no mayonnaise then. One of my friends loved salad cream so much that she went back to Italy with six bottles of it. I never took any salad cream with me, nor indeed any tomato soup – only the memory of it, so inextricably linked with that chance encounter with Oliver on that winter's day.

~

I WAS DESTINED to eat Heinz tomato soup once again – but not until 2005. Our three children had rented a house in the Lake District for us all to spend a week together to celebrate my own and Oliver's eightieth birthdays. We were 13 people and 3 dogs. I don't like sitting down 13 at the table, so I was delighted by the presence of the dogs. It was the 1st of April and my younger son, Guy, had decided it was his turn to cook the dinner. We sat down at the table and a tomato soup arrived, with a few shrimps floating in the middle. It looked very attractive, bright red with the pale pink dots of the shrimps. Guy is a good cook, having enlarged his repertoire of English dishes by living in Italy and enjoying Italian food for twenty or so years. I took a spoonful of soup, rolled it around my mouth and declared it 'delicious'. Everyone burst out laughing. It was a tin of Heinz tomato soup, doctored by Guy with three squeezed garlic cloves, a few pinches of chilli powder, some lemon juice and the shrimps. April Fool! I tried to wriggle out of my embarrassment by saying it was improved by the additions, but without much success. As far as I remember, it tasted of garlic and chilli, and was, I am sure, far removed from the brown-sauce-tasting red liquid of the Lyons Corner House.

Minestra coi Pomodori
Pasta and Tomato Soup

My tomato soup is very different from the Heinz version. It has chewy bits in it and tastes summery and fresh.

SERVES 6

75ml extra virgin olive oil
3 garlic cloves, finely chopped
6 ripe tomatoes, skinned and coarsely chopped
2 onions, thinly sliced
3 tbsp chopped fresh parsley
salt and freshly ground black pepper
150g ditalini or any other small short-cut pasta
4 tbsp freshly grated parmesan cheese

Heat the oil in a large saucepan and sauté the garlic until just coloured.

Add the tomatoes, onions and half the chopped parsley to the pan and fry gently for 10 minutes, stirring frequently. Pour in 1.5 litres of water and add salt and plenty of pepper. Simmer, covered, for 20 minutes. Raise the heat and drop in the pasta. Stir well with a wooden spoon. Cook over a moderate heat for about 10 minutes until the pasta is al dente.

Just before serving, add the remaining parsley and the parmesan cheese. Mix well and serve.

CHAPTER 14

BILLING ROAD

Horse meat roll

O LIVER AND I RETURNED from our honeymoon in Bath and walked into our own home: a two-up, two-down and two-underneath in The Billings. The Billings was an area of three cul-de-sacs off the Fulham Road, near Stamford Bridge, now a very fashionable address. The house was our wedding present from Oliver's parents, who'd bought it for just £1,500, which was cheap even then.

Number 5 Billing Road was a workman's cottage with no bathroom but an inside loo planted in the middle of the so-called garden room downstairs at the back. The Irishman from whom Oliver's parents had bought the house was a builder, who one day decided he'd had enough of the privy in the yard and wanted an indoor loo. So he made a hole in the floor, broke into the sewer that ran under the house and plonked the loo on top. He was very proud of it.

Our house was one of only two in the Billings with no net curtains. After a few weeks I had to relent and hang some, though, because all the local children, especially the girls, who played in the street would stick their noses to our window and I felt like a fish at the aquarium. I was clearly a different specimen to the other inhabitants. I drove a car, never had curlers in my hair, spoke a strange language to my dog and had a doorbell that went 'dri-ing' and not ding-dong. I liked those children, they were fun and cheeky, but polite and never aggressive. There was only one snag; they loved pulling out the semaphore-type traffic indicators on our car and swinging on them, which did the indicators no good at all. It happened two or three times until Oliver had a word with the various parents and then it stopped. Parental discipline still existed in the 1950s.

The car, called Jessie, was Oliver's pet. My pet was a Cocker Spaniel called Tita. The car was a pre-war Morris Cabriolé which had kept Oliver happy throughout his years at Oxford. It sat outside our house, forming an almost unique fixture of the Billings.

In the two years we lived there before my first child was born, what I remember most were my frequent food shopping trips, usually to the North End Road market. There were quite a few vegetable stalls selling good-quality produce, even if the choice was limited. I learned about parsnips and swedes; I bought and cooked them, and decided I liked them, despite my brothers pointing out, during their visits, that in Italy they were only fed to the pigs. But they, too, enjoyed them, sautéed or puréed with masses of butter and parmesan. The market also boasted a very good fish stall. (My criterion for judging the freshness of fish is whether you can smell fish at a distance of, say, more than two yards. If you can, forget it.) At North End Road I used to get different types of herrings, and pilchard and sprats, all kinds of flatfish, such as sole, witches and dabs, as well as the dog fish and gurnard that other people

Billing Road with 'Jessie'.

overlooked because they didn't know what to do with them. Then in the spring and summer there were the splendid salmon trout and salmon, all wild of course (the hated farmed species hadn't yet arrived on the scene).

In the Fulham Road, just around the corner from the Billings, there was a Waitrose. Inside, it had a long counter on each side. First on the right, as I went in, was the counter with butter, margarine and blocks of white lard served by a cheerful lady with tight curls and deep red lipstick. She'd cut pieces of butter from a big slab and, with great dexterity, pat it into shape with her wooden paddles while exchanging the usual casual comments about the weather. And on I'd walk to the next counter with the sugar and all the biscuits and then round the other side and back home. I liked those shops of the

Fifties, in spite of the fact that I couldn't get unsalted butter, which wasn't available in Britain then – yet another gastronomic gap that perplexed me.

Another of the things that struck me when I first came to Britain, and to be honest I still notice it now after more than half a century, is the inability of a shop assistant to do more than one thing at a time. If you ask something which needs only a quick answer while they are serving someone else, the answer is always 'I am serving now.' For a long time I wondered if it was unwillingness rather than inability. But then somebody explained to me that it is neither. I was interrupting and therefore I appeared to be rude. But I was used to Italy where the shop assistant takes the money with one hand while with the other grabs a salame from behind the corner ready for the next customer and answers a question to a third. I suppose it is one of the fundamental dividing lines between the British and the Italians: the Italians like to serve people and are good at it, while the English don't and on the whole are not good at it. Italians also like to interrupt – and I'm a prime example, as Oliver used to point out.

Once a week, on Saturday morning, Oliver and I would get into Jessie and drive to Soho. The journey took just over a quarter of an hour and we usually parked in Brewer Street or Wardour Street, right in front of one of the well-stocked Italian delicatessens Parmigiani or Lina, Camisa or Del Monico, each of which we patronised in turn. They also supplied the few Italian restaurants in the area, such as Gennaro, Quo Vadis and, later, La Terrazza, the restaurant which put Italian cooking on the culinary map of London. I bought all sorts of cheeses and *salumi* – cured pork meats – pasta and rice, olive oil in five-litre tins, proper coffee and all manner of goodies.

Next, we'd go to the vegetable market in Berwick Street. There were no pseudo leather bags and belts and purses then, but gorgeous peppers, courgettes, proper artichokes and fennel, depending on the season. We'd round off our shopping with fish from Richards and meat from Randell & Aubin or Bifulco. Meat was rationed until 1954, so for the first four years of my married life I bought hearts and tongue, pig's trotters, brawn, tripe, rabbit and all the things I loved, and that Oliver learnt to love too.

Afterwards, we'd have coffee at the Bar Italia, one of the very few bars where you could get a real espresso that slowly descended in a cloud of steam from the Gaggia machine, the first espresso machine in the UK. Occasionally, we had lunch in Soho before going to the cinema. Quo Vadis, Bianchi, Gennaro were our favourite restaurants and, later, in the Sixties, La Terrazza. But, for financial reasons, we didn't eat out much, especially not around our home in Billing Road where the only place that served reasonably good food was a Cypriot restaurant in the Fulham Road called Salamis.

Even on the rare occasions when we went to a smart restaurant, I found that the quality of the food did not match the high prices. The cheaper places were dreadful, though – the smell alone put me off. And some of my worst experiences were of the food on cross-Channel ferries. As we boarded the English ferry at Calais, on our way back from Italy, my nostrils and my stomach were assaulted by what I called the English smell: frying fat, recycled ad infinitum, mixed with Bisto made up with washing-up water. After the excellent food in Italy and in France where we'd stop to eat at those delightful little bistros in the provincial towns, the shock of the food on the ferry was all the greater. The same smell seemed also to pervade many corners of London at the time, especially Leicester Square and Shaftesbury Avenue.

At home in Billing Road, I enjoyed cooking for Oliver and for the friends that visited us, who always asked for pasta, which I dressed with all sorts of sauces unfamiliar to them. The only pasta dish, apart from macaroni cheese, that was familiar in Britain then was spaghetti with meatballs, which confounded me. In Italy no one ate pasta with meatballs, least of all spaghetti. It was all down to the Americans who fell in love with the spaghetti that the Italian immigrants brought with them, but, of course, they had to have their meat as well. So the dish was created in the American–Italian restaurants and from there it came to Britain, just like any other American fad. I cooked *bucatini alla carbonara* – *bucatini* being spaghetti with a hole running down the centre and which has just become the 'it' pasta in Italy. Another favourite was *penne ai quattro formaggi*, or my version of the macaroni cheese which my English friends knew from their childhood, albeit tasting rather different from what they recalled which was maybe more as the writer Saki described macaroni cheese, 'similar to a bad production of an Ibsen play, melancholy and boring'.

But my dinner party successes were not confined to pasta. One dish that all our friends loved was my crusty meat rissoles that, when cut, exuded a Mediterranean aroma of herbs and garlic. I called it *le polpette della mia Mamma*, but that was not the whole truth. I should have called it 'the horse meat *polpette* of my mother'. But how could you tell a British person that he or she was eating – and enjoying – horse meat? I mixed a few other ingredients into the *polpette* so nobody could detect the slight sweetness of the horse meat (although what British person would know what horse meat tasted like anyway?). I was not as honest as Clement Freud, who confessed on a TV programme about food in the Fifties that, when some diners at his restaurant asked him what that excellent steak was, he replied frankly 'horse meat'. Nobody believed him.

My recipe was so good that it is still in my repertoire, but I make it with beef and pork now. In the early 1950s, though, beef and pork were rationed, while horse meat was not. At the splendid Boucherie Chevaline in the Fulham Road, just around the corner from our house, the French butchers behind the counter were most obliging. I could get anything I wanted, cut the right way or minced, chopped or cubed. I would have liked them to sell donkey and mule meat, too, which I prefer, and all sorts of salami, just like the horse meat butcher in Milan that I always visited on my trips back home. A few years ago, I was in Mantova for the Gonzaga exhibition, and I had a memorable stew of donkey with polenta. The meat, cut into morsels then flavoured with vegetables and herbs, was cooked in dry Lambrusco wine for eight hours. It was just as wonderful as the Gonzaga exhibits.

My dinners were, if nothing else, different from those we had at our friends' houses. As well as pasta, I cooked *risotti*, fish and vegetables in various guises, but I was weak on puddings, as we only had them on special occasions in my childhood. At my friends' dinner parties in London, however, pudding was the best course. Often two or three puds were passed round, one always a mousse of some sort – usually chocolate or lemon – and then a pavlova or other creamy concoction. The main courses, though, were predictable: in the spring and summer it would be salmon with a row of cucumber down its back, or coronation chicken, a recipe created for the Queen's coronation in 1953. In the winter, it was roast pheasant or partridge with all the trimmings. All very nice and formal – and a bit dull.

~

MY LIFE OF leisure came to an abrupt halt with the arrival of my son Paul. At five o'clock in the afternoon on the 15th of December 1952, Oliver drove me to Westminster Hospital, where I'd chosen to have my baby because of its proximity to Oliver's parents' house. When my contractions started more seriously I was put in one of the labour rooms and told to ring the bell if I needed help. My pains started to get stronger, so I rang. The nurse came and told me the baby wasn't due yet and left me again. My pains grew and my panic grew. I rang again. The same nurse came in, had a look at me and, once more, told me that the baby was not coming yet. Before leaving, she added, 'If you ring again we'll cut the bell off,' and slammed the door behind her. I am not one of those who look back nostalgically to the 'good old days' of the National Health Service. Eventually, a house doctor and a midwife arrived and, after a few false alarms, so did Paul at eleven o'clock that night. It certainly was not a long labour for a first baby, but it had seemed an eternity. Paul was immediately whisked away to the nursery and was brought back only at regular intervals, every four hours, for his feed. He never slept, and I thought I could hear him screaming at all hours of the day and night. But he was in safe hands in the nursery with all the other babies and no mums, which was the English way in those days.

After one week in hospital, I went home with my little baby, happy at last not to have to listen to his screams without being able to go to him, happy to be able to take him for walks in his pram (one of those old-fashioned Rolls-Royce types) and happy not to have to eat any more hospital food.

My mother came to stay with us to help me with the baby and that was the most joyous and precious time we had together. I was depending on her and she could help without bossy me getting in the way and taking my revenge on her for having criticised me far too often when I was a teenager. She took over the house and the cooking so that I could dedicate myself to the baby and learn my new role in life. Paul was what was then called a colicky baby. What that meant was that Oliver spent all the hours he was at home after work walking up and down with a screaming Paul in his arms. I fed Paul by the clock, never mind if after two hours my little hungry bird was crying again. We were indoctrinated with the dogma that babies should be left to cry for at least the first 15 minutes or they would become spoilt, nor should they be fed before the four-hour interval was up. My days were spent listening to a screaming Paul or walking up and down the sitting room cuddling him in my arms while singing all the songs that came to my mind. I even managed to compose one, quite good in fact, so much so that Oliver, when he first heard it, said that it was quite Mozartian. I am afraid Doctor Spock had yet to arrive on the mother–baby scene. Looking back, I cannot believe how daft the whole thing was. Mamma tried to convince me to be less rigid and more Italian, but to no avail. My mother also disapproved of the British custom of putting the baby out on the pavement in the middle of a cold winter, but I strongly believed in the wisdom of the British race. Mamma stayed with us a fortnight and then had to go back home. That was one of my saddest goodbyes, of which I'd had too many in my life.

So Paul's pram joined the other prams sitting outside the front doors of the Billings. Cars were a rarity, but prams were not. Babies, and there seemed to be a lot of them in those post-war years, were put out of doors in their prams. Every day Paul was duly put out in the so-called fresh air. That winter, the worst smog ever was recorded. It was indeed the last year of the famous London pea-souper because, soon after that, the Clean Air Act was passed and things got much better. I remember my lovely baby all decked up in beautiful white clothes and blankets speckled with black soot after a morning in the 'fresh air' (the Billings are not far from Lotts Road power station with its belching chimneys). It was as if I'd seasoned his little face with black pepper. Pea-souper or not, Paul survived the four months we were there, before we moved to the leafier and healthier Holland Park.

Tortino di Sardine
Baked Sprats

In 1950, in London, sardines were only available in tins and
fresh ones were unknown. But I discovered sprats, a fish of the
same family, and found it an excellent substitute for its
Mediterranean cousin. Fresh sprats are usually easier to find
than fresh sardines.

SERVES 4

750g fresh sardines or sprats
6 tbsp extra virgin olive oil
6 tbsp fresh breadcrumbs
2 tbsp wine vinegar
2 tbsp capers
2 garlic cloves, chopped
1 tbsp chopped marjoram
1 tbsp chopped flat leaf parsley
1 chilli, seeded and chopped
salt and pepper

Preheat the oven to 200°C/gas mark 6.

Pull off the head of the fish – as you do this, most of the
inners will come out too. Open the fish from the belly cavity
and lay them flat on a chopping board, skin-side up. Press
gently down along the backbone and then slip your forefinger
and thumb under it and loosen it from the flesh. Pull the

backbone out towards the tail. Wash the fish and leave them to drain on a slanting board.

Reserve 1 tablespoon of the oil and heat the rest in a frying pan. When hot, add the breadcrumbs and fry them until golden. Add all the other ingredients and continue frying for about 2 minutes, stirring the whole time.

Brush a 20cm (8in) round oven dish with a little of the remaining oil and cover the bottom of the dish with a layer of fish, skin-side down, arranged like the petals of a daisy. Spread half the breadcrumbs mixture evenly over the fish, cover with the remaining fish, skin-side up, and top with the remaining breadcrumbs mixture. Douse the dish all over with the rest of the oil and bake in the oven for 15 minutes.

This dish can be served hot – but not piping hot – warm or cold.

~

Polpette alla Casalinga
Beef Rissoles

SERVES 3–4

400g best lean minced beef
100g mortadella, finely chopped
50g grated parmesan cheese
3 tbsp ricotta cheese
3 tbsp dried breadcrumbs
1 free-range egg
2 tbsp chopped flat leaf parsley

1 garlic clove, chopped
salt and pepper
seasoned flour for dusting
4 tbsp olive oil
25g unsalted butter
4 tbsp Marsala
100ml meat stock

In a bowl mix together the minced beef, mortadella, parmesan, ricotta, breadcrumbs, egg, parsley and garlic. Season with a little salt and plenty of pepper and mix again, using your hands.

Divide the meat mixture into 8 portions of roughly the same size and then shape each portion into a ball. Pat the balls thoroughly to let out any air bubbles and lightly flatten them a little so they look like small hamburgers. Put the rissoles in the fridge for at least 30 minutes.

Dust each rissole with a little seasoned flour. Heat the oil and butter in a non-stick frying pan and, when the butter foam begins to subside, add the rissoles and fry them for 5 minutes. Turn them over very carefully and fry the other side for 3 minutes, until a lovely dark crust has formed on each side. Pour the Marsala over them, cook for 1 minute and add the meat stock. Cook over a gentle heat for 10–15 minutes, then check the cooking liquid seasoning and serve.

and my parents-in-law sold their eighteenth-century Georgian house in Lord North Street in Westminster. They had been finding the house increasingly difficult to run and live in, with its five floors and numerous stairs. And my father-in-law no longer had to go to his office nearby, having just retired from the Treasury, although he remained on the board of various companies. So, 25 Holland Villas Road seemed a good solution for all of us.

But I wasn't particularly happy in that house. It was far too grand for me, with its huge drawing room of 30 feet by 15, in which our modest furniture looked lost and out of place. Only the grand piano, on which my mother-in-law used to accompany Oliver's violin-playing when he was a child, was in harmony with its surroundings. And then there was the problem of how to heat rooms that are 12 feet high with only gas or electric fires. Of course, there were many advantages to living in a large house: plenty of space to store everything, although we didn't have much to store at the time, space to move around and for children to play in, and room to have friends from Italy to stay, which happened very often.

My brother Marco was the most frequent guest. He came to learn English and he stayed with us for a full year, during which time he often drove me mad. He was late for dinner, he never seemed to work, he always forgot to do what I asked him to. I called him all sorts of names, and yet fiercely defended him in front of others, even Oliver, the family bonds coming to the fore. Marco was eighteen and his favourite pastime was chasing girls and, being a very attractive young man, the chase usually ended with satisfactory results. After Marco left us, he found a job straight away in advertising, then

Holland Villas Road.

in printing and went on to have quite a successful career. He married an English girl, Sarah, an attractive blonde who worked as a model in Milan for one of the grand couture houses. They had two children, but Sarah eventually left him so, at the age of seventy-five, Mamma took over Marco's family when his children, Alex and Nicky, were eight and seven respectively, and brought them up with the help of Angela, her faithful daily from Puglia. Hard work, but I am sure that was what kept my mother fit and very alive.

ONE OF THE best features of the house in Holland Villas Road was its large garden, which backed on to those of the houses behind. But they were a good 200 feet away and there was a barrier of green trees between us. Oliver's father, Sigi, looked after the garden and he'd spend hours hoeing, digging, fertilising, planting and transplanting. As soon as he came home from one of his board meetings, he'd change into his gardening clothes and out he went, never put off by rain or cold. In fact he liked to garden in the fine English rain; when it was sunny he preferred to sit down and read.

Sigi was a fascinating man, with a large intellect and a small ego. He spoke a handful of languages, the snag being his English intonation. So when he spoke Italian or French to my parents, they didn't even bother to listen because it sounded like English, which they couldn't understand. There was one occasion, he told Oliver, when he'd had a meeting with a Polish man and they discovered the only language they had in common was Latin, and so they proceeded to converse in that ancient tongue. In spite of his considerable intellect, he didn't have a good ear, either musical or linguistic. He used to say that he only knew when the National Anthem was being played because everybody stood up.

Sigi was the elder brother of Arthur Waley, the famous sinologist who translated Chinese and Japanese poetry and novels into English, thus introducing the unknown Far Eastern literature to the western world. Arthur used to have tea with Oliver's parents in Holland Villas Road. He came with his companion of many years, Beryl de Zoete, a diminutive woman who wrote books about Indonesian dances, on which she was an expert. She talked the whole time, while Arthur sat there, gazing into the distance. At Oxford, Oliver had resented being introduced as Arthur Waley's nephew, instead of a person in his own right. And, at one of my parents-in-law's cocktail parties, I too was introduced to Harold Macmillan as

Arthur Waley's niece, but as soon as Macmillan realised I was only a niece-in-law, he politely made some excuse, then turned on his heel and moved on.

On the 4th of April 1954, our second child, Guy, arrived. He was an angelic baby from the start, with deep chestnut eyes shadowed by long eyelashes and a ready smile that enchanted everyone. He was even considerate enough to arrive at 10 p.m. on the last day of the financial year so that we could collect the Government's child allowance for the preceding year.

Holland Villas Road in the Fifties was full of married couples like us, with young children and we soon made friends with the neighbours. There were the Bostons at Number 30; Jim and Bunny Tanner, the best party-givers, at 22; the Butlers at 28; and the Eleys across the road. My first meeting with Penelope Eley was extremely unorthodox. It took place on a small rock off the island of Giglio in the Tuscan Archipelago. I was swimming towards that very rock, towing with my teeth a rubber dinghy containing Paul and Guy, then aged six and five. On the rock I saw a woman with a young girl. Between one splutter and another I said, 'I'm Anna Waley, I live opposite you in Holland Villas Road. Aren't you Lady Eley?' In that clipped accent of the English upper class, she replied, 'Oh, how do you do?'

Some of the houses were divided into flats, like the one opposite. In the ground floor flat lived the comedian Frankie Howerd of *Up Pompeii* fame. Paul and Guy were delighted when he gave them his autograph and they proudly showed it to their friends at school. And in the house next door, in the top floor flat, lived Shirley Tudor Pole who, with her blonde hair flying in the wind as she drove her two-seater Morris

Cabriolé, looked more like Lauren Bacall than the girl next door. When she left her husband, she and her son Edward lived with us for two or three weeks. Years later, when we were recalling her stay at Number 25, she told me that, whatever her problems during that difficult time of her life, she had the pleasure of looking forward every night to sitting at a table where good food was served. I was amazed when I heard that, because I'd never paid much attention to what I was cooking while we were living in Holland Villas Road; I was too busy adjusting to my new English life.

I only remember that, at one stage, I wanted to learn how to make some Spanish dishes from our au-pair, Angelines. Angelines was in her thirties, the same age as me, and she was quite happy to share the cooking. I was even happier, since I could learn two things in one go: the language and the cooking of Spain. Angelines came from Santander and, like most people from Galicia, she was a talented cook with a large repertoire. We would compare notes on the cooking of chickpeas or *bacalao* – dried salted cod – and when she returned from her holidays in Spain, she would bring back pimentón – paprika – and chorizo, which were non-existent in London then. She taught me how to make a good paella; I taught her how to make a decent risotto. While she made gazpacho, I made *pappa col pomodoro* – bread and tomato soup. Paul and Guy were the judges of our culinary efforts and I have to confess that Angelines' dishes often won hands down.

Paul and Guy were happy in Holland Villas Road, helping grandpa in the garden, playing upstairs with granny in her sitting room or being taken to Holland Park by one of the many au-pairs that arrived over the years. Paul had started at a nursery school in Allen Street, but only spent a year there, as I discovered he was being bullied by two American toughies who made him eat soap. At least that was what he told me years later. Paul was rather small and enjoyed reading books more than kicking a ball, which made him a target for bullies. I knew he wasn't happy there, so it was a blessing when I was asked by an acquaintance, Mrs Geddy, who used to teach at the Norland School, if she could hold a playgroup in our nursery downstairs. It was a large room, with an upright piano, a huge collection of Dinky cars, donated by my friend Carla, and plenty of space for the children to run around. It was an ideal arrangement for the children and for me. I felt like a nineteenth-century mother with lots of children. I loved to hear them dancing and singing and jumping around, being looked after by someone else. I'd be in the kitchen next door, cooking or experimenting with new dishes, or baking little biscuits or cakes for the children's elevenses. One of everybody's favourites were the polenta biscuits whose bright yellow colour and gritty texture intrigued them. I used to walk into the nursery and all those little faces looked up at me with greedy eyes, ready to grasp one of the biscuits or a piece of cake. I remember chubby Charlie Boston, the most interested in food, who used to ask me what was that lovely smell, his interest I am sure nurtured by his mother, a good cook ready to discuss food with her children, something unfashionable at the time.

Mrs Geddy arrived at 8.30 a.m., driving her grey Baby Austin, always smart and trim, modelling herself on Claudette Colbert, the 1940s Hollywood actress, whom, with her dark fringe and scarlet cupid's-bow mouth, she resembled. The children arrived at 9 o'clock: Ruth, Roger, Peter, Nina Grunfeld in her smart blue coat and velvet collar, accompanied by Nanny Smith (who years later was the protagonist of the television series 'Nanny Knows Best') and, always last, Charlie followed by the harassed Mrs Hampson, the Bostons' housekeeper. Charlie was always running away, and between Number 30, where he lived, and Number 25 he managed to find hundreds of hiding places.

Mrs Hampson was a remarkable woman, who died aged ninety-four only a few years ago. She grew up in South Wales where her father found work as a miner, having walked all the way from London when he lost his job in a brewery. Back in London, Hampy, the nickname Charlie gave her and which we all adopted, became a nurse and found work in Guy's Hospital as a young woman. Hampy was interested in everything and everybody. Her dream was to go to Egypt, about which she knew a lot, as she did about the Hittites and the Romans. She was an avid reader and surprised me early on by asking if I was related to Arthur Waley; she loved his poetry and his *Tales of Genji*.

So life went on, punctuated by the yearly change of au-pairs – except for Angelines, who stayed for two years in a vain attempt to learn English. One of her favourite lines on the telephone was, 'Sorry, Mrs Waley on the streets, again.' The advantage was that we all learned Spanish, even our budgerigar, which repeated over and over again *'Muy bien, muy bien. Adios'*. (His cage was next to the telephone.)

Eventually, Paul and Guy went to school at Faulkner House in Notting Hill, which was good enough to prepare the boys successfully for their entrance exam to Colet Court, the prep school for St Paul's School. Soon they had grown out of the small Holland Park and wanted to go to Richmond Park to play football or have fun stalking us while hiding behind trees. We often drove there with our neighbours, the Bostons, so I had my friend Tchillie to talk to and they had their friends, Julia and mischievous Charlie, to play with. During the mushroom season I'd drag Tchillie, Julia, Charlie and their English bulldog to hunt for mushrooms on Wimbledon Common, which we found a far better fungi ground than Richmond Park.

Another companion on the mushroom hunt was my Italian friend Luciana Farchy, with her daughter Sandra. Small and extremely agile, Luciana managed to get into the thickest of bushes and her basket was always the fullest. She used to drive a Baby Austin or a large Jaguar with the same panache. The snag was that when she sat in her Jaguar she could only see the road through the arc of the steering wheel. That didn't stop her from driving it. Now aged eighty-six, she still drives with the same panache. The Farchys lived in a large flat at Number 8 Addison Road nearby, an immense house which was demolished in 1970, together with all the other houses up to Number 9 when the leases came to an end. In their place hundreds of quite small pseudo-Georgian houses were built. Those beautiful nineteenth-century houses, with their enormous gardens, made way for what came to be known as Millionaire's Slum of Abbotsbury Road.

～

IN HOLLAND VILLAS ROAD I gradually began to feel more at home in England. I also began to understand the English better, although I still didn't feel I had much in common with them. I realised that we Italians were closer even to the Scandinavians than the English. Continental Europe is indeed a continent, with people sharing quite a few social and cultural habits. Those twenty-two miles of water, the English Channel, are far longer than the Atlantic Ocean. The English, I discovered, were not Europeans. They are still not today.

Paul and Guy were a great help in providing an anchor for me and there was a time during that period of my life when I needed it badly. Once the boys were both at school, I had taken a part-time job in 1959, interpreting and translating at Robson Lowe, the philatelic firm in Pall Mall. And then I fell in love with a Portuguese man I met through my work. José, a dark-eyed Frank Sinatra look-alike, was divorced and, after a few illicit meetings on business trips to philatelic conferences, he asked me to leave Oliver, marry him and go to live in Lisbon with him. I didn't have to think for long. I realised that I could not possibly take Paul and Guy, then aged seven and six, away from their devoted father and grandparents, and all their friends, to a country where they could neither understand nor speak the language. Nor would I ever leave them behind.

Language was indeed a great barrier between me and José, too. José had only a smattering of English and no Italian, and my knowledge of Portuguese was nil. So we spoke French together; he fluently, I falteringly, which made communication rather difficult at times – even in bed one needs to communicate. After some furtive passionate encounters in London, Rome, Lisbon, or wherever we could steal two or three days away on a business trip, our affair died an early and natural death, and I went back to being a faithful wife. I had

With Paul and Guy.

been unhappy with my double life, however short-lived. I was very good at weaving a web of intricate lies, but my conscience and my sense of duty managed to spoil what delights I had during that brief affair. Luckily, Oliver never knew of this transgression, although he did find out about two other minor affairs I had later that had meant very little to me, which was why I was not careful enough to cover my tracks.

I dedicated myself with new vigour to my domestic life at Holland Villas Road. Oliver's deep love for me and mine for him somehow became even stronger after this escapade. I began to feel a greater sense of connection with my newly adopted country, although I felt I never totally belonged, in the way that Paul and Guy would have liked me to. They were sometimes embarrassed by me, like the time when Paul told me, as he came out of Colet Court one day, that he had won a scholarship to St Paul's school, and I jumped with joy and hugged him. Guy said, 'Mummy, you shouldn't do that in public.' But then I heard the little voice of one of his friends in the back of the car saying, 'My Mummy would have behaved much worse.'

I enjoyed my boys' company, especially in the kitchen, where I cooked endless meals for them. They were always asking for potato gnocchi, spaghetti with Marmite, *pasta al ragù* or *cotolette*, just as my grandchildren do today.

But the thing they liked best in the kitchen was to sort out, clean, slice and cook the mushrooms we picked on Wimbledon Common. First, we piled them on the kitchen table, then Paul fetched the two fungi books we had, both Italian, because English ones were hard to come by. We started by throwing away the fungi that, after a second look, we knew were not edible, and made piles of the different species that remained. And then the fun started with the looking, discussing and turning each one over and over to try to give them a name. While Paul, the more academic, was reading the description in the book, Guy was more interested in studying the worms, of which there were many, wriggling out of the spongy undersides of the old Boletus or the craggy stems of Lactari.

And finally the decision on how to cook them. The boys always wanted them *a cotoletta* – breaded and fried in golden butter. How they enjoyed sinking their teeth through the golden crust into the softness of the mushrooms, just as I did at their age. So the best large caps of the porcini and parasols were prepared like that and the rest were cooked, all together, *in umido* (with a little tomato sauce) or *trifolati* (sautéed with garlic and parsley) or in the oven with anchovies, parsley, garlic and breadcrumbs. This is still the way I like to cook them now when I have lots of different types that my grandchildren have picked.

RECIPES

Spaghetti with Marmite

This is hardly a recipe, but I want to include it because I haven't as yet found a child who doesn't like it.

350–380g dried spaghetti
50g unsalted butter
1 tsp Marmite
freshly grated parmesan cheese for serving

Cook the spaghetti in plenty of boiling salted water.

While the pasta is cooking, melt the butter in a small sauce-pan and add the Marmite and 1 tablespoon of the pasta water. Mix thoroughly to dissolve, then pour over the drained spaghetti. Serve with plenty of grated parmesan cheese.

~

Polentine
Polenta biscuits

These were the favourite biscuits of the children who came to the play group. In the spring I used to add a few crunched-up elder flowers, as we do in Lombardy for the feast of Saint George on the 23rd of April. Sometimes the children went into the garden to help me pick the flowers, and then they liked the biscuits even more.

MAKES 50–60 BISCUITS

120g coarse polenta flour
60g Italian 00 flour

½tsp baking powder
Pinch of salt
130g icing sugar, sifted
100g unsalted butter, at room temperature
grated zest of 1 organic lemon

Mix thoroughly the two flours, the baking powder and salt in a bowl and then transfer the mixture onto a work surface. Shape it into a mound and make a well in the centre. Put all the other ingredients into the well and mix them together until you form a ball. You can do all this in a food processor.

Dust the work surface with some flour, and roll the ball out to a thickness of about 1cm. Cut into rectangles of 2 x 5cm and place them, wide apart, on two lightly buttered baking trays. Now place the trays in the fridge and chill for 30 minutes or so.

Preheat the oven to 150°C/gas mark 4. After the 30 minutes, remove the trays from the fridge, place them in the oven and bake for about 8 minutes, until they become dry to the touch and a deeper golden colour. Remove the biscuits from the trays with the help of a spatula – they are rather brittle – and line them up on a wire rack to cool. When cold, store them in a tin.

CHAPTER 16

CORNIA

Hare in a sweet and sour sauce

IN THE AUTUMN OF 1972 I went to Brussels for the inter-national philatelic exhibition as an interpreter on the stand of Robson Lowe. I quite enjoyed that part of my work, as it involved meeting lots of people of different nationalities and, even better, eating in good restaurants. And Brussels had good restaurants aplenty. Their typically rich food with masses of butter, cream and wine was a change from my uncomplicated Mediterranean cooking.

It was a Friday and Oliver was due to join me after I had finished work. We were going to spend the weekend together in Brussels, just the two us, with no children. He rang me and, instead of giving me his flight number, he said: 'Catch a plane to Pisa and we'll meet there. Myriam has found us a house.'

'Marvellous,' I answered. 'See you in Pisa tomorrow.'

Myriam, a good friend of ours, was in Tuscany in search of a house for herself and we had entrusted her to look out for us, too. She had found two houses in Chianti, quite close to each other, which sounded promising. So on that Saturday in September, Oliver and I drove from Pisa airport to Gaiole-in-Chianti and on to Castello di Cacchiano to meet the Baron

Alberto Ricasoli Firidolfi, owner of Cacchiano and the land around. He was selling some of his farmhouses, most of which were derelict, their inhabitants having left them after the war when the Italian land reform took place.

In late September, Chianti was at its best: the hills all different hues of red and yellow and the vineyards alive with workers harvesting the grapes. We turned left onto a precipitous gravel road with holes and boulders and stones, and drove on and on along the lane which was now weaving its way up through big white rocks and small thickets of scrub oaks and sloe bushes. After what seemed an endless bumpy ride, the track ended in a field with a magnificent walnut tree on the left and, a little further ahead, on the right, a modest farmhouse of perfect proportions: Cornia. The house, and its setting, painted a picture of rural paradise, with fine views over the Tuscan countryside, and I immediately knew we were going to buy it.

Alberto Ricasoli was there to show us around. There were stables on the ground floor, and the rooms upstairs were reached by an outside stone staircase in traditional Tuscan style. Jutting out from one corner were tumbledown pigsties covered with bramble and old-man's beard. The autumnal colours were glowing strongly in the still summery sun and the large fig tree at the back was heavy with fruit, its branches bent by their weight, inviting us to pick. The well, just under the tree, gave the final touch to this image of bucolic bliss. No matter if there was no supply of water other than the well, nor any electricity and certainly no 'easy access'. First thing Monday morning we were with the notary in Siena to sign the *compromesso* – the document that bound us to buying the property and to paying the deposit of ten per cent of the agreed price. We found a builder, gave him instructions and, three days later, flew back to London.

I went back in the spring with the children in our Renault 14 loaded with chattels. The house, we were told, was habitable, although the builders were still working in it. We arrived in the dark and, after the winter months, the track was far more treacherous than I remembered. The holes had become craters, full of water, and the mud was thick and gluey. It was also extremely cold and wet, as spring can often be in Tuscany.

We decided to leave the car and walk the last 100 metres, carrying the few things we needed for the night. Once inside, I was gripped with panic when I saw that the bathroom wasn't finished and there was no loo. But with the rapidity and efficiency that Italians can display when they want to, the bathroom was installed the next day and we were able to move in. Gradually, the house began to look more like a home. We had decided to leave the stables as they were, and to make only the first floor habitable. Here, we had three bedrooms, one bathroom and a tiny kitchen off the living room. I immediately fell in love with the living room which, the house being on top of a hill, had a panoramic view over the surrounding valleys broken up only by even higher hills.

Myriam's rather grander house was on the slope of the hill, and Myriam and I often got together. Like me, she was a passionate cook and an equally passionate eater. We'd go to the restaurant on the Badia a Coltibuono estate, which later became famous under the baton of Emanuela Stucchi, daughter of cookery writer Lorenza de'Medici. In those early days, though, the cook was a local woman who made

Cornia in Tuscany.

Myriam's favourite pasta dish, *pici alla senese*, a Tuscan tagliatelle with a palate-shooting chilli sauce. Chilli was rather uncommon in Italy then and there were only three areas where it was used a lot: Calabria and Basilicata in the South and the province of Siena in the North, where indeed we were. The dish I liked most at the Badia was an assortment of roast meats: veal, guinea-fowl, pork, chicken, wild boar, and sometimes kid, served in a small pool of the roasting juices surrounded by segments of roasted potatoes perfectly crusted outside and mellowy soft inside.

We also dined at Carlo and Carloni, both situated under the imposing Ricasoli castle of Brolio. Myriam insisted that Carloni was the better of the two especially for its *pici* with fungi sauce, while I swore by Carlo, partly because the proprietor had been so kind to us on one occasion. We'd gone there one Easter Sunday and Carlo told us, apologetically, that the restaurant was full. I begged him to let us in, saying we didn't have any food at home, having just arrived the night before, which was true. Carlo saw our sad predicament of an Easter Sunday without lunch. He squeezed an extra table in the corner of the room, which he loaded with *finocchiona* (Tuscan salame) mountain prosciutto and *coppa di testa* (brawn), saying, 'This is to keep you happy for the moment; I'll be back.' And back he was with mountains of *tagliatelle al sugo*, roast kid with *insalatina di stagione* – seasonal salad – and pecorino with raw broad beans, the first of the season.

Oliver and I had many happy holidays at Cornia, making friends with a few other *villeggianti* – people who, like us, had holiday homes there decades before it became fashionable – and often dined in each other's houses. One day we were asked to 'a Sicilian supper' by some friends from Milan, to be cooked by Claudia, their Sicilian guest. The dinner was truly Sicilian and excellent. For one night, I could forget the sober simplicity of Tuscan food and indulge in the flamboyant Sicilian opulence, its scent and richness so reminiscent of Arab cooking. The smell took me back to the markets of Vucciria and Ballarò in Palermo, where I'd walk around for hours, stopping occasionally to sample a fried aubergine, or a boiled octopus tentacle, one or two chickpea fritters, a few luscious olives or a handful of fat pistachios from Bronte, the town near Mount Etna where the best pistachios in the world grow. Sicilian fare has always fascinated me because I firmly believe it is in Sicily that European food was born, in that melting pot of different cultures and cuisines, beginning with the Greek and the Roman and on through the Arab, Norman, French and Spanish to become Italian and then, with the Renaissance, to spread all over Western Europe.

The Sicilian–Chiantigiano dinner started with the richest *caponata* I had ever eaten – a magnificent pile of fried aubergines, topped with lobster. This was followed by a refreshingly simple *ziti* – a long, hollow pasta – with courgettes. Then we had *farsumagru* – a meat roulade stuffed with prosciutto, spinach, eggs and ricotta – and, at the end, a spectacular Cassata Siciliana was placed in the middle of the table, covered in beautiful pistachio green icing and studded with Sicilian candied fruits.

I'd loved Sicilian food ever since I got to know that enchanting island, thanks mainly to the San Giulianos, whom Oliver and I had known for about forty years. We went there, and I still go, often as guests of enchanting Michi in her comfortable converted barn, and of her brother Giuseppe, in the *casa reale* – royal house – as his house is jokingly called. It is indeed a grand house set in a magnificent garden, a green pool in the middle of the flat, dusty boring countryside between Catania and Siracusa. We'd sit around the swimming pool, as blue and large as that made famous by David Hockney, and chat and read and reminisce of our youth and our exploits.

Giuseppe, now 75, is still as devastatingly charming as when he descended upon us in London for a few weeks to learn English. Oliver always suspected I had an affair with him and, much later, when he asked me, I'd told him (truthfully) no. He commented, 'What a pity!' When I told the story to Giuseppe, he said, 'But I would never go to bed with my host's wife.' 'But I know you did on another occasion,' I reiterated. 'Ah, but there I was not a guest but a member of the staff.' Dear Giuseppe, always the perfect gentleman. After a few weeks, Giuseppe left us to take up a post as a valet to some minister in a minor British colony. He enjoyed his 'downstairs' experience, and every time he returned to London he would come to see us, driving his master's Rolls or Cadillac in black uniform and cap. He always had some amusing story to tell, like the time the ex king of Italy, Umberto II, was dining at the minister's house. When the king discovered that the minister had an Italian on his staff, he insisted on meeting him and, on hearing Giuseppe's surname, got up from the table, walked up to Giuseppe and embraced him, saying, *'Cugino'* – cousin – as they call each other within the top stratas of the aristocracy – to the utter amazement of the guests.

The lunches and dinners at San Giuliano were always memorable; sometimes for their utter simplicity and at other times for their well-balanced richness, like the wild rabbit dish I had there on the night Giuseppe was entertaining a group of Scandinavian wine merchants. The merchants were there to taste the San Giuliano wines – Giuseppe's new enterprise – from the vineyards he'd planted next to the citrus groves established by his ancestors. The wild rabbits, which had been shot on the estate, were cooked in local Malvasia wine and enriched by *zibibbo* – special dried grapes – and pine nuts. It was so different from the wild rabbit I had in Chianti, a simpler but equally delicious offering, cooked in the local wine.

~

IN TUSCANY it was always at the tables of the locals that we had the best meals. Soon after we settled in our primitive

Cornia we were asked to lunch at the home of the Resti, who had a flat in the splendid fortress of Cacchiano. Remo Resti, one of the Ricasoli workers, looked after our house when we were away, and his wife, Anna, got it ready for us before we arrived and closed it after we left. They were a delightful couple, she always ready with her domestic tips, he always curious about what was going on in the world. He was particularly fascinated by Mrs Thatcher, who was an endless source of conversation between us.

And then there was Rossella who ran the general store in Monti, a nearby village. She was extremely pretty, like a blonde Claudia Cardinale, and full of life and giggles. In between serving her customers she'd sometimes give a demonstration of the latest dance she'd learned at the *balera* – an open air disco – on the previous Saturday night. She'd move up and down the shop singing, dancing and darting flirtatious glances at any man around. And she cooked excellent ragù.

But it was with Aldo, the carpenter, and his wife that we had the finest food. At first, Oliver was amazed that all these people would ask us to lunch or dinner. But it was part of the local tradition for them to open their houses and offer us, the 'foreigners', their warm welcome in the shape of food and wine. I liked Aldo; I found him very attractive, although he was certainly no Adonis. He reminded me of a ferret, with his sharp features and speed of movement. And he was fun. But Aldo had one black spot, as far as I was concerned. He was an inveterate and indiscriminate hunter, a typical Tuscan whose motto seemed to be 'if it moves, shoot it'. When the hunting season started, he was off, and never mind if a bullet strayed into our windowless house or through our front door which would not shut properly. Many times he asked me if I would allow him to build, on our land, one of those huts made of tree branches for him to hide inside and shoot any bird that happened to pass by. In spite of my soft spot for Aldo, I always said no, although I was quite sure that as soon as we packed our bags and left Cornia in the middle of September, he'd be there building his hut. There were already few enough birds; perhaps they'd learnt that Tuscany was an out-of-bounds region and flown somewhere else.

One day I was driving with Aldo in his old Fiat Seicento when he suddenly veered violently to the right and started careering down the field, zig-zagging between the olive trees. *'Ma che diavolo stai facendo?'* – 'What the hell are you doing?' – I screamed, and we came to a halt. 'I am very sorry,' he answered. 'I forgot I was in the car. I saw that lovely hare running across the field . . . and off I went. Did you see it?'

Aldo was a good carpenter and an even better cook. One day he asked us to supper to eat the hare he'd caught that day. The table was laid on the terrace of their house high up in Lecchi, with a view all round. Aldo and his wife had also invited two of our English neighbours, Tim and Henrietta Behren. We started with chunks of local salame with focaccia, followed by home-made *pici al ragù*. The main dish was the splendid hare – the victim of our indiscriminate hunter – which Aldo had cooked Tuscan-style in a sweet and sour sauce. I had to admit that it was even nicer than the jugged hare my mother used to make at home. Maybe only the best hares crossed Aldo's path.

Chianti was still Chianti then. Slowly, throughout the decade we were there, we saw the change: more and more cocktail parties in more and more artistically done-up farmhouses. We were even asked to a 'masque' one year, the sort of entertainment I always connected with Oxford colleges. Our American hostess, beautiful in shimmering white, arrived in a boat drawn across the lake looking just like the Lohengrin I had seen at La Scala years before, but without the swan. However, the food was much better than at any Oxford college or, indeed, any other cocktail party I'd been to. No tiny, insipid canapés or sticks of pineapple and cheddar puncturing a large grapefruit; no palate-sticking sausage rolls, or the omnipresent salmon or cucumber sandwiches. Just a prodigal assortment of all sorts of salami, prosciutti and *coppe*, the uniformity of their colour broken here and there by round bread loaves, long bread sticks, flat *schiacciate*, puffed *focacce* and rounds and rounds of pecorini of different ages and provenances. In the middle of the table, as always, were the splendid *trionfi* – triumphs – of fruit and vegetables, so temptingly appetising that you had to quickly dismantle them.

But then one day I counted no less than seven cars with British number plates in Gaiole, our village. Chianti had become Chiantishire and we didn't like it any more. We sold our farmhouse, a great mistake since, twenty years later, Cornia – still in the same fairly primitive condition as when we sold it – was snapped up by a German buyer for £400,000. He divided it up in mini-flats to be let to foreigners at an astronomical rent.

When I went back to Chianti in 2001, Cornia wasn't my Cornia any more. It had been totally refurbished – practically rebuilt – and I left with no regrets, apart from the money I'd missed out on. I kept Aldo's recipe, which I still cook whenever I can find a hare. Hares are becoming a rarity even in a 'shooting' county like Dorset and, if Aldo ever came to visit, I doubt I'd be in any danger from his careering down the green pastures of Dorset instead of the olive groves of Tuscany.

RECIPES

Tagliatelle Verdi e Zucchine al Sugo di Pistacchio e Basilico

Spinach Tagliatelle and Courgettes with a Pistachio and Basil Sauce

SERVES 4–5

200ml extra virgin olive oil
4 garlic cloves, peeled and finely chopped
600g courgettes, cut into matchsticks
120 shelled pistachio nuts
50g fresh basil
30g flat leaf parsley
250g dried green tagliatelle
25g unsalted butter
salt and freshly ground black pepper

Heat 2 tablespoons of the oil with the garlic in a frying pan and, when hot, add the courgettes and fry at a lively heat until they are golden brown all over. Shake the pan frequently and mix well with a fork – a fork is better than a spoon, because it helps to keep the matchsticks separated. Fry until cooked but still slightly crunchy, about 10 minutes. Season with salt and pepper.

While the courgettes are cooking, put the pistachios into a small saucepan, cover with water and bring to the boil. Boil for 20 seconds, and then peel them straight away – wear gloves because it is much easier to peel the nuts at this stage. Dry them thoroughly and put them in a food processor with the basil and parsley. Whiz, while adding the remaining oil through the funnel. Scoop out the mixture into an ovenproof serving bowl, season with salt and pepper and place the bowl in a low oven, 100°C/gas mark 1.

Cook the pasta in boiling salted water. Drain, reserving a cupful of the pasta water, and immediately turn the pasta into the bowl containing the nuts and herbs. Add the butter and toss thoroughly, adding 3 or 4 tablespoonfuls of the pasta water. When well mixed, spoon the courgettes over the top and serve at once.

$\sim$

Lepre in Agrodolce
Hare in a Sweet and Sour Sauce

For this recipe, you must have the joints of the hare cut into small pieces. Ask your butcher to chop them or do it yourself, which is not difficult. The pieces should be small so that more of the delicious sauce can penetrate easily into the meat.

1 hare (about 1.3kg), cut into pieces
30g sultanas
6 tbsp olive oil
1 carrot, chopped
2 celery sticks, chopped
2 garlic cloves, chopped
small bunch of flat leaf parsley, chopped
1 tbsp rosemary needles, chopped
50g unsmoked pancetta, chopped
1 tbsp plain flour
250ml meat stock
200ml red wine vinegar
25g candied peel, cut into small pieces
30g bitter chocolate, broken into small pieces
40g pine nuts
1½ tbsp muscovado sugar
salt and pepper

Wash the hare pieces and dry thoroughly.

Soak the sultanas in hot water for about 20 minutes, then drain and dry them.

Put the oil in a heavy casserole and, when hot, sauté the hare pieces, turning them over and over until brown. Add the chopped vegetables, garlic, herbs and pancetta and fry for a few minutes. Sprinkle with the flour, add the stock and the seasoning and cook for about 1½ hours.

Meanwhile, prepare the sweet and sour sauce. Put the dried sultanas into a small saucepan and add the vinegar, candied peel, chocolate, pine nuts and sugar. Cook on a very gentle heat, stirring constantly, until the chocolate and sugar have melted and then pour over the hare. Turn the pieces over and over, and cook for a further 30 minutes, until the hare is cooked through. Check the seasoning and serve with polenta.

CHAPTER 17

BARNES

Carbonara must be eaten hot

IN THE SPRING OF 1962 we moved to Vine Road in Barnes. 'But where is Barnes?' our friends asked, astonished by our daring move to this unknown south-western suburb. But I'd never really felt at ease in Holland Villas Road and we wanted to move further out of the centre to an area with more open space than Holland Park.

So we bought the smaller half of an attractive 1830s house overlooking Barnes Common which had a granny cottage at the end of the garden. It was the perfect arrangement to be close to, but not actually living with, Oliver's mother, who had recently become a widow.

It was my dream home; light and sunny with plenty of rooms and a secluded garden at the back. And my dream was complete when, seven months after moving in, Julia arrived – a daughter at last. She was born at 6 a.m. on the 10th of January 1963 after a very long night of labour, during one of the coldest winters on record. The temperature stayed below freezing until the beginning of March. But Number 12 Vine Road was never cold, thanks to Julia, who, being three weeks premature, had to be kept very, very warm. All our friends came not only to see the new baby but also to get warm, they told us. Julia was the perfect baby: pretty, good, amenable and cheerful, as indeed she still is, despite the worries she gave us when she was a teenager.

I remember one day when I was feeding Julia, in my large sunny bedroom with my dog at my feet, I looked out of the window on to our beautiful garden, and thought, 'I am quite happy now.'

Paul and Guy were in heaven too, tobogganing in Richmond Park and, later, when the snow at long last disappeared, kicking a ball around Barnes Common with their new friends from around the corner in Woodlands Road. Woodlands Road was the most 'fun' road I have ever come across, inhabited by a mixture of actors, journalists, artists and the like who threw a lot of good parties, and who loved gossiping and borrowing from each other, everything from the milk to the wife.

I particularly enjoyed the Hoggs' parties. Liz used to send an invitation to a 'plonk and blotting paper party'. The wine was just one up from real plonk and the 'blotting paper' consisted of little square sandwiches, made with sliced white bread, and some sort of filling which varied from smoked salmon and Gentleman's Relish to other spreads of various flavours and denominations and not much glory. But the guests more than made up for the lack of culinary imagination.

At one party, I met Roy Plomley, who had just created *Desert Island Discs* for the BBC. He was a charming, unassuming man who seemed delighted to hear that I was a fan of his programme. He asked me what items I would choose. I cannot

Julia's christening.

recall all the ten records, but I do remember that I chose the 'Love Duet' from Verdi's *Otello*, one of Beethoven's late quartets, and 'When I'm Sixty-Four' by the Beatles. 'And for the book, I think Dante's *La Divina Commedia* with all the appendixes and notes I can lay my hands on, so that at long last I would be able to understand it all,' I finished. Now, forty years on, I might choose the same records but certainly not *The Divine Comedy*. I feel that, having reached the venerable age of eighty, I can survive the rest of my life without a complete understanding of it. As for a luxury, I would choose an endless supply of the best olive oil so that I can enjoy the fish which I will catch and cook on a hot stone and the vegetables, grass and roots that I will pick. In fact I can live on steamed or grilled or raw vegetables as long as they are dressed with olive oil. I cannot bear to have them naked, as they are still served in some country pubs in my adopted country.

When we first arrived in Vine Road, the other half of our house was let to an American General. He had an alcoholic wife (or so it was said, since we never set eyes on her) and a fierce Alsatian dog. The dog had apparently been trained by the Japanese on the same lines as they trained the dogs that guarded the prisoner of war camps during the war. And, indeed, he guarded his master's garden in the same way. In our garden I had a small plot of land where I grew a few vegetables which I loved to tend. But, as soon as I bent down to work I could feel the hot breath of the beast on the other side of the fence. This ruined all my agricultural efforts and I always blamed the dog if my French beans were too few or my tomatoes too tasteless. Thank goodness, the General soon left, and so did the beast.

After a short period with another American General, the house was bought by Marguerite and Harry Woolf, a young lawyer who later became Lord Woolf of Barnes, the Lord Chief Justice. Marguerite used to give marvellous dinner parties. They were very formal, as that was still the time when we 'ladies' would go upstairs to powder our noses, a habit that by then I'd got used to. Everyone dressed smartly and the food was good, if still predictable, and the puddings were superb. But one day, Marguerite surprised us all by cooking a spectacular Middle-Eastern dinner. Marguerite was a Sephardi Jew of Iraqi origin and on that occasion the intense aromas of the Middle East came alive. I shall always remember the delicious Persian rice with its crunchy crust, so different from my risotto but with the same intensity of flavours.

IT WAS IN Barnes that I started my cookery writing career. We were all sitting around the table in the dining room, pushing a large bowl of *bucatini alla carbonara* from one to the other on a rainy evening in the spring of 1973, when the telephone rang. Carbonara is one of the few pasta dishes that must be eaten hot – very hot. Even I, who prefer my food warm, heat the plates up for it. 'Blast!' I said, 'you go,' hoping that Oliver or one of the children would do just that. But no. 'It's always for you at this time of day,' they argued, and continued tucking in. So I answered, and that telephone call changed my life.

An American voice said: 'I am John Marqusee and I'm very interested in your idea of writing a book on pasta. Splendid idea, but I want a book on the history of pasta – the shapes, the making, the people – everything – not just recipes.' It happened so fast that I'd forgotten that, only that afternoon, I had mentioned this idea to Joanna Marqusee, whose father, John, had a small publishing house called Paddington Press.

The idea of writing a book about pasta was first sown in my mind by a friend, Geraldine Gartrell, and by my two brothers who could never understand why spaghetti and macaroni, which were popular in the US, were still ignored in Britain, or, when not ignored, badly cooked. Both Guido and Marco came to London quite often and were depressed, just as I was, by the gastronomic scene. They thought it was about time the British knew about good food, and pasta in particular. I feel it was a great pity that neither of my brothers took the radical step of becoming a chef – radical, because at the time no offspring of a bourgeoisie family would even contemplate choosing such a 'demeaning' career. Guido cooked very well, but tended to be too creative, often mixing too many different flavours for the sake of mixing. He took cooking very seriously and went to cookery school for quite a few years. Marco, too, is a keen cook, but with a less adventurous approach. He prefers to follow recipes, often mine, which sometimes leads to language problems, even though his English is very good. When that happens, he rings me and I have to go through the recipe step by step and search for the Italian for parsnip, carraway or cardamom.

Geraldine was a journalist with a natural feel for what the public wanted and needed. She was a good cook and extremely interested in food. We used to go for long walks together with our dogs in Richmond Park and exchange recipes and ideas. She supplied me with many classic English recipes, like the one for her apple chutney which I've been making now for the past thirty years; or for her fudge with its sticky toffee and intense vanilla flavour. She, on the other hand, was always asking me for new recipes for pasta sauces or *risotti*, which she passed on to her friends.

Later, Geraldine became my most faithful champion, always producing one or more of my dishes at her dinner parties, some of which I'd completely forgotten I'd created. Many times, I have successfully tested a recipe and written it up, and then put it out of my mind. I've even been served dishes at dinner parties and, on tasting them, commented, 'This is very good,' to be told 'Oh, I do hope so; it's one of yours.' I'm always delighted to see that my recipes really work, as indeed every recipe should.

At the time of that telephone call, I was giving some private Italian lessons to prepare students, like Joanna Marqusee, for their A levels. I was also doing some teaching at Westfield College, part of London University, and, occasionally, at the London Opera Centre. By then, alongside my part-time job with Robson Lowe, I had been teaching on and off for about twenty years and was finally able to choose where and whom I taught. Out of the window had gone the Linguists' Club in Campden Hill and the College of Adult Education in Kensington. Most of the students there were middle-aged Kensington ladies in the afternoons and a handful of accountants and the like in the evenings – people who only wanted to learn Italian so they could go to Sorrento and exchange a few words with the locals. Their minds were already full of shopping lists and bank statements and there was little room for Italian. But my private students, and those at Westfield College or the Opera Centre, were young people interested in developing a real understanding of the language, and everything I said was imprinted on their minds.

At Westfield College, I was known as *la falsa Signora Waley* – the false Mrs Waley – because the true one was, in fact, Doctor Pamela Waley, wife of one of Oliver's cousins, and she was their real lecturer. All I had to do was listen to their reading and talk with them to check that their Italian was pronounced correctly. At the Opera Centre it was the same, although instead of reading Manzoni or Italo Calvino we read librettos. I was in heaven. To be able to indulge my love of opera, and even be paid for it, was more than I'd ever hoped for. I was surrounded by young people discussing how to interpret the characters of Radames in *Aida* or Mimi in *La Boheme*.

I also had some older private pupils, some of whom became close friends, like Tom and Thesa Ingram who introduced me to the part of Dorset where I live today. They had a cottage there where Oliver and I spent many weekends, little realising that I would end up seeing my life out there. Had somebody told me at the time that Dorset would be my resting place, I would have thought they were insane. I loved London, and Barnes, and for me the country was worthy of consideration only in the summer and only for a few days.

My most entertaining pupil was Oliver Knox, with whom I had endless discussions on the best Italian translation of an English word or phrase and vice versa. My star pupil was David William, a friend from Oliver's Oxford days. These two men, and my dear husband of course, guided me through the intricacies of the English language and became my mentors on literary matters.

⁓

THAT EVENING IN 1973, after my telephone conversation with John Marqusee, I immediately decided to give up my teaching job. It took up a lot of my time, not just the hours spent teaching, but also in driving from Barnes to Finchley Road, where Westfield College is situated, or to Commercial Road in the East End for the Opera Centre.

So I packed up teaching, packed my suitcase and set off for Italy to start the research for my book. I loved interviewing people and writing, both of which were new to me. And I certainly loved cooking. So, once back at home again, I started to 'cook' in earnest. I spent my day weighing, cooking, testing, shopping, eating and writing. I lived food and talked food. I was no longer going into the kitchen just to make dinner or whatever, but spending my day there with pen, paper, books, scales, measuring spoons and cups and jugs. I realised how lucky I was to have a career I enjoyed as much as my family did, and in which Oliver and the children participated with enthusiasm.

Oliver was the ideal taster and tester. He did not have a very discerning palate, never having been taught to appreciate or criticise what he was eating. So if he described a dish as 'rather bland', I knew it would not be appreciated by the average English eater. But if he approved with enthusiasm, I was quite sure the dish was just right, and I would jot down the recipe. Oliver liked classic English dishes, such as baked beans, although he preferred my version of them to the tinned ones and adored my sausages and mash: I fried the sausages gently with onion then finished off with red wine and added lots of butter to the mash. More importantly, Oliver also helped me as a ghost writer. He wrote the historical part of my first book from the research I had carried out in Italy and in London. He also used to check all my writing – and correct it, though we often squabbled over punctuation. He placed the adverbs in the right place, added the correct preposition and shortened my sentences, since I tended to write in the rather rhetorical style the Italians use. We were a great team.

My book, *Portrait of Pasta*, was published both in the UK and the US in 1976 by Paddington Press. As luck would have it, Caroline Hobhouse, the best cookery editor in the UK at the time, liked it. So things began to happen straight afterwards, and I was 'in'. Nobody in Britain knew much about Italian food then. Pasta generally meant tinned Heinz spaghetti, olive oil was still used to settle your stomach and hardly anybody knew what salame, prosciutto and Parmigiano were.

I always hoped to meet one of my new fans, but it happened only three times: once on a plane to Rome, next on a cruise in the Baltic and, the last time, in a village in Kent. On the plane it was a Japanese artist who sat next to me. She lived in Perugia and was ecstatic when she realised who I was. She immediately gave me her card and we promised to meet again. Of course, we didn't. But the second person became a good friend. Rosemary Roche and her husband, Alec, had sat at our table on board the *Minerva*. Rosemary, a warm, cheerful Australian, had not only heard my name, but even had some of my books. At last, I thought, I am famous. We got on well and Oliver and I went to see the Roches in their splendid flat in Rome overlooking the Tiber where Rosemary produced a seriously good dinner *all'italiana* – four courses accompanied by three different wines. The third occasion happened much later when I was spending a few days with my friend Geoffrey

Sharp in Kent. While walking Poppy, my gentle lurcher, in the woods, I tripped over a tree root and gashed my leg – a common problem that people face in old age. Dripping with blood, I rushed to Geoffrey's doctor and was seen immediately by a pretty blonde nurse. After bandaging my leg, she started taking notes and, on hearing my name, she stopped dead, looked up at me and gasped, 'not *the* Anna Del Conte?' 'Yes, why not?' I retorted. 'Oh, I have been a great admirer of yours for a long time. You've not made my day but my year.' I drove back gleaming all over.

Although I never met any other fans, I have been lucky enough to meet many people who were happy to talk about food and swap recipes and ideas, like the man who sat next to me on a flight to Bologna. He was a handsome man of forty-something who told me, after he'd finished describing his lectures at the University of Bologna where he taught astrology: 'Sí, I do cook, but only for my two-year-old daughter. She is extremely fussy and only eats roasted sea bass with sautéed courgettes, risotto with vegetables, and most pasta, but not tagliatelle. Very un-bolognese.' I certainly do not share that little girl's taste.

~

PASTA WAS, and still is, my favourite food, and carbonara one of my favourite sauces. I make it quite often, with many variations. Sometimes I add white wine, sometimes cream, or sage or rosemary, or I use only the yolks of the eggs. I love it in any guise, but the *bucatini alla carbonara* on the evening I was asked to write my first book will always remain the best.

RECIPES

Bucatini alla Carbonara
Bucatini Carbonara

SERVES 4

---

1 tbsp extra virgin olive oil
3 garlic cloves, peeled and bruised
150g unsmoked pancetta, cut into short strips or small cubes
400g dried bucatini or spaghetti
1 egg and 2 yolks
50g freshly grated Parmigiano-Reggiano
50g grated pecorino cheese
15g unsalted butter
salt and black pepper

Put the oil and the garlic into a large frying pan over a high heat. Sauté the garlic until it is coloured but not brown, then lift it out and discard. Add the pancetta and sauté for 10–15 minutes, stirring frequently.

Meanwhile, cook the pasta in boiling salted water. While the pasta is cooking, lightly beat the egg and the 2 yolks in an ovenproof bowl, then mix in the cheeses, butter and a generous grinding of black pepper. Place the bowl in a very low oven to warm.

When cooked, drain the pasta, reserving 1 cupful of the pasta water. Transfer the pasta to the frying pan and stir fry for 2 or 3 minutes. Mix 3 or 4 tablespoons of the reserved pasta water into the bowl containing the egg and cheese mixture, then tip in the bucatini. Toss very thoroughly, adding a little more water, if necessary. Serve immediately.

~

Pasticcio di Tagliatelle e Salmone Affumicato
Baked Tagliatelle with Smoked Salmon

This is one of the most successful dishes I have created. It is based on a recipe allegedly written by the chef of Tsar Nicolas II, and is one of the recipes from ancient cookbooks that I found and included in my first book, *Portrait of Pasta*.

SERVES 4–6

250g dried egg tagliatelle
50g unsalted butter
200g smoked salmon, cut into strips
100g gruyère cheese, cut into thin slices
50g grated parmesan cheese
dried breadcrumbs
salt

For the béchamel sauce
750ml full-fat milk
60g unsalted butter
50g Italian 00 flour
½ tsp cayenne pepper

First, make the béchamel sauce. Heat the milk in a saucepan

until it begins to bubble at the edge. Meanwhile, melt the butter in a heavy saucepan over a low heat, then blend in the flour, stirring vigorously. Now draw the pan off the heat and add the hot milk, a few tablespoons at a time. You must let the flour mixture absorb each addition thoroughly before going on to the next stage. When all the milk has been absorbed, return the pan to the heat and bring to the boil. Cook over the gentlest heat for 5 minutes, stirring frequently, then remove from the heat and stir in the cayenne pepper.

Preheat the oven to 200°C/gas mark 6.

Cook the tagliatelle in plenty of boiling salted water. Drain, reserving 1 cupful of the pasta water. Return the pasta to the pan and add about two-thirds of the butter, cut into small pieces. Toss thoroughly.

Spoon 2 tablespoons of the béchamel sauce into a buttered oven dish and then spread about a third of the pasta over it. Cover with half the salmon strips, half the gruyère slices and a little béchamel sauce. Sprinkle with a little parmesan. Now, cover with a layer of pasta and then the remaining salmon and gruyère slices, 2 tablespoons of béchamel sauce and a little parmesan. Top with the remaining tagliatelle, pour 4 tablespoons of the reserved pasta water over the dish and top with the remaining béchamel.

Mix the breadcrumbs with the remaining parmesan and sprinkle over the top. Dot with the remaining butter and bake in the oven for 15 minutes until the top is beautifully gold.

Leave the dish to cool out of the oven for 5 minutes or so before serving.

CHAPTER 18

TOKYO

Spaghetti with tomato sauce

Iᴺ 1978 I ᴡᴇɴᴛ ᴛᴏ visit my son Paul in Tokyo, where I had the best spaghetti with tomato sauce ever. Or so it seemed, although nostalgia may well have played a part.

At that time, I was still working part-time as a translator and interpreter for Robson Lowe, now part of Christie's. I'd decided to hold on to this job until I could see how my cookery writing career was going to develop. Robson Lowe, the founder of the firm, was a far-sighted businessman who saw Britain as part of Europe long before Ted Heath took it into the Common Market, and he organised philatelic auctions in Switzerland, Italy and France and employed a handful of bilingual women to deal with the overseas markets. While my German and French colleagues were fully-fledged auctioneers, I was never able to grasp the speed at which auctions progressed.

It was at an auction in Basle that I finally realised that my abilities lay behind a desk with a pencil and not high up on a rostrum with a hammer. I had to conduct the sale in three languages, two in which I was fluent, but the third, French, became a nightmare, especially when the number I had to call contained a 'soixante-dix', 'quatre-vingts' or 'quatre-vingt-dix'. (Why couldn't they use 'septante', 'huitante' and 'neuvante'?) I tried to 'jump' past these tricky numbers, but the jump was too high and I could see the puzzled stares of the would-be bidders. So, after what was the longest ten minutes of my life, I was taken down and replaced by my German colleague, who carried on as though nothing had happened. And that was the beginning and the end of my auctioneering career.

Robson Lowe was selling a number of valuable stamps and letters of particular interest to collectors in Japan and Hong Kong. Mr Lowe, knowing that I was thinking of visiting my son in Tokyo, suggested that I could take these lots to be viewed there. So, always a thoughtful employer, he could pay my fare.

At Heathrow I was given a black attaché case containing stamps and letters to the value of £54,000. That bag was to stay with me at all times until I could hand it over to the right people in Hong Kong and in Tokyo. It became a particular worry in Hong Kong where I had a stopover, since I arrived on a bank holiday and I was unable to deliver it directly to the bank as instructed. Frankly, I was not going to spend the rest of the day shut up in the little room where I was staying, nor was I going to traipse round Hong Kong clutching the heavy black bag. So, I hid it in the shower and off I went. Thankfully, it was still there when I got back, and I was able to deliver the stamps destined for the Hong Kong bank the following day.

I arrived in Tokyo, clutching my precious bag, but Paul was not there to meet me as planned. I waited and waited, with my heart pounding faster and faster. What should I do? How could I make the Tokyo delivery? Eventually, Paul appeared, smiling apologetically. I needn't have worried, after all. I should have remembered that Paul is always late – and we managed to deliver Mr Lowe's stamps.

After finishing his Oxford degree in Oriental studies, Paul had taken a job in Tokyo as an editor on an English newspaper while researching his PhD and a book about the city. He had a small flat in Monzen-Nakachō, which was apparently quite large by Japanese standards. It consisted of two straw mat rooms – a living room and a bedroom – plus a tiny kitchen and a bathroom. It was on one of the upper floors of a block of flats in a poor district of Tokyo, near the port, overlooking some busy canals. I was fascinated by the life on the water – the barges, the boats and all the activities that went on down below.

But I was even more fascinated by the neighbours. The block of flats was like a beehive, most flats being inhabited by families with two or three – or even more – children, or so it seemed to me. I'd see the children going to school in the morning, impeccably turned out in their blue aprons and their yellow caps over their shock of ebony hair. All quiet and orderly and well behaved. In the three weeks I was there I never heard a single cry or shout, and this was in September when all the windows were flung open to let in the last of the summer sun. Too well-behaved even, I thought.

Paul was my personal guide and interpreter, taking me not only to the tourist parts of town like Ginza, but also to the 'real' Tokyo because those were the areas Paul was interested in for his PhD. As always, the first thing I did each morning was to go shopping for groceries. There was a local market nearby with stalls full of vegetables, fruit and fish, of all shapes, sizes and colours, most of which were unfamiliar to me. And, to my delight, I also found a shop that sold bread, without which, for me, no meal is complete. It was an amazing find in the middle of Tokyo. (The owner was apparently Danish, but the two shop assistants were Japanese.) It reminded me of the baker's in Pianella, a village near Siena, where we often went to buy their delicious bread when we had our house in Chianti. It had the same smell, the same dusting of white flour everywhere, similar large shelves on which the bread was laid out. The only difference in Tokyo was the lack of variety; in Pianella I never mastered the names of all the different shapes. The Japanese woman who served me had on a spotless white apron and a cap on her head, her jet black hair lightly powdered with flour, just like an eighteenth-century lady's wig.

Sometimes we ate in, but mostly we went to Japanese restaurants that were anything but smart. Tokyo at that time was a very expensive city compared with Europe. But a meal in a 'soba' or a 'tempura' restaurant was financially and gastronomically sound. These are in fact the only two Japanese dishes I like; sushi and sashimi leave me cold. For me, part of the pleasure of food is its smell, and raw food does not smell. There was one particular soba restaurant we went to two or three times where the food was very good. We all sat cross-legged at low tables, which gave the place a feeling of peace and calm, although I felt distinctly uncomfortable after about half an hour.

As I didn't know much about Japanese food, I let Paul choose the dishes, and he chose well. On one occasion, the dinner was particularly memorable, or perhaps it was the atmosphere or our dining companions, who are often a very important condiment to the dishes themselves. I particularly enjoyed the *zaru soba* – noodles in a basket – where the noodles, usually made with buckwheat in this particular recipe, are served cold – or at least chilled – with some clean spicy condiments. I'm very fussy about cold pasta, yet there I was enjoying a dish which fundamentally was very similar.

I also liked the idea of going to restaurants where only one type of food is served; they are like symphonies with a single theme – like the 'tempura' restaurants where the food is deep-fried, enveloped in the tastiest batter imaginable. Tempura is thought to have been introduced to Japan by the Portuguese and Spanish missionaries and traders in the sixteenth century. But the difference between tempura and a Spanish *frito* is that the batter for tempura is not smooth and fluid as in European fritters; instead the flour and liquid are loosely folded together so that the result is a lacy, fried coating. The various shrimp and squid or aubergines and green beans look – and taste – different from Mediterranean fritters when they come out of the wok. I realised that the food I liked best in Japan was that with a similar relative in Italy. That's not so odd; after all, we all love the food we were brought up with, the food we know from our childhood. As long as, that is, we had good food in our childhood. I have a theory that the palate, just like the eye and the ear, must be educated – if not in the cradle, then very soon afterwards.

Every now and then in Tokyo, I needed an Italian food fix. This, I have to admit to my shame, because I have always derided the diehard Italians who would come to London and complain about the food. I once took an Italian friend to a

Chinese restaurant. She was insisting on having bread with her meal, and she got quite cross with me when I told her there was no way I was asking for bread in a Chinese restaurant. The upshot was that she got up and left.

Fortunately, there was a small Italian restaurant near Paul's flat in Tokyo. Giuseppina in the kitchen and Mario in the front welcomed us with open arms and treated us like bosom friends. It was like entering garlic-scented sunshine. They both came from Campania, near Naples. How they finished up in Tokyo I never understood, but thank goodness they did, and opened this tiny restaurant in that out-of-the-way part of Tokyo inhabited mostly by Japanese. The restaurant didn't advertise; it simply had a notice outside in Italian which, translated, said: 'Here, real Italian spaghetti'. And it was indeed real, its gutsy tomato sauce strengthened with just the right amount of garlic and enlivened by a few herbs.

A tomato sauce in Japan can indeed taste of real tomatoes, as tomatoes grow well in the fertile volcanic soil of the islands. Giuseppina cooked her *sugo* – tomato sauce – at length in the traditional way. Forty minutes would suffice in a hurry, she said, and one hour was just right. And, like her compatriots in Campania, during the winter and spring months, when no local tomatoes were available, she used tinned tomatoes. But, whether tinned or fresh tomatoes, it was an unforgettable *spaghetti al sugo*.

In spite of Giuseppina and Mario's wonderful spaghetti, and all the sobas and tempuras, I never quite took to Japan. I found it an alien country, far beyond my comprehension. How could the people who built places of such utter spiritual peace as the Zen Gardens in Kyoto and the Todaiji Temple in Nara have embraced some of the worst aspects of western commercialisation? I found Ginza district, with its blaring western noises and lights, far worse than London's Oxford Street and Broadway put together.

When I saw the film *Lost in Translation*, in which Scarlett Johansson portrays the utter loneliness that a foreigner can feel in Tokyo, I could well understand her feelings, even if I had my son for company. And yet, once you turn off the noisy, psychedelic avenues, and walk for five minutes, you are in old Japan with its narrow streets lined with tiny houses and their even tinier, well-kept gardens where the only sound is the clip-clop of the few passers-by.

So I said goodbye to Japan without much regret, flew back to Hong Kong and fell deeply in love with that city and its people. Hong Kong is more Naples than Naples. Its unfamiliar noises are noisier, its dirt is dirtier, its urchins are more urchin-like, its people are more shoving and pushing and the food is more colourful, more plentiful. It was such a contrast after Tokyo and a joy to able to communicate with people. Almost everyone spoke English, or at least spoke very well with their hand and body gestures. And then there was the sea. All I wanted to do was to get on one of those ferry boats and lose myself amongst the endless islands that crown the harbour.

But what I loved most was the extraordinary display of all sorts of food, and the pleasure of eating it. Paul took me to the popular eateries of the Chinese where very few tourists went. I tried everything, or everything but the fried scorpions. One evening we went to Aberdeen, just across the water, all lights and reflections and lanterns. We ate in an enormous restaurant, which was full of screaming Chinese families. We had fish and fish and fish. I remember the spiced-salt prawns, so incredibly tasty as if somebody had stirred spices into the sea – you pick up the large prawns with your hands, crack them with your teeth and suck all the juices out.

I had that same dish some years later in London at a dinner party at the house of cookery writer Yan-Kit So, whose books put Chinese cooking on the culinary map of Britain. The surroundings were very different, but the prawns were just as good. Yan-Kit was an excellent cook and an attentive hostess. We sat around her table while she set to work in the kitchen, just a few feet away, cooking while contributing to the conversation. How did she do it? I admired her. I am hopeless at doing the two at once; when I cook I cook and when I talk I talk.

THE DAY I shall never forget from that faraway holiday is the one we spent in Macau, a fascinating place that manages to strike such a harmonious note between East and West, China and Portugal. We had a magnificent fish lunch on the veranda of a rather run-down restaurant in the port and then sat there savouring the colonial past. We walked barefoot along the pebble beach and up to St George's Church, with its symbols of Christianity and Buddhism mixed together in a mosaic of faiths, and then continued through the Portuguese side of the island, where it felt as if I was in a sort of distorted Lisbon. I saw a photograph of Macau recently and was dismayed; it is no longer a distorted Lisbon but more like a bad reproduction of Las Vegas.

We caught the hydrofoil back to Hong Kong with only two

minutes to spare and the next day I flew back home. It was an eventful flight because one of the jumbo jet engines decided to pack up somewhere over Iraq. It was dawn and I realised that the sun was coming through the port side of the plane, although flying north and west it should have been on the starboard side. Just at that time, the pilot announced that we were flying back to Bahrain. And there we stayed for two days. I hated those two days; they were a surprise and I don't like surprises. I like to plan everything in advance, and I was at a loose end. The only good thing I got out of the incident of the failed engine was that, inexplicably, it cured me of my fear of flying.

Three days later, back at home in Barnes, I cooked Giuseppina's *spaghetti al sugo*. It was good, but it was not the same. Was it the different tomatoes, the different hands or the different ambience? Who knows?

Spaghetti al Sugo di Pomodoro
Spaghetti with Tomato Sauce

MAKES ENOUGH FOR 5–6

1kg ripe tomatoes, cut into quarters
1 small celery stick, cut into chunks
1 small carrot, coarsely cut
1 medium onion, coarsely chopped
2 garlic cloves, crushed
small bunch of parsley, chopped
1 tsp tomato concentrate
1 tsp sugar
6 tbsp extra virgin olive oil
salt and freshly ground black pepper
500g dried spaghetti

Put the tomatoes in a heavy saucepan and cook over a high heat for about 5 minutes. Add the celery, carrot, onion, garlic, parsley, concentrated tomato, salt and sugar. Cook at a steady simmer for about 40 minutes, stirring occasionally. Keep a watch on it and, if necessary, add a little hot water.

When cooked, purée the sauce through a food mill and return it to the pan. Add the oil and cook for a further 10–15 minutes. Check for salt and season with ground pepper.

Meanwhile cook the spaghetti in plenty of boiling salted water. Drain the spaghetti and mix in the sauce. Serve at once.

CHAPTER 19

GASTRONOMY AND TRAVELS

Truffles with everything

AFTER THE PUBLICATION of my first book, *Portrait of Pasta*, things had taken a rapid turn. Caroline Hobhouse, cookery editor at Macmillan, asked me to adapt the American edition of Marcella Hazan's first book, *The Classic Italian Cookbook*, for the British market. I was delighted because I thought it was the best book on Italian cooking in the English language. When her second book came out in the US, I was again asked to do the adaptation for the British edition. So back I was at the scales, cursing the American system of cups and spoons, while thinking of good old Napoleon who set the metric system, so easy to grasp and divide and multiply. I also decided that I needed an agent to deal with the intricacies of contracts, royalties, and the *dos* and *don'ts* involved in the publication of a book. Vivien Green came into my life and she has been my literary rock ever since. Whenever I feel down and unsure, I ring her up and she makes me feel able to write again.

More or less at the same time I was asked by Ebury Press to write a book on Italian cooking for the popular *Good Housekeeping* Cookery Club series. To this day, some of my friends still use quite a few of the recipes. The complaint I had from them was over the cooking times. 'Far too short,' they told me. Well, I have the idiosyncratic belief that cooking times are extremely personal and, ideally, should not be specified, but I have learned to be more precise. The book had a long introduction on the different regions of Italy, pointing out for the first time to the English reader, the incredible variety of Italian cuisine.

It was in 1984 that my writing career really took off, thanks to the publication of my next book, *Gastronomy of Italy*, which was not a cookery book but an encyclopaedia of Italian food: the produce, products, tools, methods of cooking and its history from Roman time to the present day. The book was the brainchild of Phoebe Phillips, who had a small packaging firm which produced good-quality books. I loved the idea without realising the full extent of my commitment. Writing the historical part, with Oliver's help, was straightforward enough, as I was able to consult a number of authoritative books both in London and in Italy. But the modern section was a nightmare. Italian gastronomy is a labyrinth into which you don't want to be drawn. You are bombarded with contrasting information. Every Italian thinks he or she knows everything about food and is longing to dispense his or her knowledge to you. Usually that knowledge is limited to what their mother or grandmother has told them and for them this is the Bible. That is perfectly acceptable when it comes to recipes – Mamma's or Nonna's recipes can indeed be the best ever – but it does not make any sense when their sayings about food in general are passed on as undisputed historical truth.

The research trips for *Gastronomy* took me all over the peninsula but mostly to Milan and Venice for their libraries and to my mentor, Massimo Alberini, always the most reliable source of information. He was the great gastronomic historian of the twentieth century, who also gave me very sound advice. Massimo was a fascinating man and a good friend, whom I miss a lot since his death in 2000.

Gastronomy of Italy was published by Bantam Books in the UK and by HarperCollins in the US, as well as in Germany and Holland, which was exciting enough. But I was thrilled when it was awarded the prestigious Gran Duchessa Maria Luigia di Parma prize. I bought a new suit and went to Parma with my proud husband for the ceremony, which was followed by a banquet, as grand as any that Marie Louise herself (she was the sovereign of the State of Parma and Napoleon's second wife) would have given. It opened with an array of local antipasti followed by a soothing and elegant soup of *anolini in brodo* – small meat ravioli in capon stock. After the sea-bass, two young lads in striped jackets, white berets and clogs, paraded around the long trestle table carrying a large tray on which sat a glistening roasted wild boar surrounded by a crown of bay leaves – a triumph to the eye and the palate.

(*Gastronomy of Italy* was re-published less auspiciously years later, in September 2001, by Pavilion and a launch lunch party was arranged at the Neal Street Restaurant, on that tragic day of 9/11. There were about two dozen of us having a sumptuous lunch, when, at the end, as we were relaxing and chatting away, Priscilla Carluccio came into the room and gave us the terrible news. We were all so stunned that I did not at once take in the seriousness of the situation; it was only later, when I got home, that I realised the significance of the catastrophic events which were to change our lives.)

Launching Gastronomy *with Alvaro of La Famiglia.*

After the success of the first edition of *Gastronomy of Italy*, I immediately went on to write two more books: *Secrets from an Italian Kitchen* and *Entertaining all'Italiana*, both of which were published in the US and in other countries, such as Brazil, from where, up to two years ago, I still received royalties. It was then that I began to be confident enough to create recipes. I was able to 'taste' the final dish just by writing about it. Some of my best recipes, I think, were written for those two books, like the *risotto al limone* and chicken in sweet and sour sauce which were based on recipes I found in seventeenth- and eighteenth-century cookbooks. I loved researching in old books, adapting the recipes and bringing to our tables dishes that existed in the past.

More books followed, thanks to the selling skills of my

agent, Vivien Green. Among them was another I really enjoyed writing, or I should say researching: *The Classic Food of Northern Italy*, published by Pavilion in 1994. For this book, I wanted to talk to as many people as possible, to eat in restaurants, *trattorie* and *osterie* where *cucina casalinga* (home cooking) was served, to visit food factories and markets, to discover first-hand the kind of background colour and detail that I couldn't find in libraries. So Oliver and I got into our small grey Clio and drove across France to start our eating in earnest in Valle d' Aosta, the border region between France and Italy, and then slowly travelling around the top half of the peninsula to places I wanted to visit, like Goro, a big fishing port in Romagna, where we were present at the most fascinating auction I ever saw. The auction went on in total silence, the bidder whispering his bid in the ear of the auctioneer – and tons and tons of fish were sold. Four weeks later, we ended up at the Trattoria Da Rosa at Macerata in Le Marche with a splendid plate of *vincisgrassi*, the local speciality.

Oliver was the driver and my reliable sounding-board, always there patiently in the background. But in South Tyrol he took on the lead role, when I discovered the locals would rather talk to him, an Englishman, than to me, an Italian. Seventy years after the Treaty of Versailles, the Tyrolese still felt Austrian, having never really come to terms with the handover of Sud-Tirolo to Italy.

It was in South Tyrol, on Lake Caldaro, that I guessed what was wrong with Oliver. For the last few days he had been complaining of tummy pains. We were having breakfast on a spectacularly clear and sunny morning on the terrace of our pension when I suddenly noticed that Oliver's face had turned that ghostly grey-green colour which I have always associated with cancer. It was a terrible shock; I felt sure I was right. When we arrived back in London, he had all the tests and found he did indeed have cancer – of the prostate – and underwent an operation from which he recovered well. In the last fifteen years of his life Oliver was plagued by many life-threatening diseases, from a heart malfunction to a brain aneurysm which nearly killed in 1990. And yet, right up to the end, he hardly complained, simply saying, 'I am such a nuisance.'

He definitely thought he was 'a nuisance' when I had to cancel a book-signing tour in the US for the publication of *Secrets from an Italian Kitchen*. My editor at HarperCollins, Susan Friedman, had arranged a coast-to-coast trip from New York all the way to San Francisco and Los Angeles, stopping at various places, and then returning to Washington via Denver and New Orleans. About a fortnight before we were due to leave, Oliver suffered some angina pains. He had an electrocardiogram and the cardiologist was quite frank. 'From the little I can see already,' he said, 'I can tell you one thing straight away: you cannot go to America.' So my trip was curtailed and I went to New York by myself for a short week. I got the red carpet treatment, but it was not the same without Oliver. I'd been looking forward so much to travelling triumphantly around the US with him and visiting many places we didn't know, places that I shall never know now.

The Classic Food of Northern Italy received two awards: the Guild of Food Writers' Book of the Year Award and the Premio Orio Vergani of the Accademia della Cucina Italiana. I am very proud of both, especially of the second, because it meant that my book was recognised by my compatriots. But I was even happier when, in 1996, I received the Verdicchio d'Oro prize for 'the contribution to the dissemination of the knowledge of authentic Italian cooking'.

~

AT THAT TIME I was also regularly contributing to *Sainsbury's Magazine*, owned then by Delia Smith. At the beginning I had been commissioned to write a series of articles for its monthly feature 'Anatomy of an Ingredient', which took me to Sardinia for the pecorino, to Parma for the prosciutto, to Lombardy for the Gorgonzola, to Veneto for the polenta and to various other places. The food photographer and, sometimes, the food editor, would accompany me and we would have three or four days of utter pleasure (the hard work came later, back at home, when I had to write the articles). We were taken to the best restaurants and *trattorie*, where the meals were prepared around the particular ingredient I was writing about. So, in Umbria, where I was researching black truffles, we had truffles with everything, a great pleasure which compensated for the discomfort of the hotel we stayed in. It was lugubriously vast and miserably cold, so cold that I felt that the only way to keep warm would have been to creep into the photographer's assistant's bed (he was rather sexy), but I didn't dare – one of my regrets, of which I don't have many. In Emilia-Romagna for my articles on dried porcini, the hotel proprietor had gone to such incredible efforts to give us porcini with everything that, at the end of the dinner, he even produced a liqueur made with dried porcini. I took a sip and, as soon as he turned his back, poured it into the aspidistra pot plant in the corner of the dining room. I always wondered if the aspidistra survived.

On another trip, I went with Jason Lowe, the food photographer with the cherub looks and the wicked wit, to Tuscany, high up in the Casentino mountains, to see the harvesting of the juniper berries. We were met by our hosts, a German producer (the 'spice king' of Europe) and his wife. They were a delightful couple, full of fun and laughter, in what seemed to me a most un-Germanic way. The weather was superb, as was the food and all the places we managed to see between the beating of one juniper bush and the next.

A few years later, I suggested to Delia Smith that I should write a series of articles combining travels with food for *Sainsbury's Magazine*. She liked the idea and decided to call the series 'Travels at Table'. We agreed that each article would feature a local feast. The first was to be on Manzanilla, the dry sherry, a challenge for me, since I don't usually write about wines nor do I speak Spanish, or at least not very well. So I flew to Seville with Jane Curran, the food and drink editor, and the photographer Debbie Patterson. At the airport we were met by our Manzanilla-producer hosts and driven to Sanlucar de Barrameda, one of the three cities which forms the 'Golden triangle', the so-called small area in Western Andalusia where sherry is produced. And there, for four days we had our feast of iced Manzanilla and seafood. A sherry *feria* – feast – was taking place the week we were there, which culminated on the Saturday night with flamenco dancing in the streets. That night, Debbie and I retired to our rooms with stinking colds, while Jane walked out of the hotel a blonde Carmen in a flame-coloured dress, playing the castanets with Sevillean aplomb.

One Easter, my 'travels at table' took me to Sicily and, again, I was accompanied by Debbie and by Helen, the assistant food editor of *Sainsbury's Magazine*. On Good Friday we went to Trapani to see The Procession of the Mysteries, a moving procession of twenty floats commemorating the Passion of Christ, an annual tradition which started in the seventeenth century when Sicily was under Spanish rule. But the day we enjoyed most was Easter Sunday when we drove south from Palermo through Mafia country to a small town near Agrigento where a model village made of bamboo cane and bread dough had been built the previous night in preparation for Easter. On the day itself, we sat at the bar, in brilliant sunshine and summer temperature, to watch the statues of Christ and the Virgin Mary being carried around, followed by the old women in black dresses and shawls reciting their rosary. The cortege was closed by their daughters in mink coats and high heels, accompanied by young men in designer beards, Armani shades and beautifully cut black suits. My English friends, in T-shirts, jeans and sneakers were hysterical with laughter.

~

IN 2006 CLARE BLAMPIED of the UK branch of Saclà (the Italian sauce manufacturer, which I knew from my Italian days as a successful producer of olives, *sottaceti* – pickles – and cherries preserved in alcohol), for whom I had been a consultant for some years, asked me to write a book on six Italian regions. So, in 2007, *The Painter, the Cook and the Art of Cucina* was published by Conran Octopus. It was beautifully illustrated with paintings by Val Archer, with whom I spent many happy days travelling in Italy. Val and I made six trips in all to the six different regions. Most of our days were spent in the car, deciding where to go, what to see, where to eat and whom to meet at what time. We discussed the merits of the Sardinian roast *porceddu* – piglet – against the roast black piglet of Puglia, the delicate yet intense flavour of the Ligurian artichokes, the richness of the peaches grown in Le Marche; I introduced Val and Roger, her husband, to *burrata* (one of my favourite cheeses) and to *fregola* (the Sardinian pasta); we shared trays of *galani* (Carnival fritters) in Venice and we forged a close friendship, when, usually in similar situations, friendships are buried. Roger was often our competent driver and he kept us entertained with his sense of humour, his enthusiastic appetite and his knowledgeable palate.

I MADE MANY good friends throughout my cookery career, and only two enemies, which is not bad considering the fierce competition in this field. My professional successes were due in part, I am sure, to my writing about Italian cooking in a country at the very time that its people were ready to embrace pasta, *risotti* and all things Italian. And the achievement I will always feel most proud of is that I was the first cookery writer to put authentic Italian pasta on the British plate.

RECIPES

Risotto al Limone
Risotto with Lemon

This is one of my most popular dishes. Everybody loves it – all my colleagues and friends, including the ones who tasted it in Barnes where I launched my professional cooking career. The first time I made it, though, Oliver looked very dubious at the idea of a risotto with lemon. He thought it sounded 'rather white and insipid'. From his first mouthful, however, he was a convert, and later declared it his favourite risotto.

SERVES 3–4

60g unsalted butter
1 tbsp extra virgin olive oil
2 shallots, very finely chopped
1 celery stick, very finely chopped
300g Italian rice, such as Carnaroli
1 litre light meat stock or vegetable stock
1 organic lemon
5 or 6 fresh sage leaves
a small sprig of rosemary
1 free-range egg yolk
4 tbsp freshly grated parmesan
4 tbsp double cream
sea salt and freshly ground black pepper

Heat half the butter, the oil, the shallots and the celery in a heavy saucepan and cook until the *soffritto* of shallot and celery is done (about 7 minutes). Mix in the rice and continue cooking and stirring until the rice is well coated in the fats and partly translucent.

Meanwhile heat the stock and keep it simmering all through the preparation of the dish.

When the rice becomes shiny and partly translucent, pour in about 150ml of the stock. Stir very thoroughly and cook until the rice has absorbed most of the stock. Add another small ladleful of simmering stock, and continue in this manner until the rice is ready. You may not need all the stock. Good-quality Italian rice for risotto takes about 20 minutes to cook.

While the rice is cooking chop up together the rind of the lemon and the herbs, and mix them into the rice halfway through the cooking.

In a small bowl, combine the egg yolk, the juice of half the lemon, the parmesan, the cream and a very generous grinding of black pepper. Mix well with a fork.

When the risotto is al dente draw the pan off the heat and stir in the egg and cream mixture and the remaining butter. Cover the pan and leave to rest for 2 minutes or so. Then give the risotto an energetic stir, transfer to a heated dish or bowl and serve at once, with more grated parmesan in a little bowl if you wish.

$\sim$

Capriolo alla Alto Atesina
Stewed Venison

I had this dish when went to the Dolomites in the winter of 1969, and have made my version of it ever since. Now venison is easily available and it has become a favourite with my friends in Dorset.

1.5kg boneless venison
4 tbsp olive oil
2 tbsp flour
50g smoked pancetta, diced
50g pork fat, diced or 4 tbsp olive oil
1 or 2 Spanish onions, about 225g total, very thinly sliced
¼ tsp ground cinnamon
¼ tsp ground cloves
300ml soured cream
salt and freshly ground black pepper

For the marinade
1 carrot, cut into pieces
1½ onions, coarsely sliced
1 celery stick, cut into pieces
1 tbsp rock salt (coarse sea salt)
12 juniper berries, bruised
8 black peppercorns, crushed
3 cloves
sprig of fresh rosemary
2 or 3 sprigs of fresh thyme

sprig of fresh sage
3 tbsp olive oil
3 bay leaves
3 garlic cloves
1 bottle of good full-bodied red wine

Heat all the ingredients for the marinade in a large saucepan until just boiling. Allow to cool.

Cut the venison into pieces, about 5cm thick. Put them in a bowl and add the marinade. Cover the bowl and leave for 2 days, preferably in a cool place other than the refrigerator.

Lift the meat from the marinade and pat dry with kitchen paper. Strain the marinade, saving only the liquid.

Preheat the oven to 170°C/gas mark 3.

Heat 2 tablespoons of the olive oil in a large, cast iron frying pan. Add the meat, in 2 batches, and brown very thoroughly on all sides. Transfer the meat to a plate.

Add the flour to the frying pan and cook until brown, stirring and scraping the bottom of the pan with a metal spoon. Add about half the reserved marinade liquid and bring to the boil, stirring constantly and breaking down any lumps of flour with the back of the spoon.

Put the rest of the oil, the pancetta and pork fat in a flame-proof casserole and cook for 5 minutes. Add the onion slices and a pinch of salt and continue cooking until the onion is really soft. Add a couple of tablespoons of hot water to prevent the onion from burning.

Now add the meat, with all the juices that have leaked out, the thickened marinade from the frying pan and about 150ml of the remaining marinade to the casserole. Season with salt, pepper and the spices and bring slowly to the boil. Cover the casserole and place in the oven. Cook for about 1 hour, adding a little more marinade twice during cooking.

Heat the soured cream in a small pan and add to the casserole. Return the pot to the oven and cook for a further half an hour or until the meat is very tender. The cooking time will vary according to the quality and age of the animal.

CHAPTER 20

SHOWING AND TELLING

Bollito misto

IN BETWEEN WRITING and researching, I also did ancillary work, some more successful than others.

The one that certainly was not successful, since it didn't even start, was my television career. In 1981 Jenny Stevens, producer of the first Delia Smith series on BBC Two, asked if I'd be interested in doing a similar one on Italian cooking. I was flattered, of course, but unsure of my acting ability. I asked her whether I should see a TV director and have some tips on how to perform in front of a camera. 'Oh, no,' she said, 'I think you are a natural and it might spoil your style.' So I went in for a test and my so-called style was a disaster. I saw the test later and quite understood why I was dropped. Eventually Antonio Carluccio was offered the series and went on to build a successful career as a chef and restaurateur. But that was not the only time I failed. I was tested again for a short programme for BBC One's *Breakfast Time* and even the warm charm of Selina Scott did not manage to defrost me. Like Elizabeth David and Jane Grigson before me, I was of a generation that did not respond to the camera. I still shiver when I think of entering that huge dark room, a long table in the middle covered with saucepans and spoons and frying pans and pots and jars and cups surrounded by monster goggles looming down at me. I was in such a state before any of the tests (I had two or three more which I managed to erase from my mind) that my son Guy told me he'd hoped I would not be chosen. 'Mummy,' he said, 'you would hate to have to do it and you would get ill into the bargain.' I am sure he was right. So I had to delete a few noughts from the number of books I was likely to sell and many pounds from my bank account.

SOME YEARS LATER I had the idea of running some gastronomic tours, which now select travel agencies are successfully doing. I decided that I needed a partner and thought of my old friend Carlo Saverio Balsamo. (We had seen each other on and off over the years and, although I knew he was still half in love with me even long after I was married, he never talked about it, apart from one occasion. After a gargantuan dinner, which he'd cooked, he made a pass at me, 'for the sake of our youth', he said. I did not take him up on it and I don't regret it, since it might later have got in the way of the plan I wanted to discuss with him.) By now Carlo Saverio was living in Milan happily married to a charming woman. I went to see him and we drew up a plan for our first venture: a tour of the Renaissance cities of the Po Valley, where the food is almost as great as the art. I would fly to Verona – with a select group of students, no more than a dozen – where I'd meet Carlo Saverio with a mini-bus. We would take them to the Opera at the Arena and to dinner at the famous restaurant Dodici Apostoli, and next day drive to Mantova to visit the splendid Gonzaga Palace and eat at Il Cigno and other choice restaurants. Then we'd move to Parma with all its art treasures and its famous food, followed by Modena, Bologna and finish the tour in Ferrara, which is famous, among many things, for the most varied types of bread in Italy. I was to be the guide for the gastronomic side and Carlo Saverio for the art and the wine, about which he was very knowledgeable. In addition, he would ask some of his aristocratic friends to open their *palazzi* and castles for our lucky students, an added attraction, especially for the Americans. We decided to have a trial tour and set off in his Alfa Romeo Coupé for a week of eating and drinking in the choicest places of those regions, which we both knew so well. It was a heavenly week. We found some wonderful restaurants, like the one of Massimo Spigaroli between Mantova and Parma, where we ate the best *culatello* (culatello is a kind of prosciutto, but even better, that is only made north of Parma), or the delightful Hotel del Leone in Pomponesco, near Mantova, where the owner prepared for us a miniature Renaissance banquet.

The tour never happened because, in 1992, Carlo Saverio was killed in a car accident while being driven in a friend's Ferrari to a country trattoria for Sunday lunch. The gods seemed to have directed their ire towards the Balsamo family. Carlo Saverio's father, the Marchese Balsamo, had been murdered by the Fascists in the terrible way I've described earlier in my chapter, 'Machine Guns'; his mother was struck down with a form of incurable arthritis in her early thirties, which made her an invalid for the rest of her life. Marica, his sister, died giving birth to her first child; and his first wife killed herself at the wheel of her car while trying to avoid a dog that had jumped into her path. And now it was Carlo Saverio's turn. I still miss him.

Another idea which never materialised was to open my own Italian restaurant somewhere in Barnes or Putney, both districts where more and more food-oriented people with money were coming to live. Some of our friends were very supportive of the idea, but not Geoffrey Sharp, an old friend from Oliver's Oxford days. Geoffrey owned and ran three extremely successful restaurants in London: Le Carrosse, The Garden, and The Grange. Oliver and I were often asked to go and taste a new menu or some dish or other cooked by a new chef. Geoffrey himself trained as a chef when French cuisine was paramount in Britain, yet he was able to create new signature dishes of his own, such as his Lamb Shrewsbury, Chicken with Apricot and Avocado and his spicy Celery and Apple Cocktail. Like many chefs at the time, Geoffrey was inspired by Elizabeth David, and he adapted some of her recipes to produce, among others, a perfect, delicately flavoured avgolomeno and a succulent *boeuf à la mode*.

One day we'd taken the boys for dinner at Le Carrosse for Guy's eighth birthday. They looked so smart in their school blazers and ties and sat down with straight backs at the table which was ready for us, near the window. I looked at them and felt very proud of my two handsome boys. Guy ordered a steak 'well done, please, and with lots of chips'. The steak arrived with a garnish of watercress, which Guy proceeded to cut and shove into his mouth. And then, to my horror, I saw him sticking half his hand into his mouth and, after a short search, pulling out an elastic band. He was horrified. But the chef was forgiven when he produced a magnificent birthday cake with eight candles and Geoffrey appeared at the table to sing Happy Birthday.

Geoffrey strongly advised me against doing 'such a mad thing', as running a restaurant, pointing out all the disadvantages, not least that my family life and my social life would be ruined. I knew he was not exaggerating. Geoffrey was, without fail, in one or other of his restaurants every night and that, he said, was what made them successful. Was I prepared to lead that sort of life? I knew perfectly well that, having so many different interests, I would have been incapable of thinking and dealing only with food at the expense of my children, my home, my friends, the theatre, the exhibitions, the dinner parties, the cinema and all the things that made my life a pleasure. So the idea of my running a restaurant died and I decided that writing about cooking, as I was doing, and cooking just for family and friends was a happier – and more realistic – prospect for a mother of three.

BY THE LATE 1980s, I was well established enough in the food world to be asked to do some cookery demonstrations. Frankly, I never enjoyed doing them. I don't like to be on a podium or addressing a number of people. But I thought it would be good for my image.

At one of these demonstrations I saw a beautiful girl in the front row, listening attentively to every word and, at the end, she came up and introduced herself. It was Nigella Lawson, who became a great champion of mine. I felt honoured. Nigella knows Italian food better than any other British-born cookery writer and is able to describe it so well. A few years later I told her the same words that Sir Walter Scott said to his great admirer, Alessandro Manzoni: 'Now the pupil has eclipsed the master.'

More or less at the same time, I was asked by Sainsbury's to hold a few seminars for their buyers, organised by Robin Weir, and this too I found quite daunting. Not only did I have to stand up in front and talk to groups of about eighty people, I had also to cook and produce something edible which resembled the authentic Italian dish. I rather dreaded those seminars and yet I went on doing them because I could never refuse a challenge (and, to be honest, the money was good).

I also did some consultancy work for Sainsbury's which involved supplying original Italian dishes that their manufacturers could produce industrially as close as possible to the original. I found this work very rewarding; it was challenging both for me and for the manufacturer. First, I had to find dishes which would best suit British eaters and then dishes which would be good when industrially made. Not easy. One of the product developers rang me one day to ask if I would create a recipe for risotto with mushrooms. I told her I couldn't possibly conceive of a risotto dish to be made in advance and warmed up in the microwave days later; it went against all my instincts and my strong belief in proper cooking. Sainsbury's went ahead without me and then rang me afterwards to tell me that the Risotto with Mushrooms had turned out to be one of their bestsellers. No comment.

I worked on quite a number of pasta dishes with Steven Poole, who was then one of Sainsbury's ready meals manufacturers. I liked Steven and it was a pleasure to work with him. He understood what I meant. He wanted to learn more and wisely decided that I should take him and his chef to Italy to taste 'the real McCoy'. I was free to go to the places I wanted and take them to the restaurants of my choice. We tucked into delicious meals in some of the best restaurants which I had chosen with great care for the authenticity of their cuisine. It also gave me the opportunity to revisit some of my old haunts – to drop into certain churches, walk down a particular street or pop into the local museum for a quick look at a painting I admired. On the last days of the trip I made a point of taking Steven to see the displays of food in the best shops and in my beloved markets so that I could come back home with a salame, a good chunk of cheese, my favourite bread and lots of fresh fruit and vegetables.

Some of my English companions caused me embarrassing moments, such as the day we had lunch with the late Giorgio Fini at his smart restaurant in Modena and they ordered orange juice with their *fritto misto all'emiliana* – a mixture of fried chicken, apple, liver, courgette and lamb. The waiter looked rather nonplussed, but Giorgio Fini, who spent half his time in New York, seemed to have seen it all before. In fact the most disgusting pairing of drink and food I ever saw was on the island of Ischia when an American couple sitting at the next table ordered cappuccino with their fish soup, and proceeded to sip it at regular intervals while eating the soup.

But the travelling companion with whom I had most fun was Pietro Pesce, an importer of Italian choice products. Pietro was from Venice and proud of it, so much so that he used to say 'No, I am not Italian, I am Venetian.' He was *simpatico* and considerate and, above all, we shared many values, including the same political beliefs, which meant we could discuss at length the incomprehensible decision of our compatriots to elect Berlusconi as prime minister. We also shared the same tastes in food. Like me, Pietro was a purist who could not bear what we called the Britalian food which was fashionable in the UK. I learned a lot from him and I hope he learned a lot from me. We were totally at ease with one another and only once did he make a sort of a pass at me. We were in Umbria, in the romantic valley of the river Nera, so beautiful that it was on the route of the Grands Tours. I had to write a piece on the lentils of Castelluccio (the best lentils I know) and we soon discovered that the hotel we were put up in was a real dump. I went into my room, took a horrified look around, got out again and knocked at Pietro's door. 'Avanti,' he said and, as soon as I opened the door, I fell straight onto the bed where he was lying – the room was so small, there was nowhere to go. With a seductive look, he said, 'You can stay here, if you want.' I told him, 'No, thank you. I want to get out of this place and now.' So we left.

Pietro could sometimes be moody as he was during a trip to Puglia. He had invited a few select cookery writers to a splendid *masseria* – the ancient farmsteads of Puglia – in Acquaviva delle Fonti where everything we ate and drank was produced in situ. The moodiness of Pietro was probably due to his being smitten by the charms of the cookery writer Josceline Dimbleby, while the writer Alice Woodledge-Salmon and I were smitten by Primitivo, the full-bodied red wine of Puglia that we drank with great abandonment during dinner on the first night. That dinner, in the true Pugliese tradition, had started with twelve antipasti and finished with a delicious ricotta pudding with the biblical name of 'Apostoles' Fingers'.

Poor Pietro died very suddenly, at the age of sixty-eight of an aortic aneurysm, which is almost always a killer. (I realised how lucky Oliver had been in comparison, as his aneurysm was in the brain, from which you can sometimes recover, as he did.)

Philippa Davenport of the *Financial Times* was another travelling companion with whom I shared tastes and distastes. We had a marvellous week in Valtellina as guests of the region, and were treated to hand kisses, amazing food and fascinating expeditions to the various manufacturers of produce of that spectacular area of Lombardy. One beautifully sunny day, we went up high into the mountains to see a shepherd who was making *bitto*, the famous cheese of Valtellina. He had his rich milk in large bowls placed down on the ground of his hut and suddenly from the corner a little shrew came out, looked around and made a beeline for one of the bowls. It put its two front paws on the border of the bowl and began to lap up the milk, not in the least perturbed by our presence. It was obviously her daily afternoon treat. We thought of Brussels, with its stringent health and safety regulations, and laughed, and went back to our hotel with a packet of white creamy *bitto* for supper.

⌒

ONE OF MY successful enterprises was to start a cookery school in Chianti with my friend Betsy Newell. Betsy ran a very successful cookery school in Kensington and had a large farmhouse in the middle of olive groves and vineyards in Chianti. So she was the ideal partner and I think we made quite a good team. I am the easy-going Italian cook, working by instinct and confident that a lot of things in cooking do not need much explaining. Betsy, though, took the rational

American approach, with weights in one hand and pen in the other, precise and clear, just what is needed in teaching. Thanks to her teaching in London, she was far more aware than I was of the limited knowledge of our American and English students.

In the mornings we all made tagliatelle and ravioli, *risotti* and gnocchi, *ribollite* (a Tuscan vegetable and bread soup) and *caponate* (a fried aubergine relish) crowning our efforts by sitting down at the table for lunch with George Newell, Betsy's husband. George, with his great knowledge of Italian wines, was ready to discuss what he poured into the glasses with his usual generosity. He was also the fire-attendant at the barbecue, and the salame- and prosciutto-slicer. For the *pici* – Tuscan tagliatelle – and the focaccia we mobilised two splendid local women, Angelina and Livia, who made, among other things, the most delicious *focaccia con le cipolle*, which was not the usual focaccia covered with red onion, but a sort of Swiss roll of focaccia dough stuffed with red onions and black olives. I tried endlessly at home to make it, but mine always broke.

In the afternoon we took our students on different expeditions – to the Palio Museum in Siena, the Ricasoli cellars in Brolio, or let them rest and digest in preparation for the second assault of the day. This was dinner at local restaurants, which everybody, including Betsy and I, loved. It was so good to sit down and eat food cooked by somebody else. A most successful outing was a day in Florence exploring not the Uffizi Gallery or the Basilica di Santa Croce, but the Mercato Centrale – the Central Market – one of my favourite places in the world. For elevenses, we took the students to the cafe in the market, the meeting place of all the local workmen, to have the panino filled with tripe or with boiled beef, both specialities of the Mercato Centrale. I must admit that few of our students dared to venture that far into the local culinary tradition, but they all enjoyed their cappuccino with the *bombolone* – the Tuscan doughnut. At the end of the cookery course, the students complained that they had eaten too much. 'Well,' I commented, 'you don't join a cookery course in Tuscany if you are on a diet.'

IN 1991, WHEN the Italian firm of Saclà first wanted to launch its range of pasta sauces in the UK, Clare Blampied, the UK managing director, asked me to suggest some suitable sauces for the British market – all to be made in its factory in Asti, in Piedmont – and also to take her and her team to restaurants, markets and food shops in Italy that I would recommend. Nothing could have given me greater pleasure. Clare was an intelligent and lively companion with whom I shared many gastronomic experiences and my relationship with the Saclà people, both in the UK and in Italy, developed into a firm friendship. Asti, where Saclà has its head office, is one of the less memorable provincial towns in the whole of Italy, but now, thanks to the Ercole family, which owns Saclà, I enjoy going there. It was at their house that I had the best *bollito misto* of my life and, on more than one of my visits, a feast of white truffles.

In 2004 Clare asked me to interview Carlo Ercole, his brother Lorenzo and his son Giuseppe for a promotional video. I had never done anything like that and was grateful to be asked, but equally worried about my ability to handle it. The production team was English and their Italian limited

At the cookery school in Tuscany.

to only *ciao* and *arrivederci*. The shoot took place during a fiercely hot and humid week in July, which didn't help the relationship between the different parties. The Ercoles wanted to be interviewed in Italian, in spite of being able to speak English quite well. So I had to 'direct' the film, which essentially meant putting my hand up and shouting 'Cut' at the appropriate moment. I enjoyed my brief stint as a film director and everybody was pleased with the results, even the Scottish producer, who, being red-haired and pale-skinned, could barely cope with the inclemency of the weather.

It was a hard week, in which I had somehow to juggle the mood of the production team with that of the Saclà people and, worst of all, with my sadness at the death of my brother Guido.

Guido had married his lover Bibi after her divorce, but eventually they parted and Guido married Bianca, an interior decorator from Turin, where he had a cushy job in advertising which left him time to read, play golf and to cook – all of which he preferred to working. But then Guido, always so strong and good-looking, had suffered a stroke in 1986, which left him partially paralysed. He was never able to walk again and for eighteen years he'd lain in bed or sat in a chair, quite conscious until the end – eighteen years of non-living.

The day after he died at the beginning of that torrid July, I flew to Turin for his funeral. It was a very moving ceremony, totally secular, no Bible readings or prayer recitals, since Guido had always been an atheist. One of his step-daughters gave a poignant address, concluding that Guido had gone for a long, long swim, as he had done so often during his life, when he would disappear for hours into the sea. Some relatives and friends read poems by Lorca and Yeats, and by our cousin Sandro Peregalli who had been so much part of Guido's earlier life.

Saclà had sent a driver to collect me after the funeral and take me to Asti to start my week as a 'film director'. Maybe the hard work had been the ideal cure to subdue my grief. After the shoot, I went to Milan for the burial of Guido's ashes in the family tomb at the Cimitero Monumentale. It was a drab and soulless affair, with a man carrying Guido's ashes in a pot to our tomb, followed by a string of mourners, hot and exhausted under the midday sun. It was then that I, although not particularly religious, missed the comfort of religion. With Guido I buried my childhood.

Le Dita Degli Apostoli
Pancakes Stuffed with Ricotta

The odd name of this recipe from Puglia, the heel of the Italian boot, means Apostles' fingers. But why? I can only suppose that the stuffed pancakes look, very remotely, like fingers raised to give a blessing. But the name does not matter – the pudding is good.

These are eggy pancakes, more like a thin frittata and also bigger, since the traditional recipe uses a 20cm wide non-stick frying pan. Before serving, I like to warm them up a little in the oven (150°C / gas mark 3) and then eat them with pouring cream, a very un-Pugliese way.

SERVES 8–10

For the pancakes
120g Italian 00 flour
5 eggs
250ml semi-skimmed milk
30g caster sugar
butter for frying
salt

For the stuffing
600g fresh ricotta
3 tbsp double cream
250g caster sugar

grated zest of 1 organic lemon
grated zest of 1 organic orange
grated zest of 1 organic clementine
1½ tbsp chopped candied peel
50g bitter chocolate, cut into very small pieces
2 tbsp dark rum
icing sugar to decorate

Prepare the pancakes. Sieve the flour with a little salt into a bowl. Drop in the eggs and beat, while gradually adding the milk, until the surface of the batter is covered with bubbles. Stir in the sugar. Alternatively, put all the ingredients in a blender or food processor and blend until smooth. Let the batter stand for at least 30 minutes – it does not matter if you leave it for longer.

When you are ready to make the pancakes, transfer the batter into a jug from which you will find it easier to pour.

Heat a cast-iron frying pan with a 20cm diameter base and add a small knob of butter. Swirl the butter around the pan to grease all the bottom.

When the pan is hot, turn the heat down to moderate. Stir the batter and pour enough batter to cover the bottom in a very thin layer, while tipping the pan quickly in all directions. Cook until pale gold, and then turn the pancake with a spatula and cook the other side, very briefly. Slide on to a plate or board. Remove the pan from the heat before you pour more batter or it will set before it can spread. You should be able to make about 8–10 pancakes, but you may have to add a tiny knob of butter every so often when the pan appears dry.

Now make the stuffing. Sieve the ricotta in a bowl and fold

---

in the cream and caster sugar. Add all the other ingredients, mix thoroughly and put in the fridge.

When the pancakes are cold, lay each one in turn on the work surface and spread about 1 tbsp of the stuffing over each in a thin layer. Roll each pancake up tightly and then cut each 'finger' into 2 pieces.

Serve the 'fingers' at room temperature, sprinkled lavishly with icing sugar.

Bollito Misto All'Astigiana
Boiled meats Piedmontese style

This is Carlo Ercole's recipe for the classic Piedmontese bollito misto, the most delicious convivial dish I ever had. Some of the cuts of meat, such as calf's tail, might be difficult to find in this country. You can use ox tail and cook it for longer. The same applies to calf's tongue.

SERVES 8–10

2 large onions, cut into chunks
3 carrots, cuts into chunks
3 celery sticks, cut into chunks
2 bay leaves
salt
1 calf's tongue
½ calf's head, cut into chunks, if available
500g shoulder of veal
500g breast of veal

1 calf's tail, cut into pieces
1 small organic chicken
500g cotechino sausage

Divide the vegetables into 3 pots, ½ into a large and ¼ each into two smaller ones. Fill each pot with water and season with a little salt. Now put one of the smaller pots on the heat and bring to the boil. When the water boils, lower the tongue into the water and cook slowly for 2–2½ hours until you can pierce the tongue very easily with a fork. Lift it out of the water, place it on a board and remove the skin. This is easier done when the tongue is hot. So put some rubber gloves on and proceed to peel it with the help of a small knife. When you have finished, put the tongue back into its pot to keep warm.

While the tongue is cooking, bring the water in the big pot to the boil and add the shoulder and breast of veal, the calf's tail, and the calf's head if you are using it. When the water starts boiling again adjust to a gentle simmer. Cook the meat for 1½–2 hours.

Do the same with the chicken in the third pot which should simmer gently for about 1¼–1½ hours, depending on the size.

The cotechino needs a fourth pot and you cook it following the manufacturer's instructions. It usually takes only ½ hour.

If you are short of pots or of space you can cook the tongue or the cotechino earlier and then reheat it.

When everything is cooked, slice or cut enough meat to serve each person, and then put the meats back into their pots to keep warm, ready for a second helping. And remember to warm the plates, because bollito needs to be eaten really hot. Serve with one of the sauces overleaf.

TWO CLASSIC SAUCES FOR BOLLITO

Salsa Verde
Green sauce

This is the recipe for the classic salsa verde, from which you can create the salsa verde of your choice: you can substitute a spoonful or two of tarragon for the same amount of parsley; use a boiled potato instead of the breadcrumbs to thicken it; use balsamic vinegar or just give it a thought and a try.

MAKES ABOUT 200ml

30g fresh white breadcrumbs
1–1½ tsp red wine vinegar
1 garlic clove
45g flat leaf parsley
2 tbsp capers
6 cornichons
1 hard-boiled egg, shelled
6 anchovy fillets or 3 salted anchovies, boned and rinsed
2 tsp Dijon mustard
150ml extra virgin olive oil
pepper
sea salt

Put the breadcrumbs in a bowl and pour the vinegar over them. Set aside.

Peel the garlic clove, cut it in half and remove the hard

central core, if necessary. This is the part that has a pungent instead of a sweet flavour.

Chop the parsley, capers, cornichons, hard-boiled egg, anchovies and garlic together. Put this mixture into another bowl.

Squeeze out the vinegar from the bread and add the bread to the mixture in the bowl, working it in with a fork. Add the mustard and then gradually add the olive oil, beating the whole time. Season with a good deal of pepper. Taste and add salt if necessary; the anchovies and capers may have given enough salt to the sauce. You might like to add a little more vinegar; it depends on the strength of your vinegar and how you like the sauce.

The whole sauce can be made in the food processor.

～.

Salsa Rossa
Red Sauce

This sauce can be prepared up to 3 days in advance, covered and refrigerated. It also freezes very well.

MAKES ABOUT 225ml

3 tbsp olive oil
450g tomatoes, cut into quarters
1 tsp tomato purée
2 onions, coarsely chopped
1 carrot, coarsely chopped

1 celery stick, coarsely chopped
3 garlic cloves, peeled
1 or 2 dried chillies, according to taste, seeded
1 clove
sea salt
1 tbsp red wine vinegar

Put half the oil and all the other ingredients except the vinegar in a saucepan with a very heavy bottom. I use an earthenware pot of the sort you can put directly on the heat. Cook over the gentlest heat for 1–1½ hours, adding a little hot water if necessary.

Purée through a food mill or a sieve. If you use a food processor, you must skin the tomatoes before you cook them.

Return the purée to the pan and add the rest of the oil and the vinegar. Cook for a further 30 minutes, then taste and check seasoning. The sauce is now ready, but let it cool a little before you serve it. You can also serve it at room temperature.

CHAPTER 21

VENICE

La colomba pasquale

CALLE DELLA RACHETTA is an alley in Venice which runs from just off the Strada Nuova, near the Ca' d'Oro, and towards the Fondamenta Nuove, a *calle* that goes from nowhere interesting to nowhere interesting. When we bought a flat there in 1980, there were no bars and no shops, save a bookshop that catered mainly for the children walking past every morning on their way to school, and a trattoria called Adelaide, indistinguishable from the mass of other Venetian *trattorie*. Adelaide might have gone now, or might serve the most stupendous food; I wouldn't know. We sold the flat in 1990.

As with our previous holiday home in Tuscany, we bought the flat on an impulse, but it was the right impulse and we had some of our best holidays there, getting to know Venice extremely well and feeling part of it at least for the weeks we spent there. During those ten years I came to understand what Henry James meant when he wrote: 'You desire to embrace it, to caress it, to possess it, and finally a soft sense of possession grows up and your visit becomes a perpetual love affair.'

To get to our flat you went up then down over the first

bridge, and the second, passing the upholsterer bent over his sofas and armchairs, and walked down the silent *calle* flanked by dignified houses. Then, suddenly, your spirits were lifted by an opening on the left as you spotted a delightful little garden bursting with greenery and dominated by a rampant wisteria. Our flat was just opposite, and every time I looked into that garden I was reminded of what Giacomo Castelvetro wrote about runner beans in 1614 in his book *Brieve Racconto di tutte le Radici di Tutte l'Herbe e di Tutti i Frutti*: 'These beans grow quite tall and with such lovely foliage that the Venetian ladies, who are very fond of shade and greenery, grow them on the windowsills so that they can peer at the passers-by but remain unseen by them.' No flowering climbing beans now, but the same air of mystery.

Our flat was on the first floor, with a large living room and a spare room overlooking the secret garden at the front and, at the back, our bedroom and the kitchen looking down on a small canal where only the odd delivery barge, refuse barge or small motor dinghy went by.

Nothing much changes in Venice once you leave the parts of the city inundated by tourists. Oddly enough, Venice, the most popular city in Italy with tourists, is the one where you can more easily shed the tourists and feel like a local. The shrewd Venetians have managed to channel the tourists along certain well-defined routes by lining them with bars offering all possible variations of lattes and cappuccinos, ice creams of every colour and flavour and boutiques displaying the most bizarre fashions in which no Venetian woman would be seen dead. The tourists are happy, the Venetians are happy and so are the pseudo-Venetians like us. For at least six weeks each year, we felt we belonged. We knew which ironmonger had the largest assortment of screws and bolts, which haberdashery would sell the braids or tassels I wanted, where to buy buttons and tea cloths, cheeses and *salumi*, cakes and biscuits. We walked and walked, *'su dal ponte, giù dal ponte, sempre diritto'* – 'up the bridge, down the bridge, keep straight on' – as the Venetians say when giving directions, in spite of the fact that there isn't a single *calle* in Venice which is straight for more than 50 metres.

But who cares if you get lost in Venice? You can enjoy the walk and arrive late. It is perfection wherever you look. The streets and the architecture are so varied that it's impossible to be bored: a shrine of a little Madonna at the corner of some house, an imposing well in the middle of a *campiello* (square), an *altana* (terrace) at the top of another house spilling a cascade of jasmine and pelargonium, a bell tower dominating a corner of your view, and of course the bridges of all sizes and steepness. And then there are the Venetians themselves, perhaps the most closely knit group of inhabitants of any Italian city, and that's saying a lot. After all, not many people from outside Venice go to live there; and almost all of those who live there seem to have lived there for ever.

I used to *fare la spesa* – shop for food – each morning at about ten. First stop was the bar in the campo at the corner of the Strada Nuova for a caffè – just an espresso. Then I'd take the gondola-ferry at Campo Santa Sofia across the Canal Grande to the Rialto market for the *spesa*. The crossing filled me with the same excitement I felt as a child when faced by something a touch dangerous but overwhelmingly beautiful. The frisson of danger was the getting into the gondola from the jetty, coins for the fare in one hand, and then standing during the crossing while the gondolier veered left and right to avoid the other boats and, later, climbing out onto the jetty opposite. The Venetians, young and old, fat and thin, jumped on, stood still and then jumped off again with an ease that I envied but never mastered. Much as I liked water, as I looked down from the boat I could see that the Canal Grande was not for taking a dip in. Even if I were able to retrieve some incredible relics from the bottom, or a bottle or two of good wine, like the wine we should have had at the dinner for our Golden Wedding in 2000.

OLIVER AND I had decided to celebrate our 50th wedding anniversary in Venice, instead of Milan or London, because of our love for the city and our certainty that all our Italian and English friends would rather join us there than anywhere else. Indeed, most of them came and it was a great success, in spite of the weather, which was awful. In October, the weather in Venice is always unpredictable, and in 2000 even more so than usual. It rained and it rained and it rained; the *passerelle* – raised boards – were set out all over the city and we all bought boots. On the night of our party, my agent, Vivien Green, left the Hotel Danieli in a very smart dress and with flip-flops on her feet (she had a shoe bag with her). My grandchildren had a marvellous time splashing around and we all laughed – all, that is, except the Venetian ladies who got splashed.

In Venice when the weather is that bad, the whole transport system becomes even more haphazard than usual. To navigate a large barge in the canals is difficult enough, and in torrential rain it becomes even harder. But it was only when we sat down for our anniversary dinner and the waiters began to pour the wine that Oliver noticed the wine was different from the one we had chosen in advance. He called the maître d' over, who explained that our wine was at the bottom of the Canal Grande, giving Oliver the exact location: 'In front of Palazzo Balbi, just where the Rio Ca' Foscari comes into the Canal Grande.' In the torrential rain, a barge on the Canal Grande hadn't seen the barge containing our wine until the two were really close. To avoid a collision, our barge had to turn sharply, which caused the crates of wine, very slowly, one by one, to slip into the canal. Apparently, these accidents happen quite often, especially now that the water traffic has increased tenfold, from which you can deduce that the bottom of the Venetian canals must be a veritable treasure trove.

SOME DAYS, I went to the market on foot: down the Strada Nuova, higgledy-piggledy, *su dal ponte, giù dal ponte*, past my husband's barber (who still recognised Oliver when he went back ten years after we'd sold our flat), past Coin, the department store full of bargains, in the hope of picking one up, and on to the church of San Giovanni Crisostomo, a little Renaissance jewel of a church built by the great architect Mauro Coducci. I used to step inside this little known and usually empty church to say a prayer in front of the three saints on the right – a superb late panel by Bellini – and then on for another prayer in front of another favourite painting, a Sebastiano del Piombo on the altarpiece, the most beautiful work of that artist, painted in chiaroscuro.

I am not particularly religious, rather the typical Italian Catholic who goes to Mass on Sundays, often more out of habit than conviction, but it is the religious art that moves me to prayers. I feel if Catholicism has done nothing else, it has served its purpose by inspiring so many artists to paint and build all the magnificent works they left as the legacy of their spiritual allegiance.

Out of the church, I was now ready to indulge my 'worldly' passion of shopping for food. The Rialto market satisfied that wholly, with its stalls of fish, fruit and vegetables and the Venetian ladies all chatting about peas, beans, radicchio, peppers, courgettes, castraure (the young Venetian artichokes), monkfish, granceole or moleche.

One year at Rialto, I decided to buy some moleche. It must have been late March or early April, which is when the crabs shed their shells. During these few hours of 'nakedness' they are picked up by the fishermen from the *vieri* (the containers in which the fishermen keep them while waiting for the *muta*, the changing of the shell). I was told how delicious they were fried *col pien* – stuffed. I asked for the recipe and, back at the flat, set to work. As directed, I beat three eggs and some grated parmesan in a bowl, added the moleche and left them there until the evening. During those hours the poor little creatures feed desperately on the egg mixture, which they love, and when they are bloated from pleasure and egg, you pick them up, coat them in flour and fry them in olive oil. They become heavenly morsels with a delicious thin crust on the outside and a mellow fishy softness inside.

But during the afternoon, while keeping a watch on my prey, my heart melted. I could not stand the death I was going to inflict on them. I scooped them up, put them in a container and walked to the nearest bridge. And there I turned the container upside down and off they fell into the dirty water of

Carrying my shopping and looking like the archetypal bag lady, I inevitably bumped into one or more of my Venetian friends in their impeccable suits, not a crease in sight nor a hair out of place. The women in Venice are even better turned out than the women in Florence, its rival in everything from art to food. After all, they walk everywhere, in their pristine attire, and are never subjected to the indignity of being squashed into a car. And they meet up with their friends, who all do their shopping at the same time, which ends with the obligatory aperitif. I found it easy to fall into that pleasant rhythm of life, even if I never achieved that level of impeccability. I had lived in England far too long to bother about the *far bella o brutta figura* – keeping up appearances.

For my ombra – glass of wine – I would go, with a friend or with Oliver, to La Vedova, which was certainly not the smartest place in Venice for an aperitif, but it was close to our flat and patronised by locals. (The name 'ombra', by the way, comes from the old Venetian habit of having a glass of wine in the shade – ombra – of the awning of the stalls set around Piazza San Marco.) There I had my glass of Prosecco, which might have been *sporco* – spiked with Campari – with lots of the delicious *cicheti*: borlotti beans from Lamon, stuffed mussels, boiled bits of octopus shining with olive oil, sardines in *saor* (vinegary dressing), polenta bruschetta of *baccalà mantecato* – a traditional Venetian dish where the codfish is cooked in olive oil, garlic, and parsley, and creamed in a blender – all laid out in platters along the counter. The friend I usually met for my ombra was Rita Stancescu, who lived round the corner in the Campo dei Santi Apostoli. She would arrive, tall and elegant, leading Chicca, a miniature wirehaired dachshund. The two of them walking down the Strada Nuova made a hilarious sight: one of the tallest ladies in Venice holding an extremely long lead, at the end of which was one of the smallest dogs in Venice. (I'm sure Rita got Chicca on purpose, conscious of the effect it would create.) But one year I went to Rita's flat and there was no Chicca to welcome me; she had disappeared and nobody had set eyes on her. Rita was devastated, convinced the dog had been taken and killed by one of the people who objected to dogs because of their poo. The clean-up law came a few years after – too late for Chicca – so, in a typically Italian way, the Venetians took the law in their own hands. Now Venice is clear of dog mess, but not the waste that tourists leave behind – the cans, bags, foil, boxes, paper hats and all sundries, all far more visible than Chicca's contribution ever was.

Rita, who sadly died some ten years ago, was a terrific cook and dedicated most of her day to preparing the two meals which Carlo, her husband, expected and enjoyed. She had a tiny kitchen, the sort that calls for a precise organisation of time and space. Out of that tiny, spotless hole appeared the most divine dishes, from the simple *cucina povera* of Venice and the Veneto to the grand dishes of the Doge's table. Her *polpettone* – meat roll was a treat not to be missed. Her pasta pies were as regal in their presentation as in their contents which tumbled out of the crust in a scented cascade of mushrooms, truffles, brains and sweetbread, cockscombs, peas and prosciutto, They were indeed pies to compete with that most famous pie ever, the *timballo* served at the grand banquet of the Prince Salina in *The Leopard*, the novel by Giuseppe Tomasi di Lampedusa.

Rita advised me where to buy Parmigiano or Gorgonzola (two different shops), and the best stall in the Rialto market for crustaceans and octopus and which one to go to for monkfish or sea bass. Like all skilful cooks, she knew that a good dinner starts in the shop. She introduced me to the Pasticceria Gobbeti off the Campo San Barnaba for the best Veneziane and Colombe. Veneziana is the Venetian New Year cake, now made all year round, similar to a panettone, but without the sultanas, and covered in crystallised sugar. I loved to dunk it in my coffee or in my sweet ombra. The Colomba, which originated in Milan is an Easter cake in the shape of a dove, with an eggy, buttery crumb, again similar to panettone, but without the sultanas, and covered in almonds.

OLIVER AND I went to Venice for Easter each year, when the smell of Colomba emanated from every corner. In Venice, smells can pervade the whole atmosphere thanks to the absence of cars and scooters. Now, every Easter when I unwrap the cardboard box containing my Colomba, I smell Venice – in particular the area around San Barnaba and the enchanting Campo Santa Margherita, the most Venetian campo of them all. In 2000, for our Golden Wedding anniversary, we rented a fairly large flat in this campo where we stayed with our daughter Julia, her husband Charles and their brood, then only three.

When we arrived, my first priority was to inspect the sunny kitchen, with its large table in the middle for everybody to sit around. I immediately noticed that the fridge was only big enough to hold supplies for two people at most. How were the seven of us, plus Paul, Guy and their spouses, and all the friends I wanted to have around, going to manage? Easily. I quickly realised that, being in Campo Santa Margherita, we only needed the fridge for milk, butter, water and Prosecco. Each morning, Oliver would go round the corner to buy the bread for breakfast. Later, we bought the fish or meat and vegetables for lunch, and then more shopping in the campo in the evening for supper. If we needed onions, or ran out of bread, or wanted some salame and focaccia to eat with the Prosecco, down somebody went to the campo, and there it was.

In the fortnight we stayed there I made friends with all the stall holders. There were three fish stalls every morning and at least as many vegetable and fruit stalls. Once a week, the van with the cheeses would arrive to compete with the *salumeria* at the corner. Nell, Johnny and Coco, our grandchildren, played in the campo, cycling and kicking a ball and fooling around, to the delight of the Venetian ladies. But one day I looked out of the window and there was Johnny lying on the ground, arms and legs stretched out, while Nell was marking out his shape with a piece of chalk. That was too much for the two smart Venetian ladies who were standing nearby, telling them in imperious tones, '*Su, su!* You cannot lie on the street; streets are dirty. *Su, alzatevi, su!*' Then another lady joined in, saying, 'They don't understand, *sono Inglesi.*' Ah, the other exclaimed, 'that explains it.' I didn't dare show my face.

Easter was my favourite time in Venice, when the city welcomes the spring. The low mist disappears, the lagoon becomes clear, the steeple of San Giorgio Maggiore stands out as if in bas-relief, as does the marvellously imposing mass of Santa Maria della Salute. Some mornings it seems as if all the palazzi and churches around the Bacino di San Marco are slowly taking off their old clothes and revealing their grandeur, starting from the bottom, up and up, until clear and naked they shine in all their glory. I remember one day passing, in the *vaporetto*, in front of the Salute, which had just emerged from the mist, and I heard a mid-western voice cooing, 'I don't know what that is, Hank, but it sure is purrty.' Well, Santa Maria della Salute could be called many things, but pretty didn't even begin to do it justice.

~

I AM OLD enough to remember the time when Venice was just for the Venetians and a sprinkling of *forestieri* – strangers – as we, Italians and foreigners alike, were called. That was in the Thirties. For two or three years my mother and father took Guido and me to the Lido for our seaside holiday and we stayed in a *pensione* just behind the Hotel Des Bains. We would go to the beach of the Des Bains where my mother rented a *tendone* – a large tent with a cabin for changing at the back and all the deckchairs and chaises longues one could wish for – which the ladies used as their *salotto* – drawing room – to be 'at home' to receive and entertain guests.

Occasionally we'd go to Venice, crossing the lagoon in the *vaporetto*, such a thrill for Guido and me. I remember going to high Mass in San Marco on Sundays and being stunned by the overwhelming sumptuousness of the service, the scent of the incense, the vestments of the five priests at the altar, one of whom was the bishop, and by all the glitter and gold surrounding them. I had already been to high Masses in the Duomo di Milano, but the contrast between one service and the other was remarkable even to a young child. The sombre solemnity of the Gothic architecture of the Duomo, which was reflected in the ceremony, seemed to subdue it. In San Marco, however, the gold, the mosaics, the lights, the round arches, gave a feeling of joyous theatricality to the Mass. The East dominated, with all its splendour.

After Mass my parents used to take us to Caffè Florian for ice cream. There we sat, smartly dressed and beautifully behaved, in 'the most beautiful drawing room in the world' as Napoleon called it, vast and yet welcoming, with the Venetians also in their Sunday best, promenading, stopping and chatting, drinking their ombra under the awning of the stalls, the children feeding those awful pigeons, the photographers flashing from under their black hoods and the Florian band playing pieces from the fashionable operettas such as *The Merry Widow*, *Die Fledermaus* or, my favourite, *The Blue Danube*. I felt like getting up and waltzing à la Shirley Temple around the piazza to the applause of the crowd.

My choice of ice cream was always the same. I knew what I liked and never hesitated: *un gelato di crema* – *crema* being custard, not cream. It had that mellow full flavour of eggs, enhanced by a touch of vanilla. Custard has always been one of my favourite sauces – it still is – and the custardy flavour, oddly enough, seems to be intensified by the freezing. The waiter always suggested a spoonful of chocolate ice, but I refused, as I would do now.

⁓

DECADES LATER, when I was in the piazza on the day of San Marco – the 25th of April – I noticed that all the men around were proudly holding a single red rose. 'Ah,' said my friend Bruna, 'that is *il bocolo*.' Il bocolo, ma cos è? 'It is a Venetian custom that, on St Mark's feast day, all the men take home to wives, girlfriends or mistresses a *bocolo* [which in the local dialect means a bud]. The *bocolo* must be scarlet, the colour of passionate love.'

There are two legends as to the origin of the *bocolo*. The first is about the ill-starred love between Maria, a girl of noble birth, and Tancredi, a young man who, to win the consent of the noble father, joins Charlemagne's army in the war against the Moors. He fights with great valour, but he is, alas, wounded and falls on a rose bush and dies. The roses in the bush become red like his blood. The dying Tancredi asks his friend Orlando to take a bud to his beloved. Orlando arrives in Venice the day before St Mark's Day and gives the noble lady the *bocolo*. The next morning Maria is found dead with the *bocolo* across her heart.

The second legend is a less tragic story. A rose bush is planted to mark the border between the property of two brothers. The two brothers become involved in a feud that finishes with the killing of one of them. The plant stops flowering. Many years later, on the 25th of April, a boy and a girl, descendants of the families, fall in love, seeing each other through the branches of the rose bush. Love blooms and so does the bush. The boy picks a *bocolo*, hands it to his beloved and peace is restored between the two families.

On St Mark's Day every year, you see middle-aged men, in perfectly tailored double-breasted suits, silk ties and hats, walking home for lunch and holding in front of them this erect and rather petrified bud – a rather surreal scene worthy of Magritte's brush. A very Italian peculiarity of this custom is that sons, too, bring the scarlet *bocolo* to their mother.

This is one of the main charms of Venice. Its inhabitants going about their everyday activities take centre stage in this carfree city: people stopping for a chat, going to the *bacaro* for an ombra, to the *salumeria* for *un etto o due di soppressa per il pranzo* – a quarter or half a pound of special Venetian *salame* for lunch – or buying their Colomba to celebrate Easter with the family. Venice is the most democratic of Italian cities, and this is due to the absence of cars. Everybody knows everybody else, from the Marquis to the plumber, through walking instead of being shut up in their BMW or van.

On that St Mark's Day in spring, Oliver and I went back to Calle della Rachetta, Oliver incongruously holding his *bocolo* and I, a Venetian for six weeks a year, carrying my Colomba, proud that one of the two Lombard cakes (the other being panettone) had been adopted by Venice.

Polpettone Casalingo
Meat Roll

SERVES 6–8

225g minced pork
225g minced chicken
300g minced beef
4 eggs
100g freshly grated parmesan cheese
115g fresh breadcrumbs
2 tbsp chopped parsley
6 tbsp vegetable oil
sprig of rosemary
150ml meat stock
3 tbsp dry white wine
15g unsalted butter
1 tbsp plain flour
salt and freshly ground black pepper

Put the minced meats in a bowl with 3 whole eggs, the yolk of the fourth, the parmesan, 5 tablespoons of the breadcrumbs, the parsley and salt and pepper. Mix very thoroughly with your hands.

Shape the meat into a firmly packed ball, pat it to let any air out, and place it on a wooden board. Roll it out into a roll about 8cm in diameter. Brush the surface of the meat loaf with the remaining egg white and coat evenly with the remaining breadcrumbs. Refrigerate for at least 30 minutes.

Heat the oil in a large flameproof, oval-shaped casserole, add the rosemary sprig and the meat loaf and brown the loaf on all sides, until a rich dark crust is formed.

Pour the meat stock over the loaf, cover with a lid, and cook over a very low heat for about 1 hour. Turn it over very carefully every 15 minutes and baste it often.

Preheat the oven to 170°C/gas mark 3.

When the meat loaf is cooked, remove it from the pan, reserving the stock, and place on a wooden carving board. Let it cool a little before carving, then cut the loaf into 1cm slices and place them, slightly overlapping, in a warm ovenproof dish. Pour 2 tablespoons of the stock onto the meat, cover the dish with foil and put in the oven for 10–15 minutes while you make the sauce.

Strain the remaining stock into a saucepan and bring it to the boil, then add the wine and boil for 1 minute. Combine the butter and flour with a fork, and gradually add this mixture to the sauce, stirring all the time. Boil for 1–2 minutes.

Serve the meat and sauce separately. The polpettone is also good served cold with a thin mayonnaise (see page 300) or a thin salsa verde (see page 268).

CHAPTER 22

PEREGRINATIONS

Curdled mayonnaise and other disasters

A FRIEND ONCE TOLD me that there are people who change
partners, people who change houses and people who
change jobs. I moved house quite a few times during my
married life. I was happy to stay with the same partner, Oliver,
for over fifty-seven years, until death us did part, and I stuck
with my translating, interpreting and teaching for some
twenty years and to my cookery writing for over thirty. As for
houses . . . I must have itchy feet, or something.

I loved the house in Vine Road, but once the children had
left, it became too big for Oliver and me. We were also going
through a sticky patch where we were a bit short of money
and it seemed absurd to live in such a large house which was
expensive to run and maintain. Another factor which really
tilted the balance in favour of moving was that I could never
forget how lucky Oliver and I had been to have a house of our
own as soon as we needed one and we wanted to give our
children a similar start. So we sold Number 12 Vine Road and
bought a smaller house in Chiswick and a flat for the children
in Clapham.

Buying the flat proved a good move. When the children

sold it ten years later, Paul had enough money to put down a deposit on a house in Leeds, where he'd started teaching at the university, Guy bought a flat in Pavia, a town south of Milan, where he, too, was teaching at the university, and Julia bought a dilapidated farmhouse in Le Marche, in central Italy, that she sold ten years later for nearly ten times the price she'd paid. But our house in Chiswick was not a good move. I disliked Chiswick intensely. Oliver had warned me that it was very different from Barnes, but not being able to find anything suitable there, I thought Chiswick would be as pleasant, with better transport connections into town and wonderful food shops that I already used. Every Friday, I went to the butcher, the deli and the greengrocer in Turnham Green Terrace, to the fishmonger in Devonshire Place and to Adamou, an Aladdin's cave of Greek and Middle-Eastern goodies which was then presided over by the old man, with cigar in his mouth, roving eyes and a quick hand for the pretty customers, while his wife at the cash desk kept an eye on the money and on her husband.

But in spite of the shops and the convenience of the Piccadilly line, two years later we were back in my beloved Barnes, this time in a small house near the river, along which I took long walks with Pippo, our mad Border Collie cross who chased the seagulls and cormorants. It was during my walks that I'd think out recipes, paragraphs, sentences – anything that I could jot down later at home. I also rehearsed my talks for the demonstrations or lessons I gave. But, I never thought about the possibilities of culinary disasters and how to avert them.

~

THE FIRST disaster happened in 1982 when I had to make some fettuccine for Marcella Hazan, who was in London for the launch of *The Second Classic Italian Cookbook*. She was due to give a demonstration at Wollands, a smart store in Knightsbridge which has now disappeared. Marcella was going to show her audience how to make egg fettuccine and serve them *all'Alfredo*, a fashionable recipe in Italy at the time. Alfredo was a famous restaurateur in Rome, and the likes of Elizabeth Taylor, Richard Burton, Cary Grant, Sophia Loren would flock to his restaurant to enjoy his acclaimed fettuccine. He always added the final touches at the table with a grand toss of his gold fork and spoon – his signature gesture. The sauce is simple to make, consisting of butter, cream and masses of parmesan.

In her demonstration, Marcella was to focus on the making of the pasta, still a novelty then, in a country where many people's idea of pasta was spaghetti hoops. I was asked to bring some home-made fettuccine that Marcella could put straight in the pot, as the pasta dough she was to make at the demo would take too much time to dry out properly. So the day before, I made a three-egg dough, stretched it out in the pasta machine, let the sheets of dough dry, turned them over at the right time, put the sheets through the machine for the final cutting, and then folded the strands into pretty little nests, just as it should be done and as I have done a thousand times before. My fettuccine nests looked perfect, I thought, all lined up on a big tray, ready to be packed in a tin, which I did the day after, in layers with sheets of greaseproof paper in-between.

The next day, armed with my tin, I arrived at Wollands, where I met Marcella and her dashing husband Victor. And

Pasta demonstration in the 1980s.

then, half an hour before the demonstration was due to start, Marcella opened the tin and . . . I freaked out. All the nests, or most of them, had grown mildew which streaked the pasta strands in various shades of grey-green. I had obviously not let the pasta dry out properly before nesting it up, nor had I reckoned on a very damp English autumn day. And now we were faced with the problem of finding some egg pasta quickly – very quickly. Someone was despatched to Harrods and came back with a packet of a very good Italian brand of dried egg tagliatelle – not exactly fettuccine, but then who would know the difference? The demo started on time and was, thankfully, a great success. I shall never forget Marcella's kindness and consideration at the time, nor can I forget that a few years later she asked me to take over her cookery school in Bologna. She had decided to leave Bologna and concentrate on her new school at the Cipriani in Venice. I was thrilled to be asked, but I declined. I couldn't possibly follow in Marcella's steps; it was far too big a challenge, and too many comparisons would have inevitably been made.

~

DISASTER NUMBER two was worse. My friend Betsy Newell asked if I would prepare an Italian lunch for the pupils at her cookery school in Kensington which she ran with her business partner, Linda Gassenheimer. Of course, I'd be delighted, I told her. So my lunch was duly advertised with great fanfare and most of her pupils signed up to come along and learn to cook something *all'Italiana*. By then, I had gained some recognition as a cookery writer in certain circles and my books were moderately successful.

For the main course, I decided to cook *vitello tonnato,* a dish I must have made hundreds of times before. We reckoned that *vitello tonnato* was the sort of dish that Kensington ladies would like to serve at their summer dinner parties instead of the ubiquitous salmon. Veal was easily available in those pre-mad-cow days and Betsy had a very good butcher who knew how to prepare continental cuts of meat. My *vitello tonnato* was to be the version with mayonnaise. I'd been making mayonnaise since I was a child, and always successfully.

So on that spring day I drove to Linda's house, where she and Betsy were already at work peeling potatoes, chopping parsley, washing salad and hulling strawberries to be served with a balsamic vinegar dressing – another novelty in Britain. By 10 a.m. all the Kensington ladies had arrived and I began. I showed them the joint of veal, put it in the casserole with the wine, vinegar and all the flavourings to cook for an hour while

I prepared the mayonnaise. Easy, or so I thought. I cracked the first egg and began to separate the yolk from the white when a splinter of the shell fell into the bowl with the egg. I fished it out and went on with the second egg, and the second hiccup. A tiny bit of the white went into the yolk – of no great significance but rather unprofessional.

Never mind, I thought, and I started to beat the yolks while adding a pinch of salt and a pinch of mustard powder to stabilise the emulsion, or so I hoped. But the emulsion didn't stabilise and the yolks curdled soon after I started to add the oil. So I began again with another yolk, another pinch of salt and another pinch of mustard. I beat and beat, always with the same rhythmic clockwise movement, and then I began to add the curdled mayonnaise teaspoon by teaspoon to the new bowl. After a few spoonfuls, the new sauce was also *impazzita* – a fitting Italian word meaning 'gone mad', which in this case referred to both the mayonnaise and its maker. I felt a deep hatred for the occasion, the Kensington ladies, Linda, even lovely Betsy, the lot. I just wanted to drop everything and run. I apologised and asked Betsy to take over, and the mayonnaise was made. Obviously it was not my mayonnaise day and I tried to laugh it off, but it was very painful indeed. After that, I never made mayonnaise at a demonstration again.

~

DISASTER NUMBER three was laughable in comparison. It happened at a dinner party I held for some friends at our flat in Venice. It was a formal dinner party and the guests of honour were the Prince and Princess Galletti di San Cataldo, whom we'd recently met. We had also invited two other couples of Venetian friends.

If only I'd known then that Vettor and Ferdinanda, who eventually became good friends, were the least formal of all people and so relaxed that, years later, when we were staying in their Palladian villa near Treviso, Ferdinanda forgot that she had four Belgian couples coming to stay on the same day. So, at the unexpected arrival of the Belgians, we had to relinquish our room and move into Ferdinanda's bedroom, while she ended up on the divan in her study. Ferdinanda, who died recently, was an amusing woman, who, as she put it, was born well, married even better, had literary ambitions after receiving a first-class degree in English, started a splendid career as a simultaneous interpreter in three languages, and then, as she said, 'What am I now? A landlady, maybe a superior landlady, but still a landlady.' She ran a successful B & B in her splendid Villa Gradenigo. But when we first met her, we didn't know all that and I was intimidated by the string of titles and the ten red balloons, each representing a Doge, in Vettor's family tree.

So, for the Prince and the Princess the dinner that evening in Venice had to be good. As a first course, I'd decided to make *gnocchi di patate*, a daft choice in April when it would be difficult to find the right kind of old potatoes in Venice. So I spent the afternoon making the dough for the classic potato gnocchi without eggs, flicked them all against the prongs of the fork and lined them all on teacloths, taking up every surface of the not-too-large kitchen. The guests arrived, we had our Prosecco with *cicheti* and then I disappeared into the kitchen and started to drop the gnocchi into the boiling water. After a minute or two, the gnocchi had more or less vanished – they had simply disintegrated in the water. I obviously had not read Pellegrino Artusi's book properly at the time, in which he recommends that you always check the cooking beforehand by plunging a few gnocchi into the boiling water to see what happens. Something that, having learnt my lesson the hard way, I have done ever since. If necessary, I adjust the dough by adding a little more flour, or an egg – or both – until, when I test them, the gnocchi remain whole.

With my gnocchi gone, I had to come up with an alternative quickly – very quickly. It would have to be *spaghetti aglio, olio e peperoncino* – spaghetti with garlic, oil and chilli – and not to worry that the dish was certainly not the correct first course for a dinner party. Everybody loved it and I passed with flying colours the daunting task of cooking a dinner for my compatriots.

The Italians are extremely critical of what they eat (in fact the Italians are extremely critical of everything). Oliver always said that nothing would pass by me without some comment. But where food was concerned the comment often becomes sharper. At the end of a meal, Italians might say nothing, they might say *'Che buono che è'* – very high praise, or they might say *'Anche la mia mamma – o la mia nonna – lo fa, ma lo fa diverso'*, which means that your dish is a very poor version of their mother's or grandmother's, which of course is always the best. For the publication of my book *Amaretto, Apple Cake and Artichokes* in 2006, my publishers organised a launch party dinner at the Blueprint Café. Head chef Jeremy Lee cooked an excellent three-course meal using recipes from the book, starting with the chickpea soup. After dinner, my brother Marco came up to me and said: 'The soup was quite good, but Mamma's *pasta e ceci* is much better.'

~

I HAD A mini culinary disaster at Harrods where I was demonstrating pasta dishes for the launch of *Perfect Pasta*, published by Conran Octopus in 1986. An Italian cookware manufacturer had just brought out its revolutionary pasta pot and Harrods wanted to publicise it. It was a tall pot, as pasta pots should be, with a colander that fitted inside the pot, so that when the pasta was cooked, the colander could be lifted out with the pasta, leaving the water behind. It sounds like a clever idea, but in fact it is one of those gadgets that I find more bother than help.

On the day in question, I stepped up onto the demonstration counter and was greeted by a friendly audience. After my usual preliminary chat on the Arabs and Marco Polo and everything else concerning the history and the making of pasta, I put the pasta pot on the heat without the lining colander, because I wanted the water to come to the boil quickly. But I'd overfilled the pot so that when the water came to the boil and I inserted the colander, a gush of boiling water cascaded all over the ring, the work surface and all, but not, thank goodness, over my feet. Laugh it all off and carry on, had by then become my motto.

~

DISASTER NUMBER five happened a few years later, although this time it was not really my fault. Joe Earl, a friend who worked at the Victoria and Albert Museum, asked if I would cook an Italian dinner for one of the Wednesday night events at the museum. The event was called *Una Notte in Italia* and was to be held in the museum's theatre. Around eighty people were expected to attend, but I only had to make enough food for everyone to have a taste of the dishes I cooked.

I decided my dinner should have a Renaissance theme, in keeping with the venue. I planned to stick to three courses with a lot of chat on the history of Italian cooking and quotations and recipes from old books. I managed to create a menu that would suit the very limited cooking facilities at the museum – a slow oven – based on recipes by three of my favourite cookery writers: a lenten spinach pie for the first course, followed by a fish stew for the main course, and a ricotta pudding to finish. I would cook the first and last courses at home and only demonstrate the method in the theatre, and also prepare the fish for the main course in advance so that it would need only a gentle simmering in the slow oven later. Perfect. The spinach pie was my adaptation from the *Libro Novo* by Christoforo di Messisbugo, the sixteenth-century chef of Cardinal Ippollito d'Este; the fish stew came from *Opera* by Bartolomeo Scappi, chef to two Popes in the sixteenth century; and the pudding was from one of my favourite books, *L'Arte di Ben Cucinare,* by Bartolomeo Stefani, chef to the Gonzagas in the seventeenth century.

Oliver and I arrived at the V&A to the sound of piped Vivaldi and were welcomed by Joe Earl and two eager girls who were to be my helpers. We went to the theatre where a long table covered by a starched white tablecloth had been prepared for me to lay out all my bits and pieces. A big oven on wheels was waiting for me, so I proceeded to switch it on and then looked for the temperature gauge. It was nowhere to be seen. The penny dropped – the oven was not an oven but a plate warmer. There was no way I could cook my beautiful big hake in it.

Meanwhile, the theatre was filling up with people and I and the girls were desperately wondering what we could do to rescue the dinner of *Una Notte in Italia*. In fact, we could do nothing, the fish could not possibly be cooked in that antediluvian gadget on wheels. So, I explained what had happened, demonstrated the method and carried on . . . with a laugh, while cursing myself for not having checked the oven beforehand. From then on, the evening went smoothly: the talk went well and the two courses I'd brought with me also went down well. Joe Earl produced more bottles of wine and everyone went home happy.

THERE WERE many more disasters, like the dishes that didn't taste as they should have tasted or that looked a mess. On these occasions I was always reminded of the comment made by an Italian man who, on first meeting me, said: '*Oh, ecco la cuoca teoretica!*' – 'Here comes the theoretical cook!'

Vitello Tonnato alla Piemontese
Veal with Tuna Sauce Cooked the Piedmontese Way

SERVES 6

1kg veal joint
75ml dry white wine
75ml wine vinegar
1 small carrot
1 small celery stick
1 onion, stuck with a clove
sprig of parsley
2 pinches of sea salt
12 black peppercorns, bruised
200g canned best tuna, preserved in olive oil, drained
4 anchovy fillets
1 tbsp capers
300ml lemon mayonnaise

Put the veal, wine, vinegar, vegetables, salt and peppercorns in a saucepan. Add 150ml of water and bring to the boil. Simmer for about 1 hour, until the meat is tender. Lift the veal out of the pan and set aside to cool. Reserve the veal cooking stock and vegetables.

Liquidise the tuna and anchovies in a blender or food processor and mix into the mayonnaise together with the capers. Now purée the reserved veal cooking stock and vegetables and add to the mayonnaise mixture. Mix thoroughly, then taste and adjust the seasoning.

Cut the cold veal into 1cm slices and spoon the sauce over them.

~

Lemon Mayonnaise

This is how I make mayonnaise: I turn the radio on, place the bowl on a damp cloth and sit down comfortably at the table with the bowl containing the eggs in front of me. The bowl is on the cloth so that it cannot slip. I use an old fashioned wooden spoon, but you can use a hand-held electric beater or a good whisk if you prefer. I like using the spoon because it makes a soothing noise and I can judge best the thickness of the sauce. Also I like it because that is what I used when I learned to make mayonnaise as a child.

Whatever you use, the important thing is to have the eggs at room temperature and not out of the fridge. I don't keep eggs in the fridge, so I do not run this risk, but if you do and forgot to take them out in good time, follow Nigella's instructions in her invaluable *How to Eat* book: put them in a bowl of warm water for ten minutes and then start.

I use a mild olive oil – not an extra virgin which is far too strong.

2 organic egg yolks
sea salt
pinch of dry mustard
250–300ml olive oil
2– 3 tbsp lemon juice
salt and white pepper to taste

Place the egg yolks in a clean dry bowl and add a little sea salt and the pinch of mustard, which help to stabilise the mixture. Beat the mixture and then start adding the oil very slowly indeed, literally drop by drop, while beating the whole time. Go on adding the oil always drop by drop until the sauce is the consistency of double cream. Now add a little of the lemon juice which will thin out the sauce. After that, keep adding oil a little at a time to allow the oil to be properly absorbed. Then start again, adding a little more lemon juice whenever the sauce becomes too thick. The mayonnaise for a vitello tonnato should not be too thick, so around 250ml of oil is quite enough.

At the end I beat in a tablespoon of iced water and then I add salt to taste, not too much because the veal cooking stock is quite salty. The pepper is optional and white pepper is better if you are making a plain mayonnaise because the black speckles of the black pepper would spoil the look of the sauce.

CHAPTER 23

DORSET

Fungi and wild garlic

IN 1998 MY LOVE FOR my grandchildren took precedence over my love of the city. I decided to cut my losses and follow my daughter Julia and her three children to the wilderness of Dorset. Oliver and I were getting on and we were in London by ourselves – with plenty of dear friends, I agree, but no family. Oddly enough, all our three children, born and schooled in London, for one reason or another had left it. Paul, having returned from Tokyo, was teaching at Leeds University; Guy stayed in Pavia and married his Italian girlfriend Giovanna; and Julia had moved to Dorset. We chose to follow Julia because of the grandchildren.

On the 8th of June 1991, Julia had married Charles Cardozo, another Catholic, who originally came from Dorset. They married in our local parish church in Mortlake, one of the prettiest Victorian Catholic churches I know; in its graveyard lies the extraordinary, tent-shaped tomb of Isabella Burton. Julia looked stunning in her ivory satin dress, with long sleeves and ruffled neckline, and a simple crown of pale pink rosebuds in her long, dark hair holding her short veil. The reception was held at Fulham Palace, a former summer retreat of the

Bishops of London, and all went well, except for the weather. It was a rainy day and extremely cold. I tried to go out into the garden but had to come back inside. Only the young managed to survive out there, even in their flimsy summer dresses (I suspect they survived because they wanted to smoke, something they couldn't do inside the palace).

In Italy we have a saying *'sposa bagnata, sposa fortunata'* – 'wet bride, lucky bride' – which was some consolation at least. Rain or no rain, Julia had found a likeable and intelligent young man. Like her, Charles had an Oxford degree and also a master's degree in business studies from Columbia University and was working as a management consultant. They bought a house in Kennington, south London, but, three years later, Charles had felt the call of his native soil and taken his family to Dorset, depriving me of my darling granddaughter.

Grandchildren are one of the most precious gifts that old age gives to us – one which makes life pleasurable again and the future something to look forward to. I'd become a grandmother at the relatively advanced age of sixty-eight (my mother had been just forty-eight when her first grandchild appeared). By then I was feeling really broody, an emotion I'd never experienced before. My own son Paul had arrived just ten months after Oliver and I had planned to start a family, so I'd never had to wait longingly for a baby. But nobody can plan the arrival of their grandchildren.

Our two sons were both married, but with no babies on the scene. Guy and his generous and positive Giovanna from Pavia, sadly, never produced one and Paul inherited the ideal son, with curly hair and a cheeky look, when he married his attractive Serbian wife. Julia had waited till the age of thirty before deciding the time was right and so, at long last, Nell was born, and my life was transformed. I was so entranced by her arrival that I even wrote a few poems about her – in Italian of course – rather charming in their simplicity, and brimming with happiness and love. Gentle Nell was succeeded in quick succession by self-assured Johnny and by angelic Coco and, four years later, by strong-willed Kate. The perfect quartet.

I have little snaps of memories of all four, which I treasure and, when life is the misery that it sometimes becomes, I am able to recall something they have said or done, which is often more poignant and unforgettable than a photograph. A phrase or an action can sum up a person far better even than an image – like the time Coco, aged six, looked up fondly at me and said, 'Nonna, I love you very much.' 'I love you, too,' I replied. 'Ah, but I love you more, because I love you from here to the sun, not once, not twice, but a million times,' and my heart melted. Or when down-to-earth Johnny asked me, 'But Nonna, why don't you try to write something like Harry Potter instead of cookery books? You would be far richer by now.' And then there was Kate, who, when we visited Oliver's grave, knelt down and, after a few minutes of silence, said, 'I told Nonno not to be too sad because soon you will be there with him to keep him company.'

So for the love of our grandchildren, we left my beloved Barnes. Oliver, to be honest, had not been too keen to move, no doubt finding it too much of an upheaval, but, as usual, he gave in. Eventually, he settled in the countryside far better than I did and was extremely happy there for the last nine years of his life.

The decision had been swift. While I can spend days making my mind up whether or not to buy a certain dress only to buy it, return it later and buy a different one, or to plan a dinner four times over before settling on a menu, I have always taken the really important decisions of my life instinctively. Getting married to a foreign man, living in a foreign country, buying and selling houses, and changing jobs, were all decisions made impulsively, like throwing myself into inevitable voids.

We'd gone down to Dorset, seen a house which had the right number of rooms, a kitchen full of light and was close to Julia, and we bought it. I was distraught at leaving Barnes where I had lived very happily for forty years, but now, after nearly ten years in Dorset, I know we did the right thing. Alone in Barnes, I would have missed my grandchildren far more than the theatre, the exhibitions, the friends, the cinema and, especially, the lights of a city at night, all things that have been an intrinsic part of my life.

After more than fifty years in England, I am anglicised enough to appreciate the countryside at any time of the year although I still dislike the long, dark unforgiving period of winter. The country is colder than London and country houses are usually colder than town houses. One of the coldest weeks of my life was in Ayrshire where, fifty or so years ago, I stayed in a spectacularly handsome house. It was April, but it was snowing, which was unusual, apparently, for that part of western Scotland. There were palm trees in the garden and they were covered in snow – an extraordinarily enchanting sight. There was no heating in the house, or, at least, none that I could feel. Huge cheerful fires were lit downstairs which bellowed out a delicious and welcome warmth. But the rooms were large and the front rows around the fires were taken up exclusively by three large Labradors; they were well aware of where they belonged, and where we belonged – in the second and much colder row. Another cold Scottish spell was much later, in the 1990s, when I was asked to give some cookery demonstrations at the house of friends, the Williamsons, near Aviemore. This happened twice, once in May and once in October, and on both occasions it snowed. The house certainly had central heating, but it was kept low so as not to ruin the priceless furniture. The kitchen was heaven, though, with a huge Aga, and there was so much work to do that the last thing I could think of was being cold. One weekend Lyn, my hostess – who also ran an upmarket B & B – and I had to do over 100 'couverts': breakfasts (and a full Scottish breakfast, of course), lunches and dinners for everyone: this included the students of the cookery school and the B & B guests both in the house and in the rented accommodation.

~

THE PART of Dorset where I now live is the Dorset of John Betjeman's poem, the first line of which Oliver loved: 'Rime Intrinsica, Fontmell Magna, Sturminster Newton and Melbury Bubb'. We had already spent a couple of weekends each year with our great friends, the Ingrams, who had a cottage near Sturminster Newton. The whole area is extremely beautiful, classic countryside; whenever I go for walks I can't help feeling that this was the landscape Virgil had in mind when he wrote the *Bucolics*, even though he didn't know Dorset. After more than nine years, I have got used to living here (well, sort of), and I have also got used to the people, all exceedingly English and quite different from Londoners. Guy had warned me that I might never make a friend. But I have, and more than one.

One unexpected delight was the abundance of good local food, not in the restaurants or pubs, where you are still often offered gluey lasagne or fried scampi with tartar sauce in a little bag, but the food in the local shops and the farmers' markets. The choice may be more limited than in London, but the quality is undeniably better. I am surrounded by the best meat farms. I can buy all the things I love, like fresh tongue, tripe, shins of pork and best end of neck of lamb to make my Italian equivalent of Irish stew. My vegetables are all grown locally, providing I stick to roots and cabbage for seven months of the year, although recently the local farmers have learned to grow some different varieties such as cavolo nero (black cabbage) and Russian kale which flourish in northern climes. Sadly, though, nobody is growing the delicious salsify or the even better cardoons. Fish comes straight up from the coast and I can even get an eel, an octopus or some cuttlefish if I am lucky. Nearby is a mussel farm where mussels, palourdes and oysters, delivered fresh from Cornwall, are kept in huge tanks of sea water ready to be sold to restaurants in London and around. I can get oysters quite cheaply; the snag is that I cannot open them because my hands are now too weak. But the mussels are excellent and they provide a greater variety of dishes. Eggs are straight from my daughter's or my friends' chickens. But the best thing is the local lamb, and the pork – the wonderful Gloucester Old Spot or the Tamworth that actually tastes like pork and has the same succulent meat that I was used to in the old days.

Then there is the pleasure of picking food for free, as I did so often in my childhood with my family and friends. We were urban children, yet we knew all the edible wild foods, from dandelions to fungi. Often in the spring we would cycle to the *prati* – meadows – only half an hour away then from the centre of Milan. We picked wild rocket, summer savoury, dandelions, borage, hop shoots, Clematis vitalba shoots and nettles to make salads and *risotti* and soups. In the autumn, when we were on holiday at the Italian lakes, we'd go up on the mountains to pick fungi, as well as the wonderful bilberries, plus, if we were lucky, a few wild raspberries. With the flowers of acacia and elder my mother would make crunchy, crackling fritters covered in icing sugar, which looked like Valencienne lace and tasted divine. But the best treats were to be had at the seaside: the delicious mussels, the not so delicious limpets and the succulent samphire.

Now I go foraging with Nell, Johnny, Coco and Kate. I have added a new food to my search: wild garlic, which I did not know as a child and is rampant on the damp banks of Dorset. My grandchildren love it, especially when I make a pesto with it. Actually, they like anything with pasta, but they are right in this instance, as wild garlic makes an excellent spring version of basil pesto. The only 'free' food I am not so keen to eat any more, oddly enough, is fungi. I had my fungi era, which finished in triumph when I was asked by Dorling Kindersley in 1995 to write twenty recipes for a book on fungi by the Danish mycologist Thomas Lessoe. So I went on fungi forays; I sorted them, I cleaned them, I cooked them, I created recipes and, by the end, I became sick of them. (In fact, one day I had one that must have been toxic – not lethal, obviously – but toxic enough to upset my stomach and my attitude towards them.)

With Kate, Julia, Coco, Nell and Poppy, the dog.

I have always been eager to try anything that is more or less edible – plants, berries, fungi. My most daring 'try' was on a boat near Chioggia where I went to see the soft-shell crabs I had to write about for my book, *The Painter, the Cook and the Art of Cucina*. I felt compelled to eat one there and then so that I could describe the flavour accurately, and asked the fisherman's permission. 'Yes,' came the answer, 'but only have a claw, not the whole thing and, I warn you, they are not that sensational.' I looked at the crab in my hand, wrenched off two undulating claws and put them in my mouth. Certainly not at all sensational compared to their deliciousness when fried. Then I looked at the laguna; the water was the colour of murky pea soup with streaks of oil here and there. During the night I kept waking up and waiting for the first signs of food poisoning, or typhoid or the plague or worse.

I still go on mushroom forays with my grandchildren and, afterwards, help them to inspect, choose and cook our spoils. Their favourite dish, as was my children's and mine at their age, is porcini caps: a *cotoletta*, breaded and fried, or ceps baked in the oven covered with thin layers of chopped parsley, garlic and breadcrumbs. Children make good tasters, because they concentrate all their senses on the food they are eating and they have strong opinions about their likes and dislikes. Later, when they become adolescents, their concentration is diverted elsewhere. Eventually, in old age food takes precedence once more and becomes one of the greatest pleasures in life – good food, of course. I know this far too well now. The problem is that my enthusiasm at the stove has diminished as my years have increased; it is not much fun at all to cook only for oneself.

Fungi or no fungi, Dorset is for me, here with my beloved grandchildren. And now, as I go into the kitchen to make my pork stew, my musings cease to be memoirs, as they change into the present tense, and today, inexorably, becomes yesterday.

RECIPE

Pasticcio di Tagliatelle e Funghi al Forno
Baked Tagliatelle with Mushrooms

Put some dried porcini in this for the stronger flavour. The other mushrooms can be a mixed lot you have picked or some fresh cultivated mushrooms.

If you are making your own tagliatelle, turn to page 133 and follow the instructions, but remember that fresh pasta takes far less time to cook than dried pasta.

SERVES 6

500g dried egg tagliatelle, or make your own
using 3 eggs and 300g Italian 00 flour
50g dried porcini
2 slices white bread, crusts removed
100ml full-fat milk
4 tbsp olive oil
75g unsalted butter

1 garlic clove, finely sliced
350g fresh mushrooms, finely sliced
3 eggs, separated
50g gruyère cheese, sliced
50g Bel Paese cheese, sliced
50g grated Parmigiano-Reggiano
150ml double cream
salt and pepper

Soak the porcini in hot water for 20 minutes or so, then lift them out and dry them on kitchen paper. Reserve the porcini liquid – if necessary, strain it through a strainer lined with a piece of muslin.

Soak the bread in the milk for 10 minutes and squeeze out the excess.

Meanwhile heat the oil and 30g of the butter in a large sauté pan. Add the porcini and the garlic and cook for 5 minutes. Mix in the fresh mushrooms and continue cooking for about 10-15 minutes, adding 1 or 2 tablespoons of the reserved porcini liquid. Transfer to a bowl.

Break up the bread with a fork and add to the mushroom mixture together with the egg yolks.

Preheat the oven to 180°C/gas mark 4.

Cook the pasta in plenty of boiling salted water, drain and toss with half the remaining butter. Whisk the egg whites and fold gently into the mushroom mixture. Season with salt and pepper to taste.

Butter an oven dish and spoon half the tagliatelle into it. Spread the mushroom mixture over it and top with the sliced cheeses and half the Parmigiano-Reggiano. Cover with the other half of the pasta, sprinkle with the remaining parmesan, and spoon the cream over. Dot with the remaining butter.

Cover the dish with foil and bake in the oven for 15 minutes. Remove the foil, turn the oven up to 200°C/gas mark 6 and bake for a further 10 minutes until the top is brown and crusty. Allow to stand out of the oven for a few minutes before serving.

THE END

M Y LIFE, AS I'd known it for the past fifty-seven-and-a-half years, ended when Oliver died in April 2007. He went peacefully, at home, with the bedroom window wide open on to the balcony festooned with wisteria and clematis montana in full bloom, looking out towards his majestic ash tree and his beloved Fontmell Down beyond. He died of kidney failure, which I'm told is one of the best ways to die because one does not suffer. One fades away, not able to eat and eventually not able to drink.

When he was dying, which he did for over a fortnight totally conscious of it, he said to me, 'I am sorry but I procrastinate even my death.' For some reason, I thought about the moment in our marriage ceremony when I had promised that he would be my 'awful' wedded husband, and hoped it had not been a Freudian slip; Oliver was anything but awful. He was moderately selfish, as most of us are, and a great procrastinator, but he was also extremely kind and gentle and easy going and very modest. He had an unusually full sense of human nature and the many ironies in life. And this meant that he often did his talking and smiling with his eyes; indeed his eyes twinkled almost the whole time he talked. He hated rows, hassles and confrontations, something that I quite enjoy, as a matter of fact. We were very different, although we shared the same interests: theatre, books, films, classical music, and maybe that was a reason why we stayed together for over fifty years. Also it may be because our generation valued loyalty more than faithfulness and we did not like to destroy a family on the whim of a passing affair. I used to tell him that he had to thank Mamma if I stuck to him for so long, because, during my nubile years, she used to say that my husband, if I ever found one, would throw me out of the window after two months. I stuck to him just to spite her, I used to tell him. He had bags of sense of humour, so much that some rubbed off on me, his 'literary-minded po-faced Milanese', as he called me on one occasion.

About a month before he died, he'd been taken to Dorchester Hospital for all the tests, against his wishes. He knew perfectly well, as we all did, that there was nothing to be done. So he told the consultant to stop giving him drugs and to let him go home to die. He came back and lay in bed, listening to music, occasionally talking to me or one of the children and sipping drops of tea or ice cream. One day he asked for Campari Soda. He wanted the little bottles of Campari Soda, not Campari in a big bottle. I feel sure that he wanted simply to try to recapture the pleasure of sitting in the sun in a square somewhere in Italy, drinking Campari Soda, one of his favourite holiday pursuits. So Julia ordered some of the little bottles. They arrived, he had a sip of Campari Soda and that was all. But I think it brought back treasured memories of Italy. In the last few years of his life, he didn't want to go anywhere else but Italy. He was happy there, happier even than in Dorset.

He planned his funeral service, and his burial in the graveyard of the local church. He chose the music he wanted to be played and the poetry he wanted to be read. The music was two adagios from Haydn and the poetry was the soliloquy from *Richard II*, Act 5, Scene 5.

The day he died, he knew it was going to be his last with us. In the evening he sent Julia and me away by silently retrieving his hand from mine and turning his head away. He did not want us to keep him any longer; he'd had enough and was ready to go. We went downstairs to have supper and, when Julia went up after we'd finished, she found him dead. She picked a clematis flower from the balcony and laid it on his chest. That morning he had told me to finish this book as quickly as I could; I think he was worried that I, too, could die before it was published. He was so proud – and I use this overused word with great discretion – that I'd been asked to write it. After all, it was he who had taught me how to write in English. Recipes were easy, but now, he said, in my very small way, I had achieved what Conrad did!

It is odd that, while Oliver was so finicky about my writing, he did not seem to care much about my speaking. He certainly did not care about my accent. I can only presume that he thought it a lost cause to try to improve it, or maybe he liked it. I never asked him. There are so many things I forgot to ask him, like how does it feel when one knows one is dying. Now it is all too late and I have to come to terms with the three big Ss in my life: *silenzio*, *solitudine* and *stanchezza*. Silence and solitude are self-explanatory, but tiredness is an

odd feeling. I am not tired in the physical sense, but everything I do, think, feel seems to have a negative edge which tires me. And of the three big Ss, *stanchezza* is the one which I find most difficult to fight, because I don't know how.

I lived with Oliver for more than fifty years; that they were all happy is immaterial. Half a century is a very long time and it has conditioned my thinking, my behaviour, my eating and sleeping habits – my whole living in fact – and, of course, my writing. Now I get cross with myself when I cannot find the right word or the right expression. They usually come to my mind in the wrong language, if they come at all. In the past, I used to ask Oliver; it was so easy. I also had a sounding board in him: 'Oliver, do you think that this is of interest to anybody?' Now, there is only Poppy, my pretty lurcher, to ask and she looks at me with those beautiful brown eyes and I am still in doubt.

There is nobody to tell me what article I must not miss in today's newspaper, what television programme I must watch; nobody to switch on the radio for me so I can listen to my favourite piece of music while I'm cooking; nobody to let me know that the composer of the week on Radio Three is my favourite, or who is the guest on Radio Four's *Desert Island Discs*. And, worst of all, nobody to deal with banks, bonds, insurance policies, and to ring up and talk to people I cannot understand. And, finally, there is nobody to find my keys. At the venerable age of eighty-two, there seems little hope of feeling less lonely, less quiet or less tired.

And then I think of my grandchildren and all the meals I have yet to cook and share with them. Suddenly, I have a reason for living.

GRAZIE

FIRST AND FOREMOST *grazie* to my editor, Alison Samuel, who asked me to write this book and then helped me to shape my diverse and diverging memories. My thanks go also to Poppy Hampson, to the copy-editor Jan Bowmer, and to all the team at Chatto & Windus, not forgetting Greg Heinimann the jacket designer and Jeff Cottenden, the photographer of the cover images which so intriguingly illustrate the contents of my book. Yet again, I thank my agent Vivien Green, for her endless support and infectious enthusiasm.

I am very grateful to my cousin, Mariateresa Peregalli Bestetti, who was 'the black box' of my childhood – helped, at times, by another cousin, Joan Allen Tuska Peregalli. Thank you, cousins, and thank you also to my other cousins, Mariella Pinelli Massola and Mariella Del Conte Scarpetta. Many of my old Italian friends have been very helpful; in particular I must thank: Giovanna Pellizzi, Giulia Valdettaro Marzotto, Michi di San Giuliano, Giuseppe di San Giuliano, Lalla Ramazzotti Morassutti, Carla Sacchi Toffoloni, Grazia Gay, Camillo and Myriam de' Castiglioni, my nephews Luca and Nicholas Del Conte, my niece, Alexandra Del Conte, and, especially, my brother Marco, who, apart from fitting in some missing pieces of my memory jigsaw, with his partner Rossella Aicardi always welcomed me in Milan and put me up whenever I went. Among my English friends, my deepest thanks are for David Williams, who had endlessly encouraged me with my writing, but also for Michelle Berriedale-Johnson, Bill and Margaretta Dacombe, Penny Escombe and Henry Staveley-Hill, Roger and Val Jupe, Geoffrey Sharp and Ronnie and Gay Wilson.

But, most of all, I thank with all my heart my children, Paul, Guy and Julia, all of whom have endlessly been bombarded with my questioning and have always been happy to read and comment on my writing. And just to close, thanks also to my grandchildren, Nell, Johnny, Coco and Kate, for being so patient whenever I could not play with them because 'I have to work'.

GENERAL INDEX

Aberdeen, Hong Kong 232–3
Abyssinia *see* Ethiopia
Alberini, Massimo 238
Albinea, Emilia-Romagna 89, 90, 91, 93, 95–6,
    101–3, 106, 129, 139
    Villa Calvi 101, 105–6
    Villa Crocioni 96–8
    Villa Rossi 105–6
    Villa Viani 89–90, 91, 95, 96
Alfredo (restaurateur) 290
Amaretto, Apple Cake and Artichokes (Del Conte)
    295
Archer, Roger 245
Archer, Val 244–5
Arton twins 143
Artusi, Pellegrino 38, 295

Badia a Coltibuono, Tuscany: restaurant 200–1
Badoglio, Marshal Pietro 92, 93–4
Balsamo, Carlo Saverio 93, 94, 102, 118, 129–30,
    252–3, 254
Balsamo, Marchese 101–2, 253
Balsamo, Marica Saverio 93, 94, 102, 103–4, 253
Barnes, London 212, 213, 215–16, 288, 289, 304, 305
Behren, Henrietta and Tim 206
Betjeman, John: 'Dorset' 306
Bianchi, Cetto 166
Billing Road, London 170–1, *172*, 174, 175, 183
Blampied, Clare 244, 261
Blueprint Café, London 295
Bocca di Magra, Liguria 102
bocolo, il 283–4
Bologna 108, 253
Bordighera, Italian Riviera 49
    Pallanca Exotic Garden 50
Boston, Charlie 187, 189, 190
Brolio, Tuscany
    Ricasoli cellars 260
Bronte, Sicily 202

Cacchiano, Castello di, Tuscany 198–9
Camogli, Liguria 53
Caotorta, Giulia Marzotto 14, 15
Carluccio, Antonio 251
Carluccio, Priscilla 238
Carrosse, Le (restaurant), London 254–5

Carso mountains 76
Casentino mountains 243
Castelvetro, Giacomo: *Brieve Racconto di tutte le
    Radici...* 272
Cavalli-Sforza, Luca 148–9
Cavalli-Sforza, Pupa 148, 149
Cavi di Lavagna, Liguria 78–9, 81–3
Chianti (region) 198–202, 204–7, 259–61
    cookery school 259–61, *262*
Chiswick, London 288–9
Christoff, Boris 6
Classic Food of Northern Italy, The (Del Conte) 240,
    241–2
Clausetti, Carlo 5, 8, 9, 16
Clausetti, Margherita 5, 6, 9, 16
Clooney, George 140
Coducci, Mauro: San Giovanni Crisostomo 275
Como, Lake 74, 138–41
Cornia, Tuscany 199–200, 201, 202, 204–5, 206,
    207
Crocioni, Signora 96–8
Curran, Jane 243

Davenport, Philippa 259
David, Elizabeth 251, 254
de' Castiglioni, Myriam 198, 200–1
de Zoete, Beryl 186
Dimbleby, Josceline 258

Earl, Joe 296, 297, 298
Eisenhower, General Dwight D. 91, 93
Elena, Queen 71–2
Eley, Lady Penelope 187
Emilia-Romagna 114, 126, 240, 242–3
    see also Albinea; Puianello; Reggio Emilia
Ercole, Carlo 261–2, 266
Ercole, Giuseppe 261–2
Ercole, Lorenzo 261–2
Ethiopia, Italian invasion of 71

Farchy, Luciana 191
Farchy, Sandra 191
Fernex, Gigi de 57
Fernex, Nini de 57
Fernex, Olga de 56, 57, 58–60, 62, 63
Ferran, Major Roy 106

GENERAL INDEX

INDEX OF RECIPES AND FOOD

(Recipes in bold)